Cherie Fournier

About the Author

Corrine Kenner specializes in bringing metaphysical subjects down to earth. She's a certified tarot master and the author of ten books.

Corrine was born in Minnesota and raised on a farm in North Dakota. In her late teens and early twenties, she lived in Brazil and Los Angeles, where she earned a bachelor's degree in philosophy from California State University. For the first part of her career she worked as a newspaper reporter, magazine editor, and media relations specialist. Now she lives in Minneapolis with her husband, a software developer, and their daughters.

Corrine offers tarot classes and writing workshops on a regular basis, both in person and online. For more information, visit her website at corrinekenner.com.

Tarot for Writers

CORRINE KENNER

Llewellyn Publications
Woodbury, Minnesota

First Edition
First Printing, 2009

Cover design by Kevin R. Brown
Cover typewriter image © Shutterstock
Interior book design by Joanna Willis
Interior illustrations by Llewellyn art department
Universal Tarot cards on cover and interior are from *Universal Tarot* deck by Roberto De Angelis,
    reprinted by permission from Lo Scarabeo

Llewellyn is a registered trademark of Llewellyn Worldwide, Ltd.

Library of Congress Cataloging-in-Publication Data
Kenner, Corrine, 1964–
    Tarot for writers / Corrine Kenner.
        p.   cm.
    Includes bibliographical references and index.
    ISBN 978-0-7387-1457-8
    1. Tarot. 2. Authorship. I. Title.
    BF1879.T2.K465 2008
    133.3'2424024808   dc22

                                                        2008040196

Llewellyn Worldwide does not participate in, endorse, or have any authority or responsibility concerning private business transactions between our authors and the public.
    All mail addressed to the author is forwarded but the publisher cannot, unless specifically instructed by the author, give out an address or phone number.
    Any Internet references contained in this work are current at publication time, but the publisher cannot guarantee that a specific location will continue to be maintained. Please refer to the publisher's website for links to authors' websites and other sources.

Llewellyn Publications
A Division of Llewellyn Worldwide, Ltd.
2143 Wooddale Drive, Dept. 978-0-7387-1457-8
Woodbury, MN 55125-2989, U.S.A.
www.llewellyn.com

♻ Printed in the United States of America on recycled paper

Also by Corrine Kenner

Crystals for Beginners
The Epicurean Tarot
The Ma'at Tarot Workbook
Simple Fortunetelling with Tarot Cards
Strange But True
Tall Dark Stranger: Tarot for Love and Romance
Tarot Journaling

Forthcoming

The Wizards Tarot

Contents

Preface

This book was born in November 2006. It started as a short feature article for National Novel Writing Month—a web-based annual event in which thousands of people worldwide playfully commit to writing a full-length novel during the month of November. The organizers simply asked me an open-ended question: how can you write a novel using tarot cards to guide you? My answer ran all of four hundred words.

After that initial exchange, I decided to elaborate on the ideas and suggestions I had offered to eighty thousand writers on the NaNoWriMo website. First I simply assembled and reviewed my notes. Then I turned those notes into handouts for my own writers group. Before long, I had compiled a detailed outline for the book you're holding now.

I didn't invent many of the techniques and ideas in this book. Instead, I've simply combined old ideas in a new way. This book applies the precepts of tarot reading to standard literary principles and shows how closely they're linked. In fact, tarot reading and storytelling dovetail seamlessly, both in theory and in practice. There's a surprising similarity, for example, between standard tarot spreads and the classical story structure that Aristotle first described. There's also a remarkable parallel between the Fool's Journey through the cards and the Hero's Journey concept, popularized in our time by Joseph Campbell and now a literary model for many modern-day storytellers.

Not only can you use the tarot to brainstorm and develop story ideas, you can use it in the later steps of the writing process, too: from finding a publisher to publicizing and promoting a finished work. In fact, this book can serve as a complete course in fiction writing, as well as a comprehensive reference for writers who are just becoming familiar with a tarot deck.

If you're like most of the people reading this book, you're probably already enthusiastic about writing. You may have studied fiction and literature at the college level. With any luck, you've completed a story or two of your own. And at this point, you probably have a compelling new story idea trying to break free—and you may even dream of writing the great American novel. You'll get the most from this book if you're a short-story writer, novelist, screenwriter, or playwright—but poets, diarists, essayists, and writers of creative nonfiction can also glean inspiration from these pages. Even writers who make a living in the corporate world can use this guide to add polish and flair to their written work.

Here you should find just enough information to encourage you without overwhelming you with detail. My goal is to kick-start your creativity without confining you to rote mechanical exercises or condemning you to a strict writing regimen. In these pages you'll find a wide range of resources: simple spreads and layouts, card descriptions, and explanations of the symbols, myths, archetypal imagery, and astrological references that are built into most standard tarot decks. You'll also find inspiration for your writing practice, writing prompts, and ideas to incorporate into your work.

Feel free to explore, experiment, and entertain yourself, and let me know how well this guide works for you—especially if you're using it to write a novel in thirty days.

Corrine Kenner
Minneapolis, Minnesota
August 2008

Acknowledgments

First of all, I'd like to thank the writers and tarot enthusiasts who tried the techniques in this book and offered suggestions and ideas for bringing the cards to life in story form.

I'm especially grateful to the members of the first Tarot for Writers Workshop in Minneapolis: P. J. Doyle, Charlene Jaszewski, Carol Perkins, Andie Ryan, and Pam Thiltgen-Hester. I'm also fond of four online workshop participants who helped me develop the materials for this guide: Denise Alleva, Susanne Fritzsche, Ann Livingston, and Cynthia Tedesco.

My thanks go, as well, to John Carlson, Michael Gerleman, and Denise Hesselroth, who offered their comments on my early drafts, and to Melani Weber, who contributed the subplot development technique in chapter six.

I'm thankful for the advice of Lisa Finander, the developmental editor who suggested that I personalize this book with my own writing experiences. I'd also like to thank three editors at Llewellyn: Rebecca Zins, who showed enthusiasm for the guide even when it was barely more than an outline; Mindy Keskinen, who suggested structure and formatting improvements; and Connie Hill, who edited the manuscript. I also appreciate the work of Kevin Brown, who designed the cover, and Joanna Willis, who designed the inside pages.

And of course, I owe a huge debt of gratitude to my husband, Dan—whose unwavering support makes it possible for me to write—and my daughters Katherine, Emily, and Julia, who make it fun.

How to Use This Book

Most people think of tarot cards as a fortunetelling device—but they're also an excellent tool for writing and creative thinking. Writers from John Steinbeck to Stephen King have used tarot cards for inspiration, and Italian novelist Italo Calvino went so far as to call the tarot "a machine for writing stories."

Calvino was right. An ordinary tarot deck can help you break through writer's block, serve as a source of creative inspiration, and give you insights into your characters' past, present, and future. Tarot cards can help you generate new material or breathe new life into a project you've already started.

Backstory: A Literary History of the Tarot

Tarot card readers and storytellers share a long, rich history. The tarot itself has existed since the 1400s, when Italian royalty used tarot cards to play a trick-taking game called *tarocchi*. Their decks were hand-painted works of Renaissance art—and the cards were a treasure trove of symbolic images that incorporated a wide range of literary and mythological figures.

In fact, some of the cards might have been based on the work of a poet named Francesco Petrarca, known in English as Petrarch. His fourteenth-century masterpiece the *Trionfi* was an allegorical account of human existence. His descriptions of Love, Chastity, Death, Fame, Time, and Divinity dovetail perfectly with the images in early tarot decks. The cards themselves inspired poetry, too. As early as the sixteenth century, some *tarocchi* players used the cards to compose impromptu sonnets about each other, called *tarocchi appropriati*.

In modern times, W. B. Yeats seems to have based some of his poems on tarot imagery. In his case, the connection between writing and tarot goes both ways. In fact, some experts think Yeats' poetry actually inspired some of the imagery in modern tarot. Yeats was a friend of Arthur Edward Waite and Pamela Colman Smith, who created the best-selling Rider-Waite-Smith tarot deck in 1909. He probably discussed tarot symolism with them before they designed the cards.

The tarot's reach extends far beyond poetry. Some writers have based entire novels on the cards. In 1932, Charles Williams wrote *The Greater Trumps*—a fantasy novel that involves a magical tarot deck and a set of corresponding figurines that spin in a perpetual dance of life. In 1969, Italian author Italo Calvino used tarot decks to devise *The Castle of Crossed Destinies*, a fable about travelers who find themselves stranded in a forest, mysteriously deprived of the power of speech. They share their stories by laying out tarot cards; the book is illustrated with the cards they use.

During the late 1970s, Piers Anthony produced a three-volume set of novels set on the faraway Planet of Tarot, where the cards come to life: *God of Tarot*, *Vision of Tarot*, and *Faith of Tarot*. At least two collections of tarot-inspired short stories have been released: *Tarot Tales* and *Tarot Fantastic*, published in 1996 and 1997 respectively, both feature sixteen stories by a variety of authors—all based on the magic of the cards. And, of course, some writers use tarot cards to structure their stories. When Francesca Lia Block wrote *The Hanged Man* in 1999, she opened each chapter with a card. Lynn C. Miller followed suit with *The Fool's Journey* in 2002.

A Machine for Writing Stories

There is no better brainstorming device than a deck of tarot cards—and this book will show you how to turn those cards to your advantage. *Tarot for Writers* will guide you through every stage of a writing project, from conception to execution, and later through the rewriting and editing process. You'll even learn how tarot cards can help you market, publicize, and promote your work.

But first, you'll need to get your hands on a deck of tarot cards.

All Hands on Deck

You can use almost any tarot deck with this book, as long as it's a standard pack of seventy-eight cards. Those cards should consist of two parts: the *Major Arcana*, which is Latin for "greater secrets," and the *Minor Arcana*, or "lesser secrets." The Minor Arcana should have four suits—typically called Wands, Cups, Swords, and Pentacles—and each suit should have ten numbered cards and four Court Cards. Make sure the deck you choose has scenic illustrations on every card. If you're new to tarot, avoid decks that illustrate the suit cards of the Minor Arcana with patterned designs instead of pictures.

This book is illustrated with cards from Lo Scarabeo's *Universal Tarot* by Roberto De Angelis. It's a modern version of the Rider-Waite-Smith tarot—which will also work with this guide. The *Universal Tarot* is published in Italy by Lo Scarabeo and distributed in the United States by Llewellyn Worldwide. You can find the deck in bookstores or online at llewellyn.com.

Tips and Hints

This guide can certainly be read straight through, from beginning to end. A simple once-over will give you a comprehensive course in reading—and writing—with tarot cards. If you prefer, however, you can skip around. After all, no one expects tarot readers to keep the deck in order. Instead, they shuffle—just as you should feel free to riffle through the pages of this guide. Before long, you're bound to land on an image or idea that inspires you. You can even combine and recombine the suggestions in this book, just as you would lay out several cards in a spread. Feel free to play. After all, tarot cards had their start as a game—and they're still a lot of fun to work with. As you explore tarot as a tool for your writing, try the following techniques.

Divide the deck. If you're a beginning tarot reader, try your first few exercises with the Major Arcana cards. Just set the four suits of the Minor Arcana aside. You can work with them later, when you're comfortable with the basic principles of shuffling, spreading, and reading the cards.

Practice on real people. While you're feeling your way through the deck for the first few times, try some practice readings for friends and family members who can give you feedback.

Take a chance. Tarot cards introduce an element of chance to your work. Try to stay open to all the possibilities they offer. Let the cards fall where they may, and allow the "fickle finger of fate" to help you learn and grow as a writer.

Synchronicity and serendipity. In addition to being lovely words, synchronicity and serendipity can be a creative writer's best friends. Let meaningful coincidence and accidental discovery whisper in your ear.

Don't get too literal. Most of this book's examples and writing samples are based on traditional tarot interpretations. If you're wondering where any symbol or reference came from, check the card descriptions in part three. When you write, however, don't feel locked into a technical analysis of the cards. You can interpret the cards in any way you like; no one will be checking your work for accuracy. Unless you tell them, most of your readers won't even know that you're getting ideas from a tarot deck.

Work with a group. Tarot cards truly come alive when you use them with other people. Find a group of fellow writers so you can all brainstorm and experiment together.

Prepare to be spooked. Tarot cards have a way of revealing secrets, even when you use them casually. Don't be surprised when a random draw of the cards starts to tell your own life story. Either incorporate it in your fiction, or clarify your question and start over.

Write it down. While it might seem obvious, this is a book about writing, so you'll need to record your thoughts and observations on paper. Even though it's tempting to move quickly from one card to the next, make sure you keep a written record of all the cards you work with and the ideas they inspire.

Practice makes perfect. You'll find ideas for your writing practice and prompts throughout this book. In general, the "Writing Practice" notes present thoughtful, detailed suggestions for your work. The lists of "Writing Prompts," on the other hand, simply offer jumping-off points to get your pen moving on the page.

Write quickly. None of the practice suggestions or prompts should take long—especially on your first draft. If your writing seems to be moving in slow motion, you're thinking too hard. Relax and let your intuition—and your imagination—take control.

Create your own cards. If you plan to spend a lot of time on a story or novel, you might want to design a custom deck for the project. You can draw your own version of the cards, or assemble a collage deck from magazine photos.

How This Book Is Organized

Part I: Tarot 101. The first three chapters of this book cover everything you need to know to start working with tarot cards. You'll discover how the structure and organization of a standard tarot deck can help you interpret every card. You'll also learn some basic spreads and layouts, along with step-by-step instructions for real—and fictional—tarot readings.

Part II: The Writer's Tarot. The real heart of the book comes next, where you'll find a wide range of techniques for writing with the cards. You'll discover how tarot cards can help you with story development, character creation, plot, setting, and description.

You'll even explore ways to boost your success at editing, revising, and promoting your work.

Part III: A Writer's Guide to Tarot Cards. Finally, you'll find a handy reference guide to all seventy-eight cards in the deck, designed to jump-start your writer's imagination.

Your Future Is in the Cards

Until now, tarot cards have been the domain of mystics and seers. Once you read this book, however, you'll realize that the cards are equally at home in the hands of a writer.

After all, writers are fortunetellers, too. Writers have the mysterious ability to envision a possible future—as well as the power to describe it so clearly that it flickers into existence. Writers see the shadows of an alternate reality, and then bring it to light with the power of their words. Like the ancient oracles of Delphi, writers can peer into the human soul and communicate essential truths to an audience of readers. And writers, like tarot card readers, can seamlessly weave together the past, present, and future.

If you're ready to add tarot cards to your writing practice, all you need to do is turn the next page . . . face up.

PART I

Tarot 101

THIS SECTION COVERS EVERYTHING YOU need to know to start working with tarot cards. You'll discover how the structure of the deck can help you interpret every card. You'll also learn some basic spreads and layouts, along with instructions for real—and fictional—tarot readings.

chapter one

Tarot Basics

LE STELLE / LES ÉTOILES — XVII — THE STARS / LA ESTRELLA

DER STERN — DE STER

"Millions of miles away, a star exploded in a supernova of light and heat. Celeste looked up briefly from the lakeshore where she had been collecting her thoughts. She shuddered involuntarily, and blamed the wind."

—Writing sample based on the Star card

As a writer, you already know what it's like to hold the power of creation in your hands. With a few strokes of a pen, you can forge a universe or start a galaxy spinning in space. You can mold brave new worlds and planets, complete with mountains, plains, and seas. You can even establish nations and cities, and populate them with culture and history. Like a living god, you can determine the future of an alternate reality.

When you hold a tarot deck in your hands, you have an additional tool at your disposal—one that can make your job as a creator infinitely more rewarding. That's because the tarot is both a cosmic model of the universe and a map of the human experience. The cards reflect the physical world and the landscape of spiritual life. In other words, tarot offers a holistic view of humanity's place in the larger scheme of existence.

The cards also dovetail perfectly with other western mystery traditions, such as astrology, numerology, alchemy, and Kabbala, an ancient form of Jewish mysticism. You can find parallels between tarot and modern psychology, sociology, and anthropology, too.

Don't think the tarot is too complicated to master, though. Once you learn a few basics, you'll be ready to work with the cards—and you'll find that the tarot is flexible enough to mold and adapt to any story you have in mind.

Major Issues

Open up a new box of tarot cards, and two things will probably strike you: First, there are a lot of cards in a tarot deck—seventy-eight. Second, those tarot cards are probably bigger than playing cards you're used to handling. There are two reasons for the bulk. Individually, the large size of the cards makes it easier to spot details and symbols within each image. Collectively, the sheer number of cards makes it possible to incorporate an entire cosmology, or model of the universe, within a single deck.

A standard tarot deck has two sections: the Major Arcana, which is Latin for "greater secrets," and the Minor Arcana, or "lesser secrets." The Major Arcana cards are the big-picture cards. They're dramatic: the characters are larger than life. These are the figures you'll probably recognize from the media, or from readings you may have had in bookstores and psychic shops. You've seen the Grim Reaper, for example, in horror movies and murder mysteries. You've met the goddess of Justice standing larger than life in courthouses across the country. And you've experienced the spinning Wheel of Fortune firsthand, as you've cycled through highs and lows of personal fortune.

The figures on the Major Arcana cards are archetypes—cosmic stereotypes that serve as a framework for our understanding of the world. Archetypes transcend the limits of time and place—and for centuries, artists, writers, and musicians have used archetypal imagery to streamline their work. In classic myths and legends, archetypal heroes like Odysseus encountered archetypal villains like the one-eyed Cyclops. Today, archetypal characters like Frankenstein's monster or *Star Wars'* Luke Skywalker are the mainstays of popular books, movies, and television shows.

Technically speaking, an archetype is a primal pattern of thought—inborn, instinctive, and imprinted on every human's subconscious mind. Carl Jung, a psychotherapist and a colleague of Sigmund Freud, was the first person to popularize the theory of archetypes. He studied dreams, myths, and legends, and concluded that we're all born with an innate ability to understand archetypes. In fact, he said, we're all pre-programmed to look for archetypes in our everyday lives, because they serve as a framework for our understanding of the world. Jung's descriptions of commonly recognized archetypes include the hero, the maiden, and the wise old man. Other archetypes include the anima, the feminine aspect of a man's personality; the animus, the masculine aspect of a woman's personality; the mother, which typifies a nurturing, emotional parent; the father, a physical, protective parent; the trickster, or rebel; and the shadow, the hidden, antisocial dark side of human nature.

Every card in the Major Arcana embodies an archetypal figure.

0. **The Fool** is the happy wanderer who sees the world through the eyes of a child. Most tarot experts agree that the Fool represents each of us—naive travelers through life, off on a grand adventure, out to learn whatever experience the tarot can teach us.

1. **The Magician** is the skilled and cunning master of all he surveys. He represents an individual in control of life's tools and techniques, like those on the table in front of him. Typically, they include a cup, sword, pentacle, and wand—the four symbols of the Minor Arcana.

2. **The High Priestess** is the enigmatic keeper of spiritual secrets. Secretive and guarded, she knows the secrets life holds—but she shares them only with the wise.

3. **The Empress** is the archetypal mother who nurtures and protects all of her creation, including humankind.

4. **The Emperor** is the authoritative protector and provider who rules the known world. A father figure, he brings order out of chaos so that civilization can prosper.

5. **The Hierophant** is a symbol of traditional authority and influence. He's the head of a hierarchy, determined to maintain his religious and cultural traditions.

6. **The Lovers** embody the twin principles of opposition and attraction. While an appearance by this couple could encourage any hopeless romantic, the card also signifies a choice to be made between two equally strong desires.

7. **The Chariot** is a vehicle for forward motion and change. The young charioteer is in command of his physical and emotional drives, even when they seem to oppose each other.

8. **Strength** is the lovely lady with the heart of a lion. She gently holds the jaws of a powerful wild cat, patiently controlling a force that could otherwise eat her alive.

9. **The Hermit** is a recluse, far removed from the hustle and bustle of everyday life. He reflects on spiritual concerns, and carries the light of wisdom as a beacon for others to follow.

10. **The Wheel of Fortune** is the spinning wheel of destiny and fate. Because nothing is certain but change itself, the Wheel of Fortune reminds us all that what goes up must also come down.

11. **Justice** is both the giver and enforcer of laws. As the ultimate arbiter, she holds a two-edged sword—a reminder that fairness cuts both ways.

12. **The Hanged Man** sacrifices his comfort and passions for a time, knowing that better things will occur as a result. He is the visionary who sacrifices one life to be rewarded with another.

13. **Death** is the card of transition. Like the Grim Reaper, who clears away all that cannot survive, the card depicts the turning of a page, the completion of one chapter of life, and the exciting start of a new story.

14. **Temperance** is the archangel of balance. With dexterity and grace, Temperance demonstrates that moderation can serve as a bridge to wholeness.

15. **The Devil** is the dark and shadowy side of our existence. With tongue firmly in cheek, he demonstrates how a selfish devotion to material possessions and ill-conceived passions can tie us down and keep us from true happiness.

16. **The Tower** is a forceful clearing of pent-up energy that strikes like lightning. It's a bolt from the blue, and it can shake any overbuilt structure to its foundation.

17. **The Star** is a shining light in the darkness. Like the goddess of the night, she's the blithe spirit who offers hope, inspiration, and guidance.

18. **The Moon** is the ever-changing mirror of the sun, and a symbol of the unconscious mind. From its perch in the night sky, the moon represents secrets and mysteries that may not be understood—or even recognized.

19. **The Sun** is a symbol of consciousness and action. It's the center of the universe, and the source of heat, illumination, and life on earth.

20. **Judgement** reveals all, heralds the dawn of a new world, and stands as a reminder of the power of forgiveness.

21. **The World** depicts the never-ending, spiral dance of life. It's a card of completion and success—as well as the chance to start another round.

Minor Concerns

Set aside the twenty-two Major Arcana cards, and the remaining fifty-six cards in the deck make up the *Minor Arcana*—the "lesser secrets." These cards usually depict ordinary people going about their everyday lives.

Just as a deck of playing cards has four suits of clubs, hearts, spades, and diamonds, the Minor Arcana is divided into the four suits of wands, cups, swords, and pentacles. (Sometimes, depending on the deck, the suit names can vary. Wands may be called rods, batons, or staffs. Cups may be called chalices, and pentacles may be called coins or discs. Usually, those subtle variations don't make much difference in how the cards are read.)

Each of the tarot's four suits has numbered cards that run from ace through ten. Some people call the Minor Arcana the "pip" cards: pips are the marks that indicate the suit or numerical value of a playing card—the six hearts, for example, or seven diamonds. In some tarot decks, the Minor Arcana cards are similarly illustrated with a numbered pattern of wands, cups, swords, or pentacles. For the most part, however, modern decks portray scenic illustrations of average people engaged in commonplace activities. Sometimes they work. Sometimes they fight. Every now and then, they take time to drink, dance, or sleep.

While the images might seem random at first, there's a method to the madness. Each of the tarot's four suits represents a separate realm of life experience. Combined, they offer a complete system for contemplating human existence.

- Wands symbolize spiritual experience. Remember that wands correspond to clubs in a playing-card deck, where the three-leaf clover design is sometimes said to represent a holy trinity.

- Cups represent emotional affairs; like hearts in a deck of playing cards, they're the very picture of emotion.

- Swords illustrate thought and communication; they correspond to spades, which have a point to make.

- Pentacles embody physical, material, and financial realities; they correspond to diamonds, which are always worth money.

In fact, if you go one step further and memorize the elemental symbolism of each suit, you'll find that it's even easier to interpret the cards.

The Elements of Style

For centuries, alchemists and philosophers believed that the entire world consisted of just four elements: fire, water, air, and earth. Many believed that the human body was made up of four elements, as well. Some people, for example, have always been considered "fiery," while others can be described as "earthy." Even though modern scientists have moved into twenty-first century physics, the ancient elements still constitute a useful psychological model—as well as a handy formula for understanding the tarot. The methodology is simple: each one of the tarot's four suits corresponds to one of the four ancient elements.

The Fiery Suit of Wands

Wands are the fiery cards of spirit and initiation, which typically refer to the driving forces of work, career, and special interests that inspire passion. In most tarot decks, wands look like freshly cut branches from leafy trees; that's your cue that wands can be set on fire and burned. You might want to picture each wand as a flaming torch that can be used for light and heat, or enlightenment and inspiration.

Where there's smoke, there's fire: the wand cards can indicate that sparks are about to fly, that passions may be enflamed, and that an affair is about to heat up. Wand cards may suggest that someone is carrying a torch or burning with desire. Wand cards might even reveal that an old issue will be rekindled, or that someone is playing with fire.

The Watery World of Cups

Cups hold the watery affairs of emotional life, and they're especially well suited to issues of love and relationships. Obviously, a cup can hold water, the essence of life. For that matter, a cup can hold any liquid that has sentimental significance, such as wine or champagne. The connection to emotion is clear: We use cups to toast each other in celebration, to commune with others during religious ceremonies, and sometimes, we use cups to drown our sorrows. Because cup cards correspond to water, they serve as a reminder that the well of human emotion runs deep. Just as the human body is 75 percent water, the human psyche is driven by an overwhelmingly emotional combination of wants, needs, drives, and desires.

Don't let the water metaphors slip through your fingers. Cup cards may indicate that emotions are welling up under the surface, or that still waters run deep. One of your characters may have ice water running in her veins, or her heart may seem to be frozen. When cups are in play, a situation may be fluid, or on the rocks.

The Airy Suit of Swords

Because a sword moves through the air, the sword cards deal with the airy, heady realm of the intellect. They depict the way we think and communicate our ideas to others. The cards in the suit of swords should be near and dear to any serious writer. After all, swords cut through confusion, and they get straight to the point. They can pierce the veil of obscurity and pin down any concepts that seem unclear. The sword cards also demonstrate that language should be handled as a precision instrument. More often than not, the imagery of the sword cards demonstrates how words can be used as weapons of war. The sword cards also seem to depict the troubles we encounter when our ideas come into conflict with others, as well as the problems we impose on ourselves through negative thinking.

The imagery of the sword cards may suggest someone with a piercing glance, a rapacious wit, a sharp tongue, or a cutting remark. Elementally, swords could represent someone with his or her head in the clouds, an airhead, airy-fairy ideals, or someone who needs to come back to earth.

The Earthly Realm of Pentacles

Pentacle cards embody the tangible realities of physical and material life—the fundamental nature of earthly existence. They often represent money or property, as well as the treasures we hold dear on an emotional and spiritual level. In most tarot decks, pentacles look like coins with star-shaped designs. That pattern is symbolic of humanity's physical nature: when you stand with your arms extended and your feet apart, someone could trace the shape of a five-pointed star around your body, with one point on the top of your head, and the other four points on your outstretched hands and feet.

The suit of pentacles deals with issues that are serious and real—like real estate. The pentacle cards often refer to people who are earthy and grounded. They could suggest that a character is imbued with a certain gravity, or gravitas. The cards might even hint at grave concerns that haunt those of us on the physical plane. Don't forget the "physics" part of the physical equation, either. The pentacle cards also embody the dimensions of time and space; in readings, the pentacle cards may strongly imply that time really is money that should be well spent.

*　*　*

The elemental associations in the tarot don't stop with the four suits of the Minor Arcana. In the next section, you'll see that the court cards are linked to the four elements, too. Later, you'll discover that even the Major Arcana cards are assigned to the elements, based on their astrological correspondences.

The Four Royal Families

A traditional deck of playing cards includes three court cards in each suit: jacks, queens, and kings. The tarot maintains that tradition—but most tarot decks have *four* court cards in each suit. In addition to the kings, the queens, and the jacks—which are usually called knights in tarot—most decks also feature pages. (In some tarot decks, the court cards have other titles, like knave, prince, or princess—but those differences don't change how you'll read the cards.)

The four members of each royal family constitute an ideal family—at least on a symbolic level. They represent a father, a mother, a son, and a daughter. Some of the court cards are masculine, and some are feminine. Some are active, and some are receptive. Together, the sixteen court cards are well suited to reign over the four Minor Arcana realms of the tarot—spiritual, emotional, intellectual, and physical—and to describe the unique combinations of qualities and characteristics that make up a personality.

Pages are young and enthusiastic. They are students and messengers, children who must learn the fundamentals of the family's rule. During the Renaissance, pages were the youngest members of the royal court. It was their job to study—and to run errands, like ferrying messages from one person to another. The concept lives on in our everyday language: even now, congressmen use pages as messengers, and we can page other people when there's an important message. When pages show up in a tarot reading, they typically represent young people, students, or messages.

Knights have outgrown their roles as childlike pages: now they are young adults who must make their own way in the world. Traditionally, when pages grew to the age of knighthood, they were tested: they were expected to embark on a quest, master a challenge, and demonstrate that they were not only strong enough and smart enough to succeed, but that they also could live up to the family's heritage. Essentially, knights were rescuers and adventurers. When knights show up in a tarot reading, they may suggest that a new quest or adventure is about to begin, or that rescue is on its way.

Queens represent women who have proved themselves; they have faced their demons and shown themselves to be mature and competent adults. Each queen symbolizes an ideal woman—a perfect wife, mother, or role model. The queens also embody the qualities we associate with femininity: they are compassionate, creative, receptive, empathic, and intuitive. They know how to exert their power behind the scenes, convincing—or cajoling—others to adapt their point of view. All told, the tarot's queens can tap into their feminine qualities to safeguard, nurture, and protect their realms. When queens show up in a reading, they often suggest that a similarly caring person will be working to safeguard, nurture, and protect her realm.

Kings are protectors, providers, and seasoned, experienced leaders, who succeeded in the missions and quests they undertook as knights. They are skilled commanders who have proven themselves on the battlefield of life, and they are confident in the knowledge and wisdom they acquired during their quests. Kings are also stereotypically masculine: they are authoritarian, assertive, and alert. They can even be aggressive. They guard their kingdoms with passion and force, and they're not afraid to make executive decisions. When kings show up in a reading, they may suggest that someone is willing to mount an aggressive defense or even wage war.

The Elements of Court

The four royal families of the Minor Arcana rule over the four elements.

The suit of wands corresponds to the element of fire, so the court of wands consists of fiery personalities who rule the fiery realm of spirit and initiation. The Page of Wands usually ferries messages of a spiritual nature; in his role as a student, he might also offer a spiritual lesson. The Knight of Wands suggests a spiritual adventure or rescue. The Queen of Wands nurtures and protects the spiritual realm, and the King of Wands provides spiritual leadership and defense.

The suit of cups corresponds to the element of water, so the court of cups consists of watery personalities who concern themselves with the undercurrents of emotional life. The Page of Cups usually bears messages of an emotional nature; in his role as a student, he might also offer a lesson about understanding and controlling one's emotions. The Knight of Cups suggests an emotional adventure or rescue. The Queen of Cups nurtures and protects the world of emotions, and the King of Cups provides leadership and defense in the realm of emotions.

The suit of swords corresponds to the element of air, so the court of swords consists of heady personalities who rule the airy realm of intellect, thought, and communication. The Page of Swords usually broadcasts messages of a thoughtful nature; in his role as a student, he might also offer a lesson in logic or communication. The Knight of Swords suggests an intellectual adventure or rescue. The Queen of Swords nurtures and protects the world of ideas, and the King of Swords provides intellectual leadership and defense.

The suit of pentacles corresponds to the element of earth, so the court of pentacles consists of grounded personalities who rule the physical world. The Page of Cups usually carries messages of a physical nature; in his role as a student, he might also offer a lesson about material reality. The Knight of Cups suggests a physical adventure or rescue. The Queen of Cups nurtures and protects the physical realm, and the King of Cups provides physical leadership and defense.

By the Numbers: Beginnings, Middles, and Ends

The numbers on each card are important, too. In the Major Arcana, the numbered cards represent stations on the journey through life. That expedition begins when the Fool takes a leap of faith from the cliff, and ends when he's experienced everything the World has to offer.

The numbered cards of the Minor Arcana cards also symbolize a progression of events, laid out from one through ten: aces represent beginnings, and tens represent conclusions. The suits indicate which events are unfolding: wands symbolize spiritual experiences, cups represent emotional affairs, swords depict intellectual issues, and pentacles suggest physical realities. The Ace of Wands, for example, often symbolizes the beginning of a spiritual quest. The Five of Cups suggests the halfway point of an emotional experience, and the Ten of Swords would typically signify the conclusion of an intellectual journey.

If you can remember the significance of each suit, as well as the fact that each numbered card represents a separate step on the journey of life, you'll be able to interpret the cards without memorizing the individual meanings of all seventy-eight cards in the deck.

* * *

Now that you know how a tarot deck is constructed, you're ready for the real deal. You're ready to lay all your cards on the table and start reading . . . the next chapter.

chapter two

How to Read the Cards

IL MAGO / THE MAGICIAN
LE BATELEUR / EL MAGO
DER MAGIER / DE MAGIËR

"As the magician raised one hand over his head, lightning flashed. The tools on his table seemed to shimmer, and then they disappeared. Four tiny creatures stood in their place: a gnome, a fairy, a mermaid, and a salamander with the face of a wise old man. They were the elemental rulers of earth, air, water, and fire, and they had answered his call."

—WRITING SAMPLE BASED ON THE MAGICIAN CARD

The tarot speaks the secret language of symbols, just as writers do. Ironically, it's a language that's mostly nonverbal. Symbols, after all, are visceral. They're immediate. Most communicate at lightning speed, at a subconscious level. In fact, for most beginning tarot enthusiasts, the hardest part of reading the cards is putting symbolic images into words.

Symbolic Language

As a writer, you have a definite advantage when it comes to reading tarot cards. For one thing, you already know how to put your ideas into words. What's more, you're probably a voracious fiction reader, too, so you're well acquainted with the symbols, metaphors, and allegories that permeate the world of the cards.

Because tarot cards originated in Italy and France, most tarot symbolism is rooted in classical Western ideals, philosophy, and history. Most tarot symbolism can be traced back to Greek and Roman philosophy, Biblical principles, and democratic values and beliefs. Even so, there's plenty of room for your own understanding of the cards. After all, a symbol is simply a familiar object, gesture, or sign that suggests more than a literal meaning. An apple, for example, might represent health—or the temptation of forbidden fruit. A wild beast could symbolize someone's untamed animal nature. A hat, which covers the head, is a subtle allusion to intellect and thought.

When you use tarot cards for creative writing, you can interpret symbols on many levels. Tarot cards and symbols can represent people—protagonists, antagonists, or supporting characters. They can depict locations—rolling meadows, wooded glens, or sunny seashores. Tarot cards can inspire conflicts, plot twists, and scenes. Tarot cards can even suggest snippets of dialogues or entire conversations.

You'll find a basic guide to tarot symbolism in the back of this book. Use it as a starting point for your own interpretations, and before long, you'll also develop your own meanings for tarot symbols and images. It's all part of the fun. There's no right or wrong way to interpret tarot cards—and the creative leaps they inspire can be breathtaking.

A Room of Your Own

You've probably heard Virginia Woolf's recommendation, loosely put, that every writer needs a "room of her own." The idea is familiar to tarot readers, too, who typically establish a sacred space for their work with the cards.

You can read tarot cards anywhere you would like. A quiet room is ideal, but you can also read at a kitchen table, in a bedroom, or in your back yard. You should find a place where it's easy for you to concentrate, and where you'll be free from interruptions.

Before you begin, clear your work area of trash and any distractions that aren't related to your writing. Many tarot readers also like to clear the air in their sacred space, dispelling stale or negative energy with candles, incense, or sage. Next, delineate your reading space by laying out a spread cloth. While black silk is traditional, you might want to use fabric that matches your cards. Solid colors are best, because busy prints can distract from the images and symbols on your cards. Light a candle as a gesture of focus and attention, and picture your sacred space filled with an energizing white glow.

Prepare to Read—and Write

Most tarot readers move quickly through a series of steps designed to help them concentrate on the cards. You can use the same techniques to help clear your mind and get ready to write.

1. Cleanse. Cleansing is the process of shedding outside energy and contaminants—not only physically, but also spiritually and psychologically. Cleansing helps wash away any outside influences that could hamper your work with the cards. Start with the practical step of washing your hands with soap and water. As you do so, visualize any cosmic and psychological "dirt" running down the drain. If you aren't near a sink, you can simply imagine yourself being bathed by waves of pure white light.

2. Center. Too often, most of us spend our days scattered in a dozen different directions. We all have a long list of responsibilities, errands, and chores to complete. Those concerns, however, can interfere with your concentration; centering can help you regain control of your thoughts and emotions. The easiest way to center is through deep breathing. Sit with your feet firmly on the floor and your back straight. Take several deep breaths, consciously relaxing your body from your head to your toes. Breathe in through your nose and out through your mouth. As you exhale, consciously release any tension along with your breath. You might want to picture each one of your worries and concerns as a helium-filled balloon—then release them, one by one, and watch them float off into the sky.

3. Ground. Grounding is the process of creating a firm connection between yourself and the material world. In the physical world, an electrical current will flow through any available conductor until it reaches the ground. If you happen to be unfortunate enough to get in the way, electricity will use your body as a conductor. When you read tarot cards, you run a similar risk of getting in the way of free-flowing emotional and spiritual energy. A good grounding, however, will help energy flow through you, so you can remain relatively unaffected by other people's problems, issues, and concerns. One easy way to ground is to sit with your feet firmly on the floor. You might even want to get out of your chair and sit on the floor. Place your hands in your lap, close your eyes, and imagine that you're a tree. Send your roots down through the floor, down through layers of bedrock, and into the center of the earth. Then raise your branches up into the sky—and spend a few minutes in that alternate reality, firmly planted, with your limbs swaying gently in the breeze.

4. Shield. In today's modern world, the air is filled with electrical energy. Some of that energy is naturally occurring. Some is emitted by electrical devices and appliances. And some is transmitted, like radio waves. Each type of energy in the physical world has a counterpart in the spiritual world. If you're in the same room or the same building as other people, you will find yourself in their energy field. Some people emit their worries and concerns unconsciously, while others consciously transmit their issues to anyone within range—sometimes by shouting and slamming doors. Shielding can help you set boundaries and ensure that random outbursts from other people don't interfere with your work. One way to shield is to visualize yourself surrounded by pure, white light. Imagine that the white light works like a force field, protecting you from the distraction of other people's thoughts and emotions.

* * *

Once you've cleansed, centered, grounded, and shielded yourself, you'll be ready to write. Simply think of yourself as a clear channel for information, and be open to any thoughts or visions you get from the cards.

Question Authority

Solomon Ibn Gabirol, the Jewish philosopher, once remarked, "A wise man's question contains half the answer." Whether you're surveying the cards for a real person or a fictional character, you'll get the best answers by asking the right questions. Here are some tips for phrasing effective questions for a reading:

Be open. Try to avoid yes-or-no questions, which can be difficult to answer with tarot cards. Go for more open-ended inquiries, like "Why is my antagonist so paranoid?" or "How does 'Emily' dress?"

Be focused. Concentrate on just one issue at a time.

Be precise. Zero in on specifics, such as who, what, when, where, why, and how.

Be clear. Put your question in writing, so you can make sure it's clear. If your question is vague, the answer will probably be vague, too.

Take notes. Keep a record of the questions you ask, the cards you get in response, and your interpretations.

The Step-by-Step Reading Routine

This is where the fun really starts, with the time-honored ritual of tarot reading. Here's a step-by-step guide to the process of consulting the cards.

1. Shuffle well. You can riffle your cards poker style, drop them hand over hand, or swish them around in a slush pile. Shuffle until you think the cards are thoroughly mixed.

2. Let's deal. Pull a single card off the top of the deck, or deal several cards facedown in the spread of your choice. Alternately, you can fan the deck out, facedown, and pull cards at random for your readings.

3. Read out loud. Turn the cards face up from right to left, just as you would turn the pages in a book. As you turn over each card, say its name aloud and describe the image on the card. Note any symbolism that seems significant. If the card you're reading is from the Major Arcana, relate it to a literary archetype, recall the stories and myths associated with it, or summarize the powerful life lessons that it represents. If the card is from the Minor Arcana, summarize what you know about the suit. Wands, for example, usually relate to spiritual issues, while cups are emotional, swords are intellectual, and pentacles are physical cards. If you don't remember anything about a card, look it up in the back of this book.

4. Do the math. Look at the numbers assigned to each card. Numbers usually suggest a progression of events, so they can indicate whether an issue is in its beginning, middle, or end stage.

5. Use the power of description. Describe the characters in each card, along with their clothing, posture, expressions, and attitudes. Imagine what the characters might say if you could hear them speak. Look beyond the characters in the card, and describe the scenery that surrounds them. Look at the earth, the sky, the background, and the foreground.

6. Engage your senses. Don't stop at a visual description: use all of your senses, and describe the sounds and smells you associate with each card. Really imagine yourself inside the card.

7. Listen to the language of color. Pay attention to the color schemes in the card. What moods do the colors convey? What information does color add to a card's meaning?

8. Notice key symbols. As you study each card, you'll probably be drawn to a single image or symbol. That image might remind you of a word, a phrase, or an expression. It might trigger a related image or scene in your mind's eye. It might make you feel hot or cold, or inspire an emotional reaction. In fact, the card might activate any one of your senses: sight, sound, touch, scent, and even taste. Simply put your reaction into words. Don't worry about being right or wrong; just describe all of the impressions you get from the card.

9. Speak freely. Once you start describing the images and symbols, don't censor yourself. Go with the flow. Random words and phrases might pop into your head. Use them, even if they don't seem to make sense. That's because the cards sometimes communicate through puns and wordplay. The word "sun," for example, could sound like "son," and once you hear it or see it, the message will make perfect sense. At any rate, verbalizing your impressions will help you assess each card.

10. Clarify. If any card seems confusing or unclear, lay a clarification card over it. When you're using tarot cards to create characters and stories, you can use as many cards as you like.

Reversals of Fortune

While you can try to make sure all of your cards are pointed in the same direction when you shuffle, some cards inevitably seem to position themselves upside down when you deal—and those reversed cards can put their own spin on a reading.

Occasionally, a reversal stands the meaning of a card on its head. When the Sun card is upright, for example, it can indicate energy, warmth, renewal, and optimism. Reversed, the same card could symbolize a loss of energy. While it seems counterintuitive, however, reversals don't reverse the usual meaning of the cards; rather, most reversals simply indicate that the card's usual significance has taken a turn—for better or for worse.

When you find reversed cards in your readings, consider these possibilities:

- A reversed card could indicate a message that's blocked, either consciously or unconsciously.

- A reversed card might symbolize situations that are developing, delayed, postponed, or cancelled.

- Reversals occasionally depict a past event that's over and done, but not yet accepted or understood.

- Psychologically, reversed cards sometimes depict attitudes that are unevolved or immature, thought or energy that is either absent or excessive, or time and energy that's being wasted or misapplied.

- A reversed card could represent the shadow side of an issue—the unspoken, unacknowledged thought or observation.

- Reversals might symbolize strengths, weaknesses, gifts, or talents that are being misunderstood, misused, or misdirected.

- Reversed cards can also suggest the concept of psychological projection, an unconscious defense mechanism that propels us to attribute our own negative thoughts and feelings to other people.

- Occasionally, a reversed card simply represents a playful spirit or attitude about an issue—or a deeply private or secret activity.

- Reversed cards can even be literal. They can depict a sudden, unexpected change in direction, a surprising change in position or a new perspective, or an assumption, a concern, or a fear that's completely groundless.

* * *

Start spreading the news: now that you've experienced the reading process as a whole, you can learn some popular spreads and layouts that will streamline your search for the perfect story.

chapter three

Classic Spreads and Layouts

"The juggler had to work fast. He didn't have a permit, and the police in this town were relentless about moving guys like him along. Still, a crowd was gathering, and he could sense that they would throw a few coins his way. All he had to do was play his cards right . . . and keep his hands moving. He was working on borrowed time."

—WRITING SAMPLE BASED ON THE TWO OF PENTACLES CARD

Most tarot-card spreads—the layouts or patterns used to arrange the cards for a reading—are designed with a definite purpose in mind. Some spreads are intended to answer specific questions. Others are designed to answer general inquiries; they offer an overview of commonplace scenarios.

Spreads and layouts can be as simple or as elaborate as you like. Some layouts consist of a single card, while others incorporate ten or fifteen cards. You can even invent your own spreads, if you like.

Here are some classic spreads and layouts that can serve as a foundation for your tarot-writing practice.

One-Card Readings

Just as a journey of a thousand miles begins with a single step, your next novel can start with a single card. A single card can:

- inspire a scene or a story
- depict a location

- hint at a character's background and past
- provide a physical description
- suggest a personality trait
- offer valuable insight into a character's personality, goals, and motivation
- stimulate a dialogue
- suggest a complication, a subplot, a plot twist, or an element of surprise

Sometimes, just looking at a card can generate a rush of ideas for your work. Every now and then, however, you'll have to work a little harder for that reward. Jack London explained the process. "You can't wait for inspiration," he said. "You have to go after it with a club." The process, however, is simple. Just pick up your pen, deal a card, and start writing.

Writing Practice

Try to extract as much information as you can from a single card pulled at random from your tarot deck. Describe the card completely, or simply list the images and symbols. Here's an example of a written description of the Six of Swords:

A ferryman steers an open boat across a small body of water, from one shore to the other. The boatman is dressed in bright colors—the sunny yellow and cerulean blue of a summer day. He stands in sharp contrast to his robed and hooded passenger, who is seated and cloaked in a muted shade of earthy brown. The ferryman is young and strong; his passenger seems old, tired, and overweight. Both the sky and the water are dark; a storm is brewing. The water they've crossed is choppy, but the water in front of the ship is calm. The bottom of the boat is pierced by six long swords, which stand upright like ghostly passengers.

Even at this stage, you might find that a single card starts to trigger story ideas. It's not too early to try your hand at creative writing with the cards. Here's the start of a short story based on the same Six of Swords card:

No matter how far he traveled, David could never get away from his father.
The dead man insisted on coming along for the ride. He shadowed him through
Mexican villages and the mountains of Peru. He followed him on safari through
Africa. He popped up at the Great Wall of China, and haunted him through
castle ruins in Ireland. When he materialized on a gondola in Venice, David knew
that the time had finally come to confront the old ghost.

Two-Card Spreads

While one-card readings are enlightening and informational, most tarot readers—
and writers—find that it's more fun to work with pairs and combinations of cards. A
simple two-card spread can offer balance and contrast. Try pulling two cards when
you'd like to compare any two people, places, or things. You can think of a two-card
spread as a show of good and bad, pros and cons, do's and don'ts, light and shadow,
highs and lows, positives and negatives, or any type of conflict—even an epic battle
between good and evil.

Writing Practice

Shuffle your tarot deck and draw two cards at random to depict the best and worst
qualities of a fictional character. Here's a "Best and Worst" reading for a fictional character we'll call "Craig."

Best Quality   Worst Quality

Best Quality—The Judgement card implies forgiveness and a fresh start. Craig
is probably a forgiving soul; he readily excuses bad behavior, and he gives his
friends and associates a second, third, or fourth chance to redeem themselves.
Worst Quality—The Three of Swords seems to indicate that Craig isn't nearly so
forgiving with himself. He is plagued by paralyzing guilt and regret about his
own past mistakes.

The Power of Three

Three-card spreads are the foundation of many tarot card readings. Typically, the three cards represent the past, present, and future of a situation. Other variations include "body, mind, and spirit," or "yes, no, and maybe."

The "past, present, and future" spread is ideal when you want quick answers or a flash of insight. Simply shuffle and cut the deck into three separate piles or deal the top three cards from the deck. Read them from left to right, just as you would read words on a page: the first card represents the past, the second card depicts the present, and the third card illustrates the most likely outcome.

Writing Practice

Lay out three cards for a "past, present, and future" spread, and read them like a story. Try to find a unifying theme or pattern that connects the three cards in a single narrative thread. Here's a short three-card reading that lends itself to a simple storyline:

Past   Present   Future

Past—Ten of Cups. Once upon a time, a young couple lived in a cozy cottage
with their two children.

Present—Nine of Wands. One day, a mysterious traveler arrived at their door.
Future—Ten of Pentacles. He promised them great wealth—but first, he said,
they would have to leave their home and follow him to a distant land.

The Horseshoe Spread

The horseshoe spread is a dramatic way to explore the details of any question or situation—all in a mystical seven-card reading.

1. **Past.** The circumstances and events that led to the present situation.

2. **Present.** The current situation.

3. **Future.** The near future.

4. **Self.** The subject's attitudes, thoughts, and feelings about the situation.

5. **Friends and Family.** How other people see and affect the situation.

6. **Obstacles.** The obstacles that must be overcome.

7. **Outcome.** The most likely outcome of the current situation.

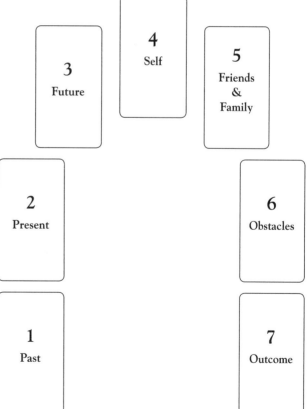

Writing Practice

When you're first learning to read tarot cards, you can practice by pulling issues and events from the news. Here's a fictional example based on a real-life news report, about a man who was found dead just five hours after his wife came home from jail. Oddly enough, the woman had actually been imprisoned for trying to kill him months earlier. When the case went to court, the man declared that he had forgiven his wife, and the judge released her on probation. Did she go home to finish the job, or was the man's death simply a bizarre twist of fate?

1. *Past—Ace of Pentacles. The woman in question, whom we'll call Josephine, tried to kill her husband by replacing his prescription medications with place-*

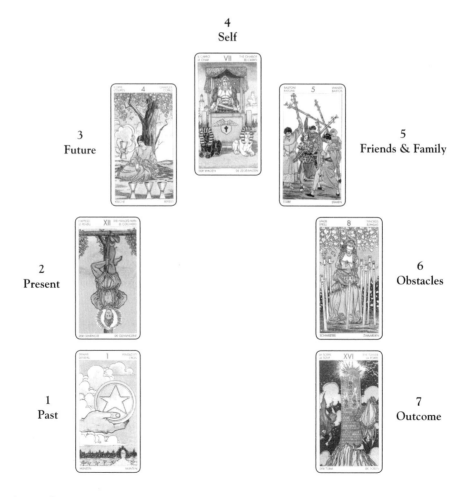

4
Self

3
Future

5
Friends & Family

2
Present

6
Obstacles

1
Past

7
Outcome

bos. The couple was struggling financially, and the husband was in poor health. The Ace of Pentacles represents new beginnings in financial and physical matters; perhaps she thought she was doing him a favor. (Oddly enough, the images does look like a hand holding a pill.)

2. *Present—Hanged Man. At the time of the news report, Josephine's probationary status was hanging on the result of an autopsy. If her husband died of natural causes, she would be off the hook.*

3. *Future—Four of Cups. When she pled guilty to attempted murder, Josephine explained that her actions stemmed in part from depression. As part of her probationary release, she was ordered to seek ongoing treatment. Now that her husband had died, she'd really need it.*

4. *Self—The Chariot. This card corresponds to the astrological sign of Cancer—a sign associated with protection and nurturing. Josephine truly does see herself as a loving, caring person.*

5. *Friends and Family—Five of Wands. This can be a card of martyrdom and self-imprisonment. No matter what the medical examiner decided, Josephine's friends and family would never agree on her role in her husband's death.*

6. *Obstacles—Eight of Swords. Believe it or not, Josephine had lived in a prison of her own making for years—and there was no release on the horizon.*

7. *Outcome—The Tower. This is the penultimate "Get out of jail free" card. Josephine was formally released from jail, and it doesn't appear that she'll be headed back there anytime soon.*

Weeks after this reading was concluded, a coroner determined that Josephine's husband died of natural causes. She was not charged with any crime or violation.

The Celtic Cross

When Arthur Edward Waite helped design the Rider-Waite-Smith tarot more than a century ago, he also introduced a corresponding spread. Since then, the Celtic Cross—pronounced "Keltic," by the way—has become a perennial favorite. Here is one popular version of the spread you can use.

1. **Significator**. The person or subject of the reading.

2. **Covering Card**. The situation surrounding the person or issue at hand.

3. **Crossing Card.**
The energy of the
moment and
current influences.

4. **Foundation Card.**
The foundation of
the situation.

5. **Recent Past.** The
last six months to
a year.

6. **Crowning Card.**
The most ideal
outcome of the
current situation.

7. **Near Future.** The
next six months
to a year.

8. **Self Image.** How
the issue looks
from the inside.

9. **Public Image.**
How others see
the issue.

	6 Highest Ideals	**11** Most Likely Outcome
	The Person	**10** Hopes and Fears
5 Recent Past	**1** **2** The Situation / **7** Near Future	
	3 Current Influences	**9** Public Image
	4 Foundation	**8** Self Image

10. **Hopes and Fears.**
Hopes and fears related to the issue.

11. **Most Likely Outcome.** The most likely outcome of the current situation.

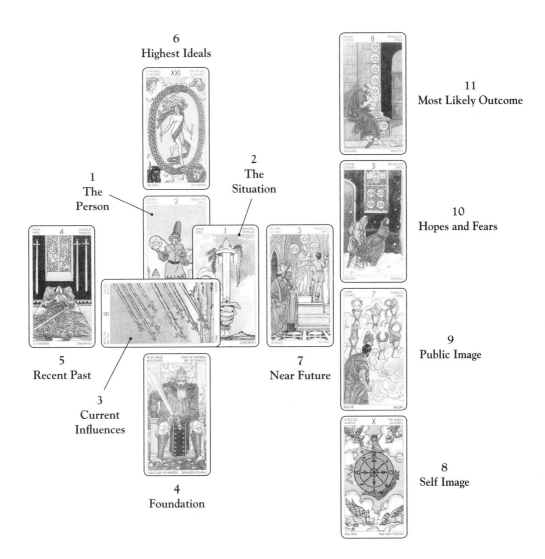

6
Highest Ideals

11
Most Likely Outcome

1
**The
Person**

2
**The
Situation**

10
Hopes and Fears

5
Recent Past

9
Public Image

3
**Current
Influences**

7
Near Future

8
Self Image

4
Foundation

Writing Practice

Lay out a Celtic Cross spread for a fictional character and diagram the reading on paper. Let your imagination run free, and record your insights. Here's a summary of a Celtic Cross reading for a fictional character we'll call "Stan."

1. *Significator/the Person—Two of Pentacles. Stan is a multitasker.*
2. *Covering Card/the Situation—Ace of Swords. He's also a recent law-school graduate.*

3. *Crossing Card/Current Influences—Eight of Wands.* Stan has been receiving a lot of strange, psychic messages lately—a fact that doesn't jibe with his scholarly and reasoned world view. The messages are urging him to pursue a new, creative path in life—but Stan thinks he might be going crazy.

4. *Foundation Card—King of Swords.* Stan's father is a lawyer, too. He expects Stan to join his practice and take over when he retires.

5. *Recent Past—Four of Swords.* Stan had been seriously ill recently. He managed to finish law school despite a year-long struggle with bone cancer.

6. *Crowning Card/Highest Ideals—The World.* Stan dreams of a long, happy life during which he'll be able to experience everything the world has to offer. He knows that a career in law promises to make him a wealthy and respected man.

7. *Near Future—Three of Pentacles.* Even so, Stan can't deny that he's being called to a career as a sculptor, not a lawyer.

8. *Self Image—Wheel of Fortune.* Despite his current doubts, Stan feels blessed and lucky to be alive.

9. *Public Image—Seven of Cups.* When Stan starts to talk of going to art school, his friends and family members think he's a little crazy. They urge him to get his head out of the clouds, take the bar exam, and follow in his father's footsteps.

10. *Hopes and Fears—Five of Pentacles.* Stan simply can't bring himself to abandon his dream, but he wonders if he's making the right decision. He fears life as a stereotypical starving artist. He also fears losing his leg—which could happen if his cancer returns.

11. *Most Likely Outcome—Eight of Pentacles.* Stan will support himself by specializing in artist's representation—part-time. And, because he's a born multitasker, he'll also apprentice himself to a professional sculptor.

Wild Cards

There will be times when you'll want more information than the cards on the table can provide. Don't panic: just add cards as you need them, at any point during a reading. Try these add-ons to any standard spread:

Wild Cards. Add a wild card to any standard spread, for information that might not have had a clear-cut place in the rest of the layout.

Clarification Cards. If you need more information to interpret an individual card, cover it with a clarification card.

Advice Cards. If you'd like to know what to do with the information in a card or a spread, deal another card for advice.

Future Cards. You don't need to conclude a reading with just one outcome card. You can add more cards, timeline-style, to see how the situation will continue to develop.

Alternate Outcomes. Deal two or three cards to see how a change in course now could change the future, too.

Hidden Cards. On occasion, you might want to peek at the "secret" cards in a tarot spread—the cards that never make it out of the deck, but stay hidden underneath. Simply pick the deck up and look at the bottom card. That's where you'll often find information that's been kept hidden or repressed.

Get Creative

Spreads are fun to invent on the fly, too. Simply pose a question and develop a custom-designed spread to help you divine the answer. Use geometric shapes that reflect the nature of your inquiry: lines, squares, circles, triangles, and stars are all popular among tarot readers.

You might be able to picture the possibilities more clearly after the next chapter, which focuses on character creation.

PART II

The Writer's Tarot

YOU'RE ABOUT TO DISCOVER HOW tarot cards can help you with every phase of story development, from character creation to satisfying conclusions. You'll even find inventive new ways to edit, revise, and promote your work.

chapter four

Character Creation

CAVALLO DI DENARI · KNIGHT OF PENTACLES
CHEVALIER DE DENIERS · CABALLO DE OROS

RITTER DER MÜNZEN · MÜNTEN RIDDER

"Nick moved slowly and methodically, gathering information with all five senses. He held his hands in front of him to get a feel for the room. He paused frequently, as he registered every sight, every sound, and every smell. Nothing escaped his practiced eye. Watching him work, Sully knew he had found the right detective for the job."

—Writing sample based on the
Knight of Pentacles card

Some writers will tell you that the best stories are character-driven. Others will tell you that plot is the most important element of a story, and that a solidly constructed storyline will keep readers hooked.

That's theory. In practice, it's almost impossible to separate well-written characters from their adventures—so we'll start with characters, because they're the easiest figures to find in a deck of tarot cards.

While tarot cards are printed on paper, the characters you'll find in the deck are more than paper dolls. They're powerful personalities that embody archetypes and symbols—and in your hands, they'll come to life with very little effort.

Cast of Characters

When you're ready to start assembling the cast of your next story, deal yourself a starting hand. Begin with one card for every character you'll need. Typically, you'll want to include:

A Protagonist. The protagonist is the hero of the story. He sees the most action—and the most conflict. The word "protagonist" is Greek; it used to mean the first actor to speak on stage in a drama. Since the protagonist is the star of the show, you'll want to develop a detailed character profile to use as a reference while you write.

An Antagonist. Every hero has an opponent—the anti-hero, or antagonist. Even though the antagonist isn't the main attraction, he or she should be just as interesting as the protagonist.

Foils. Because everyone needs a friend, many literary characters have foils—sidekicks who illustrate their strengths and weaknesses. Don Quixote's foil was Sancho Panza; Sherlock Holmes had Dr. Watson. Fred had Barney, and Lucy had Ethel. Even bad guys have henchmen, minions, and lackeys: Captain Hook had Mr. Smee, for example, and Dr. Evil had Mini-Me.

Supporting Characters. Figures who pop up throughout the course of a story without taking lead roles themselves are supporting characters. They usually have names and at least some explicatory background; you can develop character sketches for them, too.

Stock Characters. Almost every story includes stock characters, such as bartenders, taxi drivers, and mail carriers. They're usually nameless, but they step in as needed to keep the story moving.

You might be tempted to develop a proverbial cast of thousands—especially when they come so readily through tarot cards. Don't succumb. Remember to keep your minor characters locked into minor roles. Consolidate their parts when you can, and make sure that their presence adds to the story without detracting from the major players.

Writing Practice

Take a moment to pull cards for five sample characters—a protagonist, antagonist, two foils, and a supporting character. Record your impressions of each one.

A quickly shuffled deck produced these sample characters:

| Protagonist | Antagonist | Protagonist's Foil | Antagonist's Foil | Supporting Character |

Protagonist—The Sun, a heroic personality on a metaphoric white horse.

Antagonist—Knight of Cups, an insecure young man who wants to prove himself by conquering the hero.

Protagonist's Foil—King of Swords, the hero's aging father, unwilling to relinquish his throne. At some point, the hero will have to claim the kingdom for his own.

Antagonist's Foil—Two of Swords, a young woman blinded by her love for the Knight of Cups.

Supporting Character—The Star, the chatty waitress who serves up hot gossip along with hot coffee.

Personality Plus

While supporting characters may be flat, or notable for a single quality, the most memorable characters in fiction are well-rounded. They're detailed, multifaceted, and multidimensional. At the same time, flat characters tend to remain static and unchanged, but well-rounded characters are dynamic. As a story unfolds, they undergo a dramatic transformation.

Obviously, you'll want to make your characters as rounded and dynamic as you can—and the process is as simple as drawing cards from your tarot deck. As you pull new cards, you'll also pull your characters out of the two-dimensional world of cardstock and into a fictional reality that feels as real as your own. You can turn to the cards to determine almost anything about a character: physical appearance, motivation, hopes, fears, partner, family, friends, education, work experience, and hobbies. Simply shuffle your deck and start dealing.

Writing Practice

Try using the cards to answer any of the following questions. You can pull as many cards as you like to determine the answers.

- Is your character a man or a woman?
- How old is your character?
- What does your character look like?
- What does your character do for a living?
- How does your character spend his or her free time?
- Does your character have a spouse, children, or a pet?
- What are your character's hopes and dreams?
- What does your character fear most?

Here's a random draw of the cards for a fictional character we'll call "Katherine."

- *Is your character a man or a woman? Queen of Pentacles—She's a woman.*
- *How old is your character? Four of Swords—She's 44.*
- *What does your character look like? The World—She's tall, athletic, and uninhibited.*
- *What does your character do for a living? Death—She's a medical examiner.*

- *How does your character spend his or her free time? Knight of Wands—She's a horse enthusiast.*
- *Does your character have a spouse, children, or a pet? Two of Wands—She has a husband who travels internationally on business.*
- *What are your character's hopes and dreams? The Sun—She's a crusader who pursues justice on behalf of abused children. Unfortunately, she sees too many of them in her work as a medical examiner.*
- *What does your character fear most? Ace of Swords—The flaws of the legal system haunt her.*

Character Building

Fiction writers often create elaborate histories and profiles of the characters in their stories. Here are some factors you might like to consider as you transform your characters from two-dimensional concepts into full-figured fiction. Pull as many cards as you like to complete a profile for your main characters.

Physical Appearance
Age
Ethnicity
Height
Weight
Hair
Eyes
Skin
Glasses or contacts
Birthmarks, scars, tattoos
Clothing style
Health issues or concerns
General appearance
Most distinguishing feature

Personality
Sun sign
Short-term goals
Long-term goals
Strengths
Weaknesses
Phobias
Pet peeves
Gifts and talents
Bad habits
Mannerisms
Fatal flaw
Saving grace

Personal Life
Spouse
Children
Pets
Former spouses or
    romantic partners
Occupation
Annual income
Home
Car
Friends, neighbors, and
    associates
Daily routine

Personal History	Favorites
Birthdate	Clothes
Birthplace/Hometown	Shoes
Mother	Restaurants, food, and drinks
Father	Books
Siblings	Movies
Other family members	Television shows
Childhood years	Songs
Teen years	Sports
Education	Pastimes and hobbies
Work experience	Sayings and expressions
Religion	
Earliest memory	
Happiest moment	
Most embarrassing moment	

Writing Practice

Develop a character based solely on the cards, and compile a detailed character sketch. Consult as many cards as you like to develop your answers—and use your imagination, too.

Here, for example, is a physical description for "Tony," a fictional character based on the man in the Nine of Cups:

- *Age—Late 30s*
- *Ethnicity—Greek*
- *Height—5'11"*
- *Weight—260 pounds*
- *Hair—Brown, curly, shoulder-length*
- *Eyes—Brown*
- *Skin—Olive*
- *Glasses or contact lenses—No*
- *Birthmarks, scars, tattoos—No visible marks, but he does have hairy arms.*

- *Clothing style—Casual and comfortable. Tony sets himself apart just a bit by wearing jaunty hats.*
- *Health issues or concerns—Tony's weight may be a problem; he looks like he's sedentary, and he might drink too much.*
- *General appearance—Cheerful, good-natured, larger than life*
- *Most distinguishing feature—Size. Tony is a gentle giant.*

Casting Call

If you're planning a large-scale work like a novel or a screenplay, you might want to develop a full cast of characters based on the twenty-two Major Arcana cards.

Consider Shakespeare's *Romeo and Juliet*, for example: its players fall neatly into Major Arcana roles.

0. **The Fool.** The Clown, a servant of the Capulet family, isn't the hero of the story—but he does bring the hero into play. As the drama begins, Juliet's father tells the clown to invite a list of people to a banquet. The clown can't read, however, so he stops a stranger on the street to help. That stranger happens to be Romeo, a teenage Montague. When Romeo learns that the lovely young Rosaline is supposed to attend the party, he decides to go, too—in disguise, because the Montagues and Capulets are enemies.

1. **The Magician.** Mercutio, one of Romeo's best friends, is named for Mercury, the god associated with the Magician card. Like his tarot counterpart, Mercutio is a trickster who loves to pepper long speeches with puns and double entendres.

2. **The High Priestess.** The Nurse, Juliet's surrogate mother, is also her closest confidante. While she believes in love, she's practical, too. She can't believe that Juliet would sacrifice herself for a man.

3. **The Empress.** Lady Capulet, Juliet's mother, married young and gave birth to Juliet when she was just fourteen.

4. **The Emperor.** Lord Capulet, Juliet's father, is loving and generous—but he's also commanding and controlling. He demands that Juliet marry Count Paris, and he's furious when she refuses.

5. **The Hierophant.** Friar Lawrence, a Franciscan monk, secretly marries Romeo and Juliet in the hope that their union will eventually bring peace to Verona.

6. **The Lovers.** Romeo and Juliet are, of course, the star-crossed lovers whose dramatic story has thrilled audiences for centuries. They fell in love at first sight on the night of the Capulet ball.

7. **The Chariot.** The Chorus drives the narrative and directs the audience's attention to milestones along the way.

8. **Strength.** Tybalt, Juliet's hot-blooded cousin, challenges Romeo to a duel for daring to appear at the Capulets' dinner party. Later, Tybalt kills Mercutio with a low blow.

9. **The Hermit.** Rosaline, the beauty whom Romeo pursues at the beginning of the drama, never actually appears onstage. Other characters say that she has taken a vow of chastity.

10. **The Wheel of Fortune.** Friar Lawrence's friend, Friar John, is supposed to tell Romeo that Juliet is planning to stage her own death. Friar John runs into bad luck on the way to deliver the message, however, and Romeo never learns that Juliet isn't truly dead.

11. **Justice.** Escalus, the Prince of Verona, orders the Montagues and the Capulets to end their fight; he demands order in his city.

12. **The Hanged Man.** The Apothecary is the poverty-stricken druggist who sells Romeo a poisonous elixir of death, against his better judgment. He will be hanged for his crime.

13. **Death.** The unseen hand of Death looms large in this story, striking down a staggering seven characters. Tybalt kills Mercutio, Romeo kills Tybalt, and Lady Montague dies of grief. Romeo kills Paris, and then kills himself. In the end, Juliet commits suicide and the Apothecary will be executed.

14. **Temperance.** Benvolio, Romeo's cousin, tries to distract Romeo from his obsession with Rosaline, and he tries to keep the other young men in the play from fighting. His name means "goodwill" or "peacemaker."

15. **The Devil.** Gregory and Sampson are the Capulet servants who fuel an atmosphere of hatred and revenge by inciting a brawl with a series of insults and gestures of one-upmanship.

16. **The Tower.** Balthasar, Romeo's servant, brings him the devastating news that Juliet is dead. He also escorts Romeo to the dungeonlike tomb where Juliet lies.

17. **The Star.** Count Paris, a handsome, self-absorbed member of royalty, wants to marry Juliet for her wealth and social status. When Juliet's father agrees to the wedding, Paris reveals his arrogant and presumptuous nature.

18. **The Moon.** Lady Montague, Romeo's mother, is a dark and distant figure in the play. When Romeo is exiled from Verona, Lady Montague dies of grief.

19. **The Sun.** Montague, like his wife, is a relatively distant luminary. He's mated to the moon, however, and he rises to enlightenment at the end of the drama.

20. **Judgement.** The play concludes with an elegy from Prince Escalus, who also serves the role of Justice. "For never was a story of more woe," he recites, "Than this of Juliet and her Romeo."

21. **The World**. The setting of any story can be considered a character in and of itself. In *Romeo and Juliet*, the setting is the Renaissance world of Verona, Italy.

Typecasting

Another easy way to develop characters is to think of the Major Arcana cards as archetypes. Archetypes are prototypes and models—cosmic stereotypes that transcend the limits of time and place. They are the symbols and images that regularly appear in our dreams, our myths, and our stories. They're also the figurative heroes of fable and legend. In fact, many societies and cultures throughout history have shared similar stories and made use of the same symbols.

Here's an extensive list of well-known archetypes. You might want to bookmark this page, so you can refer back to this list when you're working with individual cards.

The Alchemist transforms base metals into gold, while seeking the elixir of life.

The Amazon, a strong, self-reliant, independent woman.

The Anima, the expression of a man's female or feminine qualities.

The Animus, the expression of a woman's male or masculine qualities.

The Artist, who expresses himself through his creations.

The Creator, constantly giving birth to new worlds, new life, new projects, and new ideas.

The Destroyer, who clears away anything that has outgrown or outlived its usefulness.

The Dictator, the domineering, controlling ruler.

The Divine Child, a newborn who rings in a new beginning and offers salvation.

The Earth Mother, Mother Nature, the source of all creation.

The Enchantress, a woman who charms and fascinates others during the course of her magical workings.

The Father, a leader and voice of collective authority; a provider and protector who can also be stern, powerful, and controlling.

The Fool, an innocent, inexperienced person, carefree but easily duped and misled.

The Gatekeeper or the Guardian, one who guards an entrance and controls passage from one area to the next.

The God, the ruling force of the universe.

The Goddess, the source of life.

The Guardian Angel, an agent of divine protection.

The Guide, an aide to travel in an unfamiliar area.

The Herald, a messenger who brings important news from an ambassador or a member of royalty.

The Hermit, a recluse whose solitude inspires others to join him.

The Hero or the Heroine, a ready stand-in for any mythic character who undertakes a mission or a quest; a rescuer and champion who is moral, ambitious, and highly respected.

The Innocent Child, a pure, spontaneous, trusting soul, optimistic and uncorrupted.

The Jester, a playful, fun-loving clown with just a hint of darkness.

The Judge, the enforcer of the rule of law.

The King, a sovereign ruler.

The Knight, the rescuer, the defender of the weak and innocent, and the man on a mission.

The Love Goddess, an intimate companion, but not a wife or mother.

The Lover, who burns with passion.

The Magical Helper, a supernatural being who bestows magical gifts and powers.

The Magician, who can bend the laws of nature to his own use.

The Magus, a wise man, magician, sorcerer, or astrologer.

The Maiden, innocent and inexperienced.

The Martyr, who sacrifices himself for a cause.

The Matriarch, a woman who heads an extended family.

The Medium, a psychic who channels messages from the dead to the living.

The Mentor, an older, more experienced guide, willing to share his or her knowledge and advice.

The Messenger, who carries information from place to place.

The Messiah, a savior put on earth to rescue his people.

The Midas, the successful businessperson.

The Miser, who would rather live in squalor than part with his money.

The Mother, the caring nurturer who loves her children unconditionally.

The Dark Mother, the mother who systematically destroys her children.

The Mystic, who has been initiated into the world of cosmic mystery.

The Outlaw, a rebel and a nonconformist.

The Patriarch, a man who heads an extended family.

The Poet, the Writer, or the Scribe, who transforms reality with the power of words.

The Priest, ordained to perform religious rites and qualified to make sacrificial offerings; an authority on matters of faith, with the power to speak and act on behalf of God.

The Priestess, the intuitive teacher, healer, and guardian of hidden wisdom.

The Prince or the Princess, the heir apparent to wealth and power.

The Prostitute, a woman who debases herself by selling her virtue for money.

The Psychic, who can tap into supernatural forces.

The Psychopomp, a spirit who guides the souls of the dead to the Otherworld.

The Puer Aeternus, Jung's eternal boy; a "Peter Pan" personality.

The Queen, a monarch who nurtures and protects her realm.

The Rebel, who questions his or her society and culture.

The Rescuer, who rushes into danger to save others.

The Ruler, the authority who creates a structure that others can use as a framework for their creative endeavors.

The Seeker, who searches for answers to the mysteries of life.

The Self, an individual connected to the universe and to a higher power.

The Shadow, the dark side most people project onto others, denying that it really stems from themselves.

The Shaman, someone who journeys between the physical and spiritual worlds.

The Son, a youthful rebel who simply wants to be his own person.

The Sorcerer, who harnesses the power of spirits and demons for his own ends.

The Student, who pursues learning as a vocation.

The Syzygy, Jung's "divine couple," the perfect union of masculine and feminine.

The Teacher, who passes knowledge on to successive generations.

The Thief, who steals from those who are not watchful when their guard is down.

The Trickster, who uses his power to manipulate and deceive.

The Ubermensch, the heroic superman, bigger and better than any mere mortal.

The Virgin, pure, untouched, and self-possessed.

The Visionary, who sees a brighter, better future for humanity.

The Wanderer, who leaves the known world to explore new horizons.

The Warrior, who trains and lives for battle.

The Whore, a woman who has compromised herself and her principles.

The Wise Fool, the inverse counterpart to the king; one of the privileged few with the freedom to speak truth to power, but only in the form of a joke.

The Wise Old Man, a scholar, teacher, sage, and philosopher, willing to share his knowledge, guidance, and advice.

The Witch, the dangerous woman who knows too much.

The Wizard, the wise old man who can transform reality.

The Wounded Healer, who uses the wisdom gained during his own illness and suffering to treat and help others.

Writing Practice

Decide which Major Arcana cards you associate with the most common archetypes. The Fool card, of course, falls neatly into the corresponding archetype of the Fool—but you might also see a parallel with the archetypes of the Divine Child, the Mystic, the Outlaw, or the Wounded Healer. Take some time to review the possibilities of your favorite cards.

Minor Characters

As a writer, you can find clues to your characters' personalities in Minor Arcana cards, too—especially through elemental associations. Remember that wands are the fiery cards of spiritual life, cups are the watery cards of emotional existence, swords are the airy cards of intellect and communication, and pentacles are the earthy cards of physical reality.

Writing Practice

You can gain a quick overview of a character's personality by using a four-card spread based on the four suits of the Minor Arcana—wands, cups, swords, and pentacles. The four suits correspond to spiritual, emotional, intellectual, and physical life. Here's a randomly generated spread for a fictional wife and mother we'll call "Reina."

| Spiritual Life | Emotional Life | Intellectual Life | Physical Life |

Spiritual Life—Eight of Wands. Reina processes information quickly—like the fast-moving missiles in the Eight of Wands. The card also symbolizes communication, which indicates that Reina is open and receptive to messages from the spirit world.

Emotional Life—Six of Pentacles. Reina is emotionally giving, like the generous benefactor in the card. She probably derives a lot of personal satisfaction from charity work; she might volunteer at a church, hospital, shelter, or school.

Intellectual Life—Page of Cups. Like the child in the card, Reina has not matured intellectually. She may have abandoned her formal education in order to marry and have children.

Physical Life—The Devil. This may come as a shock, because it stands in such contrast to the placid cards before it, but Reina is surprisingly sensual. She enjoys all of life's "guilty pleasures," including gourmet food, fine wine, and sex. She might even be tempted to abuse drugs and alcohol.

Bear in mind that your character's motivation and goals will blend seamlessly into your storyline—which we'll cover in chapter six. As the story unfolds, your character's conflict will become a crisis, which will lead to a climax, which will only resolve itself in the conclusion.

The Private Lives of Public Personalities

Behind the obvious personality traits of your characters are the psychological needs and desires that propel them into action.

Goals and motivation. Realistic characters have dreams and desires, just like real people. They don't move through their fictional lives in a random direction; they have goals and aspirations that guide their choices, for reasons that make sense to them. As a writer, you'll want to explore the motivations that drive your characters, and you'll need to be aware of the concrete objectives and rewards they hope to achieve.

Stakes. While we all have hopes and dreams, most of us don't face utter ruin if we fail to reach our goals. Fictional characters aren't so lucky. If they're interesting, they spend their fictional lives immersed in do-or-die moments. Their stakes are high. What's at risk for your characters if they fail to reach their goals?

Internal conflict. Most fictional characters also face nearly insurmountable obstacles in reaching their goals—and the conflict they experience is a key component of any story. Conflict can come in many forms, but the most telling conflict is often internal.

Internal conflict grows out of a character's background, personality, motivations, and goals. It's based on two opposing needs or desires. Think, for example, of the internal conflict you'll find in almost every workplace: a modern woman's desire to have both a career and a family.

Writing Practice

Pull three cards for your favorite character: the first to determine his primary goal and motivation in your story, and the second for the loss he'll face if he fails to achieve that goal. Use the third card to explore the internal conflict he'll have to conquer along the way. Here are three cards for a fictional character we'll call "George."

| Goals and Motivations | Stakes | Internal Conflict |

Goals and motivation—The Magician. George is a naturally shy person—a trait that has led, so far, to a life of loneliness and despair. He lives in a rented room, works in a cubicle, and eats by himself in a run-down diner every night. He desperately wants to learn how to talk to other people, make friends, and find someone to love.

What's at stake—Ten of Swords. George already knows what will happen if he doesn't turn his life around. He'll experience death by a thousand cuts, as each day he continues to hide from the people around him.

Internal conflict—Eight of Swords. George might not realize it, but he's actually trapped in a situation of his own making. He harbors a secret martyr complex, and his reluctance to open up to other people doesn't stem solely from a desire for self-protection. He's also a little bit selfish, a little bit superior, and a little unwilling to share his innermost self with others. He'll have to rethink his self-image to break free of his past.

Hopes and Fears

While external forces play a role in every drama, there's nothing more compelling than characters who prove to be their own worst enemy—and there's no more satisfying story than that of a character who transforms himself from the inside out. Tarot readers see a parallel drama in almost every tarot reading. In fact, tarot readers commonly choose a single card to represent two closely linked concerns: hopes and fears. That's because the two issues are virtually inseparable, like two sides of the same coin. Many people have at least one goal they fail to reach, not because it's unobtainable, but because they're afraid of change.

You can use the psychology of hope and fear to add an unforgettable element of drama to your characters. Simply use the cards to determine the one thing your character wants most in life—along with the terror that's associated with that goal. To be believable, a character's greatest fear should dovetail with the personality traits and background you're already in the process of developing.

Writing Practice

Go through your deck and pull a single card—either consciously or at random—to represent a character's innermost hopes and fears. Once you know the one thing your character dreads most, plunge him mercilessly into its depths. Force your character into the world he fears. And be ruthless: the story of an ordinary housewife doing her weekly shopping at the supermarket is dull, but the story of a housebound agoraphobic forced to find her lost child at the Mall of America could be fascinating. Here's an example based on the figure in the Four of Pentacles:

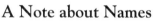

> *Senator Foreman managed to amass a huge fortune before he went into public service. Now his greatest fear is the loss of his power and prestige. When he's wrongly convicted of a sex crime, he loses his seat in Congress, his fortune, and his freedom. Will he be able to rebuild his life—and his reputation—from prison?*

A Note about Names

You can use the symbolism of the cards to inspire meaningful names for your characters. Our fictional "Senator Foreman," for example, derived his name from the "man" in the "Four" of Pentacles.

Dialogues and Interviews

Conversation can reveal a lot about a character: the words people choose provide valuable clues about their upbringing, education, and, of course, their thought processes and communication skills.

When you use tarot cards to help you develop your characters, it's surprisingly easy to get the cards to open up and tell you about themselves. You just need to use your writer's imagination. Start by choosing a card to represent your character. You can use a card you've previously selected to represent him, or you can shuffle and draw a card at random. Then imagine that the figure in the card is a real person. The figure might resemble the character you have in mind, or it might represent a dimension of your character's personality. Picture the figure in the card sitting across from you, large as life, and imagine yourself as an interviewer, conducting a simple question-and-answer session.

You can create a dialogue with any person, place, or thing—which means you can imagine a conversation with any image or symbol in a tarot card. You can talk with the defeated warriors in the Five of Swords, the black cat in the Queen of Pentacles, or the Sphinx in the Chariot card. You can even go a step further and imagine a dialogue between two characters, two cards, or two versions of the same card. All you need to do is start the conversational ball rolling—metaphorically speaking—and write down the exchange exactly as you imagine it. Write whatever pops into your mind. Follow your stream of consciousness, wherever it leads. Ask questions, get answers, and open new avenues of explanation and concentration. The process is as unlimited as your imagination.

Writing Practice

Choose a single card to represent a character in your story. Interview that character, using pen-and-paper techniques. Here are some starting ideas for your conversations with the cards:

- Ask questions. Don't start with any suppositions or expectations. Just pose a question to any card you choose, and wait for the answer.
- Begin with an open-ended question, like "Tell me about yourself," or "Describe yourself." Then write down any response that enters your mind.
- Ask follow-up questions based on the responses you receive.
- If the responses you get don't make sense, ask for clarification.

Characters often say surprising things during their tarot-card interviews. They don't hesitate to break the rules of polite conversation—or society. Here's a sample exchange with the woman in the Nine of Swords:

Q: *What are you doing up at this time of night?*
A: *I couldn't sleep. I've been having the most horrible nightmares.*
Q: *Tell me about them.*
A: *They all start simply enough. I'm home, alone, when the doorbell rings. When I try to answer the door, however, I can't get it open. I'm trapped.*
Q: *You mean the door is locked?*

A: *Locked, bolted from the outside, barricaded, bricked off . . . Night after night,*
   I realize that I'm a prisoner in my own home.
Q: *How do the nightmares end?*
A: *With me screaming. I wake myself up with my screams.*

Fill in the Blanks

You can also imagine the responses your characters might give to simple, fill-in-the-blank prompts. Try these, or invent your own:

I am the [card title or character name], and I have a secret. It is _____.

I am _____. You would never guess it by looking at me, but _____.

I am _____, and right now my biggest concern is _____.

I am _____, and I wonder about _____.

I am _____, and I want _____.

I am _____, and I feel _____.

I am _____, and I worry about _____.

I am _____, and I understand _____.

I am _____, and I always say _____.

I am _____, and I dream about _____.

I am _____, and I'm afraid of _____.

I am _____, and I hope _____.

I am _____. I often fantasize about _____.

I am _____, and my most prized possession is my _____.

I am _____. When I look back on my life, I regret _____.

I am _____, and sometimes I feel guilty about _____.

I am _____. When I look back on my life, I am proud of _____.

I am _____. The happiest day of my life was _____.

I am _____. The greatest tragedy of my life was _____.

I am _____. If I could change anything about myself, it would be _____.

I am _____, and I believe it's my destiny to _____.

I am _____, and someday, I will _____.

Compare Notes

Your work in interviewing cards isn't limited to "first-person" research with individual cards. You can get even more insight by approaching several cards for insight into your characters. Pull random cards from the deck, and ask the characters you find to describe each other. They're all neighbors, after all, and they're more intimately familiar with each other. Try asking the Queen of Swords what she thinks of your antagonist. Pull the Empress or the Queen of Cups, and get a mother's insight. Find the Hierophant, buy him a drink, and tempt him to reveal what your protagonist has confessed.

Writing Practice

Pull two cards, and ask a character in one to describe a character in the other. Here, for example, is how the warrior in the Seven of Wands might describe the wanderer in the Eight of Cups:

The Seven of   Describes the
Wands . . .   Eight of Cups

"He's a wimp. He doesn't have the courage to stay and fight when the going gets tough. He doesn't man up to do the job. He'd rather run away than face his demons. He's always talking about 'finding himself' and 'following his bliss.' One of these days he's going to wake up and realize that he broke his bliss when he left it behind, and that some guy like me has picked up the pieces and made more of those brittle shards than he ever could."

*   *   *

Character creation doesn't end with literal interpretations of the card images. You can also navigate by the stars, deriving crucial background information by combining the art of tarot with the science of astrology. Keep reading for details.

chapter five

Astrology and Tarot

"I rarely come out of my shell. It's not that I don't like to get out in the world . . . It's all the confrontation I can't stand. It seems that everywhere you go nowadays someone is waiting to snap at you. Everyone's crabby. Everyone's on edge. It's easier just to swim beneath the surface, go with the flow, and stay out of trouble—even if it means you have to hold your breath for a while."

—Writing sample based on the Moon card

It's an open secret that writers have long used astrology as a tool for character development. Writing teachers commonly suggest that their students turn to astrological texts to research the traits and characteristics of various personalities.

Tarot shares a long history with astrology—and you can use the connection to develop rich, multilayered characters. Start by referring to the artwork on the cards: many tarot artists include astrological glyphs or zodiac creatures in their illustrations. Later, you can combine that imagery with elemental correspondences and zodiac maps.

Luminary Personalities

Major Arcana correspondences. Each one of the Major Arcana cards is associated with either a sign or a planet. Check this list, and you'll see that the qualities associated with those signs and planets reinforce the traditional meaning of each card.

0. **The Fool**, who doesn't care what society thinks, is assigned to Uranus, the planet of rebellion.

1. **The Magician**, the master of banter and fast talk, is assigned to Mercury, the planet of speed and communication.

2. **The High Priestess**, the archetypal psychic, is assigned to the Moon, the luminous orb of reflection and intuition. Most depictions of the High Priestess include lunar imagery.

3. **The Empress**, wife and mother, is assigned to Venus, the planet of love and attraction. You can find the astrological glyph for Venus in many renditions of the card.

4. **The Emperor** is assigned to Aries, the sign of leadership. Look for images of the Aries ram on your Emperor card.

5. **The Hierophant**, the keeper of tradition, is assigned to Taurus, the sign of stability, luxury, and pleasure. Some Hierophant cards feature Taurus bulls or elephants.

6. **The Lovers**, who think and speak as one, are assigned to Gemini, the sign of thought and communication. The Lovers themselves are one version of the Gemini twins.

7. **The Chariot**, the protected home on wheels, is assigned to Cancer, the sign of motherhood, home, and family life. Cancer's crab carries his home on his back.

8. **Strength**, the lionesque show of force, is assigned to Leo, the sign of fatherhood, creativity, and play. Leo is also the sign of the lion.

9. **The Hermit**, the quiet leader, is assigned to Virgo, the sign of duty, responsibility, and service to others.

10. **The Wheel of Fortune** is assigned to Jupiter, the planet of luck and expansion.

11. **Justice**, the model of equality and equanimity, is assigned to Libra, the sign of balance and social grace. Libra is usually represented by a balanced set of scales.

12. **The Hanged Man**, suspended in an alternate reality, is assigned to Neptune, the planet of mysticism and illusion.

13. **Death**, the ruler of the Underworld, is assigned to Scorpio, the sign of sex, death, and other people's money. The scorpion associated with the sign has a deadly sting.

14. **Temperance**, who straddles a divide between two worlds, is assigned to Sagittarius, the sign of long-distance travel, philosophy, and higher education. The Sagittarian archer—half horse, half man—also combines two widely different experiences, while his arrow soars across long distances, on its way to new horizons.

15. **The Devil**, the embodiment of temptation, is assigned to Capricorn, the sign of business, career, and social standing.

16. **The Tower**, perpetually under attack, is assigned to Mars, the planet of energy, war, and aggression. The astrological glyph associated with Mars is a weapon-like arrow.

17. **The Star**, a glimmering light of hope and inspiration, is assigned to Aquarius, the sign of social groups and futuristic thinking.

18. **The Moon**, which rules the night, is assigned to Pisces, the sign of the mystic and subconscious.

19. **The Sun**, the sustainer of life, is assigned to the Sun, the source of energy and enlightenment.

20. **Judgement**, a representation of the last call, is assigned to Pluto, the planet of death, resurrection, and unavoidable change.

21. **The World**, our earthly home, is assigned to Saturn, the ringed planet of boundaries, limitations, and restrictions.

Minor Elements

In the Minor Arcana, each of the four suits corresponds to the fire, water, air, or earth signs of astrology.

The wands are fire cards, which correspond to the fire signs of Aries, Leo, and Sagittarius. The wand cards typically include fiery colors and a bright, sunny landscape.

The cups are water cards, which correspond to the water signs of Cancer, Scorpio, and Pisces. The cup cards usually include a lot of watery greens and blues, and they feature lakes, rivers, streams, and oceans.

The swords are air cards, which correspond to the air signs of Gemini, Libra, and Aquarius. The sword cards often incorporate a lot of yellow, which represents the element of air. The cards in the suit also feature symbols of air, such as wind-swept landscapes, clouds, and flying birds.

The pentacles are earth cards, which correspond to the earth signs of Taurus, Virgo, and Capricorn. The cards in the suit often include rich, garden-like scenes that serve as a reminder of earth's bounty.

Elemental Reference Guides

This chart summarizes the elemental associations of each sign, along with astrological symbols and imagery that you can look for in your tarot deck.

Fire Signs	Earth Signs	Air Signs	Water Signs
Aries, the Ram *Ruled by Mars* ♂	Taurus, the Bull *Ruled by Venus* ♀	Gemini, the Twins *Ruled by Mercury* ☿	Cancer, the Crab *Ruled by the Moon* ☽
Leo, the Lion *Ruled by the Sun* ☉	Virgo, the Virgin *Ruled by Mercury* ☿	Libra, the Scales *Ruled by Venus* ♀	Scorpio, the Scorpion *Ruled by Pluto* ♀ *or* ♇
Sagittarius, the Archer *Ruled by Jupiter* ♃	Capricorn, the Goat *Ruled by Saturn* ♄	Aquarius, the Water Bearer *Ruled by Uranus* ♅	Pisces, the Fish *Ruled by Neptune* ♆

The Wheel of the Zodiac

Tarot and astrology come together on the wheel of the zodiac. All of the signs and planets (and by association, tarot cards) have a place on the wheel—which is divided like a pie chart into twelve houses. Each house describes the qualities of the sign and planet that belong there.

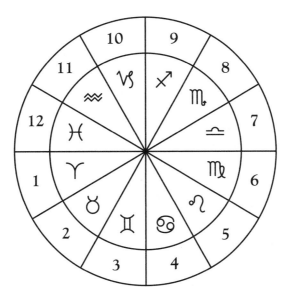

Zodiac Houses

House	Rulership	Ruling Sign	Ruling Planet
First House	Physical appearance, first impressions	Aries, the Ram; associated with leadership	Mars, planet of energy and aggression
Second House	Money, possessions, values	Taurus, the Bull; associated with property	Venus, planet of love and attraction
Third House	Communication, siblings, neighborhoods	Gemini, the Twins; associated with communication	Mercury, planet of speed and communication
Fourth House	Motherhood, home, and family	Cancer, the Crab; associated with protection and nurturing	The Moon, orb of reflection and feminine cycles
Fifth House	Fatherhood, creativity, and recreation	Leo, the Lion; associated with courage and showmanship	The Sun, source of energy and enlightenment
Sixth House	Work, duty, responsibility, service to others	Virgo, the Virgin; associated with health and cleanliness	Mercury, planet of speed and communication
Seventh House	Marriage, partnerships, intimate relationships	Libra, the Scales; associated with justice, equality, equanimity, and balance	Venus, planet of love and attraction
Eighth House	Sex, death, other people's money	Scorpio, the Scorpion; associated with the dark mysteries of life	Pluto, planet of death, resurrection, and unavoidable change
Ninth House	Philosophy, long-distance travel, higher education	Sagittarius, the Archer; associated with honesty and exploration	Jupiter, planet of luck and expansion
Tenth House	Ambition, status, career and public image	Capricorn, the Goat; associated with work and rewards	Saturn, planet of boundaries and limitations
Eleventh House	Social groups, causes, long-term thinking	Aquarius, the Water Bearer; associated with visions of a better world	Uranus, planet of independence and rebellion
Twelfth House	Psychic ability, the occult, hidden places	Pisces, the Fish; associated with intuition	Neptune, planet of mysticism and illusion

The Zodiac Spread

A tarot spread based on the zodiac wheel can help you analyze your character as an astrologer would. It's laid out exactly like a horoscope wheel: start by placing a card in the 9 o'clock position, and continue laying cards counter-clockwise.

1. **First House** *(Aries, ruled by Mars)*: Leadership, self-awareness, drive, and initiative; physical appearance and first impressions

2. **Second House** *(Taurus, ruled by Venus)*: Money, possessions, values, security, creature comforts, material resources, and treasures

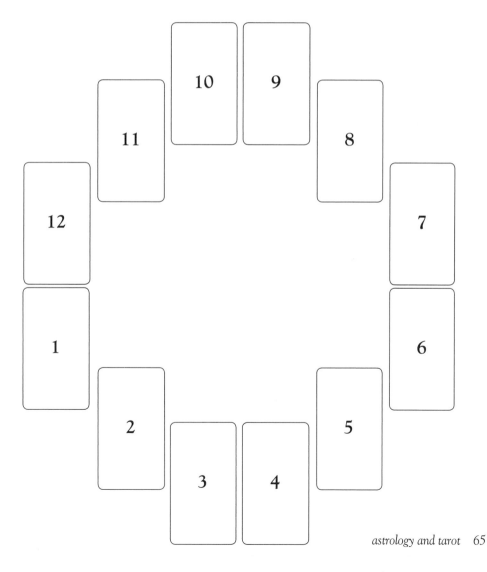

3. **Third House** (*Gemini, ruled by Mercury*): Communication skills, thought processes, logic, siblings, and neighbors

4. **Fourth House** (*Cancer, ruled by the Moon*): Mother figures, home, and family; sensitivity, emotional well-being, the ability to nurture and be nurtured, and intuition

5. **Fifth House** (*Leo, ruled by the Sun*): Creativity, self-esteem, recreation, children, and father figures

6. **Sixth House** (*Virgo, ruled by Mercury*): Work, duty, responsibility, and service to others; health, cleanliness, and attention to detail

7. **Seventh House** (*Libra, ruled by Venus*): Marriage, partnerships, intimate personal relationships; balance and social grace

8. **Eighth House** (*Scorpio, ruled by Pluto*): Sex, death, joint resources, and inheritance

9. **Ninth House** (*Sagittarius, ruled by Jupiter*): Philosophy, long-distance travel, and higher education

10. **Tenth House** (*Capricorn, ruled by Saturn*): Ambition, career goals, status, and public image

11. **Eleventh House** (*Aquarius, ruled by Uranus*): Social groups and causes, inventiveness, and long-term, futuristic thinking

12. **Twelfth House** (*Pisces, ruled by Neptune*): Psychic ability, the occult, the subconscious mind, psychological health, and hidden places

Writing Practice

Lay out a zodiac spread for one of your characters, and interpret it by comparing the images on the cards to the astrological qualities associated with each position. The card in the first position, for example, falls in the first house of the zodiac. That placement is associated with Aries, the sign of leadership, and Mars, the planet of energy and aggression.

10. Capricorn 9. Sagittarius

11. Aquarius

8. Scorpio

12. Pisces

7. Libra

1. Aries

6. Virgo

2. Taurus

5. Leo

3. Gemini   4. Cancer

Example

Here's a zodiac spread for a fictional character we'll call "Caballo," who happens to be loosely based on the figure in the Knight of Swords.

1. *Aries/Mars qualities—Page of Wands. Caballo is still young and inexperienced, but he is developing a fiery leadership style, and other people are impressed by his energy and enthusiasm.*

2. *Taurus/Venus qualities—The World. Money, property, and comfort mean the world to Caballo.*

3. *Gemini/Mercury qualities—Six of Wands. Caballo is used to being praised and rewarded for his communication skills and quick thinking.*

4. *Cancer/Moon qualities—Four of Cups. Caballo may harbor a sense of disappointment in his relationship with his mother. He does not recognize what she may have done right, but he does remember every mistake she made in his upbringing.*

5. *Leo/Sun qualities—The Star. Caballo is used to being the center of attention; he honestly believes that he is the center of the universe. It's a trait he inherited from his father.*

6. *Virgo/Mercury qualities—the Knight of Pentacles. Caballo sees himself as an adventurer and rescuer, and he's serious about his work.*

7. *Libra/Venus qualities—Ace of Wands. When it comes to close personal relationships, Caballo believes in speaking softly—but he carries a big stick.*

8. *Scorpio/Pluto qualities—Wheel of Fortune. Caballo is lucky; he has inherited great wealth. His money also makes him attractive to the opposite sex.*

9. *Sagittarius/Jupiter qualities—Ace of Swords. Caballo has a keen intelligence, which he has honed through study and travel. He loves long, philosophical debates.*

10. *Capricorn/Saturn qualities—Four of Swords. Caballo doesn't believe he has to work hard to gain power or respect. He's learned that all he has to do is get out of bed, and he achieves his goals.*

11. *Aquarius/Uranus qualities—Queen of Wands. Caballo loves to party. He has a magnetic personality that attracts both men and women, and it seems as though everyone wants to be his friend.*

12. *Pisces/Neptune qualities—Eight of Pentacles. Caballo has to work at developing his intuition.*

* * *

In the next chapter, your characters will finally get a chance to tell their stories. Get ready to take notes.

chapter six

Storylines and Plot

"For days, Brita worked on the formula, never leaving the lab. The sun rose and set, but for her, time stood still. She had seen the Intel reports. She knew that a splinter group had her formula, and they were ready to unleash it. The only thing that mattered was coming up with a cure . . . for a plague she had created herself, in the very same place where she now stood."

—WRITING SAMPLE BASED ON THE TEMPERANCE CARD

Tarot cards are an easy way to divine storyline and plot ideas. After all, tarot readers glean stories from the cards every time they give a reading. Tarot cards lend themselves naturally to outlining a sequence of fictional events, too.

The Plot's Afoot: Beginning, Middle, and End

When Aristotle taught literary theory in ancient Greece, he focused on three basic elements: beginning, middle, and end. The old philosopher's three-part plan can help you outline a timeless drama, too. Just lay a card for the beginning, middle, and end of your story. Here's an example.

Beginning   **Middle**   **End**

Beginning—Ace of Cups. A young woman finds herself pregnant and unmarried. Her boyfriend abandons her, but she refuses to relinquish the infant. Her parents died when she was a child, and now she thinks this baby is her only chance to have a family of her own.

Middle—Nine of Pentacles. The young woman goes to live with her great-aunt, an octogenarian who owns a vineyard in Northern California. Over the next few years, as she raises her child, she struggles to live up to the old woman's high expectations and strict demands. Along the way, she unexpectedly learns almost everything there is to know about winemaking—the hard way. It is a competitive and sometimes underhanded business.

End—Two of Cups. When her aunt dies, the young woman is utterly bereft; she didn't realize how frail her strong-willed mentor had become, or how much she had come to love and respect her. She inherits the vineyard, but nearly loses it to a corrupt estate attorney. At the same time, she is forced to fend off a takeover bid by the owner of a neighboring vineyard. In a surprise twist, she realizes that she has fallen in love with him—and that he has loved her since the day they met. They marry and merge their two estates.

Three-Act Structure

Aristotle's overview is a good starting point, but you can take it one step further by developing it as a three-act structure—a format favored by contemporary playwrights and screenwriters. Link the acts together with plot points—significant moments that represent turning points, plot twists, and individual points of no return. Here's a typical three-act structure:

Act I, the exposition, introduces the protagonist, the setting, and the plot. It delineates a character's ordinary world, and helps define his motivation.

Plot Point 1 marks the beginning of Act II. This is where the story really begins, with a single, clearly defined, life-changing event. It's the catalyst; it jump starts the action and propels the hero forward—either mentally or physically, because he'll either understand his mission better or find himself in another location.

Act II develops the story and the drama, as the lead character undergoes a series of challenges and overcomes obstacles that keep him from reaching his goals. On some level, those obstacles mirror his psychological issues. As the protagonist confronts each challenge, he will probably seem to fail in his mission.

Plot Point 2 represents the protagonist's greatest challenge—the key to his total success or his complete failure. Plot Point 2 leads directly to the climax, at which point the end of the story is predictable.

Act III, the resolution, resolves all of the loose ends and concludes the story.

The Three-Act Spread

The three-act structure lends itself naturally to a tarot card spread. Shuffle your deck and lay three cards side by side, to represent three acts. Then add cards to represent plot points and your story's climax. For high drama, here's an example based solely on Major Arcana cards:

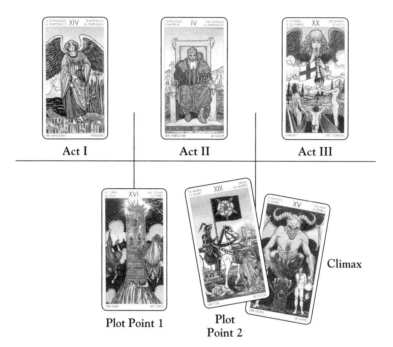

Act I   Act II   Act III

Plot Point 1   Plot Point 2   Climax

Act I—Temperance. It seems like a normal Tuesday for Malachim French, an angel who has chosen to spend a thousand years in human form. He works as a registered nurse in southern California, and he moves smoothly and efficiently through his routine morning duties at Riverside Community Hospital.

Plot Point 1—The Tower. At 10:15, however, he excuses himself and makes his way to the hospital's roof. An angelic friend has warned him that an earthquake is about to strike, and he wants to bear witness to the event. He positions himself on the helipad, and watches as the neighborhood crumbles around him.

Act II—The Emperor. Once the shaking stops, Malachim heads down to the emergency room, where he knows he'll be needed. As expected, the hospital's chief of staff has implemented the facility's disaster plan.

Plot Point 2—Death and the Devil. There's an unexpected development, however. A legion of demons have made their way up from the Underworld through fissures in the earth—and like Malachim, they're incarnating in human form. Their methods, however, are truly evil: they're taking over the dead and dying bodies of earthquake victims. In fact, one of the bodies they've appropriated is that of the hospital's chief of staff, who was grievously injured during the earthquake. In the chaos and confusion, he actually begins to murder patients who weren't seriously hurt, to make more bodies available for his minions. Only Malachim can see what's really going on—but if he reveals his true identity to anyone, he knows he'll be sent to limbo indefinitely.

Act III—Judgement. The stakes are too high. Malachim breaks his vow of silence. He confesses his secret to the hospital chaplain, and together they fight the forces of evil. While the odds are overwhelming, they work together to vanquish all of the demons—except for one. The chaplain, it seems, is a fallen angel himself—and he has a much larger objective in mind than empowering a legion of low-level demons. Just as Malachim grasps that horrifying reality, the chaplain escapes, sounding a dire warning about the future of the world. Malachim wins a reprieve from limbo to pursue the chaplain . . . in the second book of this series.

The Plot Thickens: The Structure of Your Storyline

Many adventure, mystery, suspense, and science fiction stories are plot-driven, which means the story advances more than the characters. Sometimes, the characters don't change at all; they're only along for the ride. On the other hand, a surprising number of relationship and coming-of-age stories have very little action. The characters change, but the scenery doesn't.

The best stories combine character development with an exciting plot. When the storyline is balanced, readers make an emotional connection with the characters and they enjoy the excitement of a fast-moving story. Whether your story is character- or plot-driven, you'll find that most plots follow a standard format.

The exposition introduces a story, establishes the mood, and reveals the basic facts of setting and character. Don't confuse exposition with backstory; that's something you'll want to reveal, bit by bit, throughout the course of your work. You might want to work some foreshadowing into your exposition, however, to hint at things to come.

The inciting force—also known as the problem, inciting incident, inciting event, or catalyst—triggers the action and kick-starts the story. It introduces the conflict, too, and hooks the reader.

Rising action usually includes complications, twists, and turns that completely submerge your characters—and your readers—in conflict. Throughout the course of most stories, characters should face a series of obstacles and turning points that force them to keep moving.

The climax comes when, eventually, those complications lead to crisis. At its peak, during the climax of the story, that crisis will be full-blown. Ideally, your protagonist will save the day by making full use of his or her larger-than-life qualities, including intelligence, creativity, courage, and perseverance. The victory will be even sweeter if those qualities happen to be the same traits that hurt your character in the past. Usually, the climax is the point where readers can predict the outcome. Don't trick your audience by employing a *Deus ex machina*—a ploy based on ancient Greek drama, when stagehands would lower a god to rescue the hero. A similarly contrived ending might be a convenient way to conclude a story, but it's cheating.

Falling action ensues when, after the climax, most of the action dies down, and characters start to make their way back home.

The resolution ends a story. Most stories come to a closed conclusion, which leave no questions in a reader's mind. Some resolutions, however, are open-ended, which leaves room for readers to draw their own conclusions. Some stories also end in cliffhangers, which pave the way for subsequent work in a series.

The denouement, a French term that refers to untying a knot, unravels all the complications and brings a story to its conclusion.

Freytag's Pyramid

In 1863, German novelist Gustav Freytag described the pattern he found in the storylines of successful books. He diagramed that pattern in the shape of a pyramid—a design that can serve double duty as a tarot card spread.

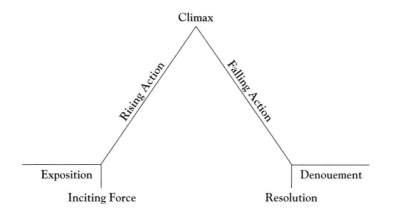

Writing Practice

Freytag's diagram makes it easy to visualize the rising and falling action of a compelling story. Try it: shuffle your deck, and develop a simple storyline based on a pyramid structure. Here's an example based on seven random cards:

Exposition—The Moon. A band of guerilla soldiers have made camp for the night.

Inciting force—The Seven of Swords. An agent provocateur sneaks into the camp and disables their communication equipment.

Rising action—The Knight of Swords. In retaliation, the group's rebel leader assassinates a high-ranking government official.

Climax—The High Priestess. He then goes into hiding, forcing his way into the countryside home of an old peasant woman. She's not surprised: she is a shamaness, and she saw his arrival in a dream. In a long series of adventures, she initiates him into the ancient mysteries of spiritual leadership.

Falling action—The Ace of Cups. She tells him about an ancient goblet, hidden in a distant jungle, that has the power to renew a long-lost utopia.

Resolution—The Eight of Cups. He embarks on a quest for the goblet—but along the way he concludes that the goblet is metaphoric, not literal.

Denouement—The Hermit. Eventually, the former guerilla becomes a shaman in his own right.

Conflicting Opinions

While the storyline may reveal the course of a story, a story itself is based on conflict—a dramatic struggle between two opposing forces. A story's conflict can be as simple as a clash of personalities, or it could detail a complicated series of interactions as characters battle over incompatible goals, actions, and desires.

There are five types of conflicts in fiction—and each one serves as a barrier that keeps characters from reaching their goals.

1. **Man versus man,** a story that pits an antagonist against a protagonist.

2. **Man versus nature,** a story that puts human life in perspective and illustrates a character's courage and strength.

3. **Man versus circumstance,** a story that forces a character to fight circumstances and fate.

4. **Man versus society,** a story that pits a single individual against society's norms, customs, expectations, values, and mores.

5. **Man versus self,** a psychological drama that teaches a character about himself.

Writing Practice

What forces are at work to keep your characters from reaching their goals? Do they face opposition from other people, or are they caught in the spinning wheel of fate? Could your character even be his or her own worst enemy?

Try using tarot cards to define a conflict for your story. First, shuffle your deck and draw two cards: one for your protagonist, and one to represent the conflict that he or she will face. Then determine how the conflict might play out in your story. Two randomly drawn cards help set the stage for this example:

Protagonist   **Conflict**

Protagonist—Knight of Cups. Young, innocent, and idealistic, Lance Knight is a young businessman who wants to heal the world with his own brand of commuter bicycles and recycled sports bottles.

Conflict—Wheel of Fortune. When he runs into financial difficulties, he tries to gamble his way clear with the "help" of an Egyptian bookie named Anwar. Before long, Lance's betting problem spins out of control.

Just for fun, try using the same two cards to develop all five types of conflict. You'll be amazed at how well the images and symbols can suggest entirely different situations.

The Writer's Celtic Cross

For more than a century, tarot enthusiasts have relied on the Celtic Cross to streamline their readings. You can readily adapt the spread for writing projects. This version, the Writer's Celtic Cross, can help you lay out a standard plot.

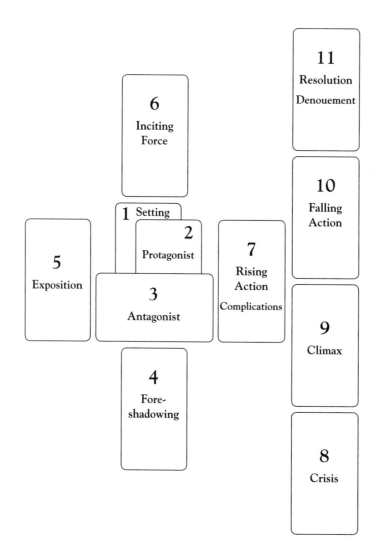

Writing Practice

Try a Writer's Celtic Cross to outline a story. You may want to put more than one card in each position, so you can delineate a series of events or add detail and dimension to your story. Feel free to use clarification cards, wild cards, and advice cards. You can also add cards, timeline style, to see how an issue will play out into the future, or play with alternate outcomes. You could even develop a tree-like matrix of related spreads, branching out from any position in the spread, to focus on individual characters, situations, or events. Here's a storyline based on ten randomly assembled cards.

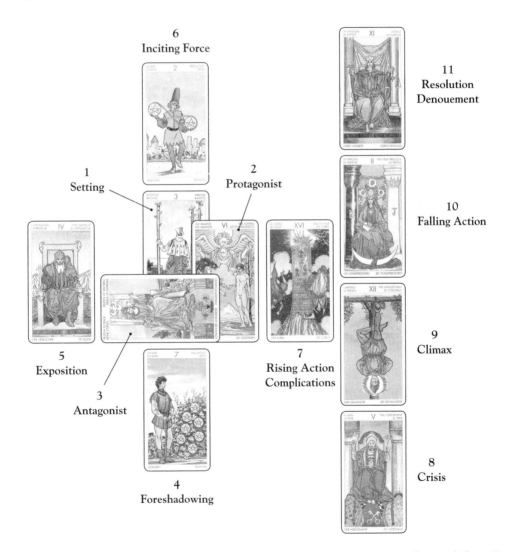

6 Inciting Force

11 Resolution Denouement

1 Setting

2 Protagonist

10 Falling Action

5 Exposition

7 Rising Action Complications

9 Climax

3 Antagonist

4 Foreshadowing

8 Crisis

1. *Setting—Three of Wands. Our story is based in a fort, a battlement, or a protected enclave of some sort. Let's look at the next card for clarification: This story will be set in the Garden of Eden.*

2. *Protagonist—The Lovers. Adam, Eve, and the Angel Raphael are the most obvious figures in the card, but let's make the serpent our protagonist. We'll call him "Samael," one of his ancient Hebrew names.*

3. *Antagonist—The Queen of Swords is sometimes said to be a divorcee. This must be Lilith, Adam's first wife.*

4. *Foreshadowing—Seven of Pentacles. Here's Adam, watching his garden grow. Little does he know that soon he'll harvest bitter fruit.*

5. *Exposition—The Emperor looks like a child's drawing of God. He'll have the first word in our story, of course, just as he does in the book of Genesis.*

6. *Inciting force—The Two of Pentacles. It looks as though Adam was trying to juggle the affections of both women at once.*

7. *Rising action/Complications—As everyone knows, Adam and Eve are thrown out of the garden. But what happens to the serpent Samael? In our story, he'll stay to claim the garden—and the abandoned Lilith—as his own.*

8. *Crisis—The Hierophant. In the new, post-Eden world, Samael assumes the guise of a spiritual authority. He begins to preach a selfish, one-sided gospel.*

9. *Climax—The Hanged Man. Samael's true identity is discovered, and he's hung upside down as a traitor to humanity.*

10. *Falling action—The High Priestess. Lilith takes Samael's place as a spiritual leader.*

11. *Resolution/Denouement—Justice. Lilith teaches a more balanced theology that combines both feminine intuition and masculine reason.*

Subplots

Subplots make long stories and novels more interesting. They're a good way to present information about supporting characters, throw complications into the main plot, or provide comic relief from a more serious storyline. Subplots can also add to the atmosphere and mood of a story.

Subplots share the same elements of a main plot, but on a smaller scale. They have a beginning, middle, and end, and they should include a crisis, a climax, and rising and falling action.

Writing Practice

To generate wild subplots at random, try a technique developed by writer Melani Weber. First, choose one card to represent your stopping point. You can deal it off the top of the deck, or you can choose a card you like. Shuffle that card back into your deck, and then start dealing new cards to incorporate into a story. Keep dealing and writing about each new card until you reach the card you originally selected—your predetermined final card—and end the story there.

Multiple Storylines

In real life, everyone has a story. In fiction, every character also has a storyline—his or her own narrative thread, which will play out alongside every other character's experience.

You might want to develop a storyline for all of your major characters, and weave them together throughout your story. On some level, each character's personal experience should parallel the larger story. Every individual's internal conflict should reflect the external conflict of your plot. The stakes should continually rise, and your characters' hopes should rise and fall with every plot twist. For your characters to be successful in overcoming both internal and external conflict, they'll need to use all the lessons they've learned during the course of the story.

As you plan your storylines and subplots, pay attention to your character arcs—the growth your characters experience over the course of the story. Explore how time and experience change them, force them to make pivotal decisions, and propel them toward their own conclusions.

Scenic Vistas

Most stories consist of a series of scenes, just like the scenes in a movie or a play. Within that series, each scene represents a single link in a storyline's chain of events. Most scenes start when characters enter a new location, and most scenes end when those characters leave. Along the way, something happens to keep the story moving. It could be action: a plane could fall out of the sky. It could be revelation, as new and surprising information comes to light: those noises in the attic aren't coming from mice. It could be a complication: a train is coming, and the car is stalled on the tracks. Every scene should introduce a surprising twist that will force the characters to respond, and compel readers to keep reading.

One easy way to construct a scene is to implement a dialectic—a three-step series of events. A dialectic opens with a single statement or position, called a thesis. As an example, let's imagine a simple story that opens with Bob, who declares his love for Betty. Bob's thesis will generate a response, or antithesis, from Betty. Let's make Bob happy, and imagine that Betty declares her love in return. Now Bob and Betty are joined together. Bob's thesis and Betty's antithesis have led to a synthesis. Their synthesis, however, doesn't freeze them in time. Instead, the synthesis they forged becomes a thesis of its own. Betty has a jealous ex-boyfriend named Buddy, and he's going to make trouble when he sees them together. In effect, Buddy is developing his own antithesis to Bob and Betty's joint thesis. Buddy will challenge Bob to a fight, and the dialectic will start over again: thesis, antithesis, synthesis.

As you build your storyline, you might want to picture a dialectic in even simpler terms. Think of the three steps as action, reaction, and movement.

The Action, Reaction, and Movement Spread

You can lay out three cards to develop a scene dialectically. Pull three cards from your tarot deck for a thesis, antithesis, and synthesis. In your mind, the cards should represent an action, a corresponding reaction, and the forward movement or change that result. Here's a three-card spread that could advance the plot of a science fiction story:

| Thesis | Antithesis | Synthesis |
| (Action) | (Reaction) | (Movement) |

Thesis/Action—The Star. After seven years alone on an interstellar transport ship, a renegade space explorer named Branch Rascal lands on the planet of Stern Ibis 17. Much to his delight, he learns that this new world is populated by unclothed Amazonian beauties.

Antithesis/Reaction—The Five of Swords. Branch doesn't announce his arrival immediately. Instead, he decides to study the women surreptitiously. His light-bending spacesuit makes him almost invisible, so he can walk among them undetected.

Synthesis/Movement—The Hermit. After familiarizing himself with their society and culture, Branch finally approaches the women in a guise he knows they can accept—that of a simple traveler from a nearby mountain range.

Storyboards

Screenwriters and moviemakers create storyboards before they start filming, so they can visualize every scene in a film. The technique lends itself to almost any style of creative writing—and it's easy to do with tarot cards. Simply arrange—and rearrange—any number of cards until they tell a story from beginning to end. Diagram their positions, and note their significance.

Writing Practice

While you're developing a storyboard, attach self-stick notes to the cards you're using. Later, you can sketch your completed storyboard and outline your thoughts in your notebook.

Variations on a Theme

When other people learn that you're writing a story or a novel, they'll probably ask the same question: What is your story about? Granted, they might want to hear a three-minute synopsis of your story—but what most people really want to know is the *theme* of your story. A theme is the underlying point of a story. Fairy tales, for example, have clearly defined themes: don't cry wolf, don't go into the woods alone, and don't share your picnic basket with strangers. Fables go so far as to include a theme in the moral of the story: slow but steady wins the race. Birds of a feather flock together. A man is known by the company he keeps.

More sophisticated authors, however, generally develop their themes in more subtle ways, through symbols, allusions, metaphors, and motifs. Their themes are thoughtful explorations of universal truths, like love, loss, and the resilience of the human spirit—the very stuff that tarot cards are made of. Like a golden thread that runs throughout your narrative, a good theme will unify the characters, the plot, and the setting. It will serve as a framework for your story, and add a layer of depth and meaning to your work.

Themes tend to develop over the course of a story, growing and changing along with the characters. From a simple series of events, a much larger concept is shaped. And as a theme reveals itself, it could surprise everyone involved—including you. Because tarot and storytelling dovetail so well, you can find any number of themes in your tarot deck. Common literary themes include:

- The hero's journey isn't always a happy one.
- It's better to have loved and lost than never to have loved at all.
- There's no place like home.
- War is hell.
- Blood is thicker than water.
- Power corrupts.

Writing Practice

Draw a card from the tarot deck to determine a theme for a practice story. If you draw the Fool, for example, you may decide that your theme will be the value of innocence, or the importance of exploration. If you draw the Empress, you might want to focus on motherhood—in both its light and shadow aspects. If you draw the Hierophant, maybe your story will explore the place of organized religion in today's society—or at any time, for that matter, past, present or future. The Ten of Pentacles could inspire a story about the legacies that parents pass on to their children.

As you continue to work with the cards, be on the lookout for images, symbols, and metaphors that will support and reinforce your theme.

* * *

If you're ready to explore story and plot at an even deeper level, try the story models in the next chapter.

chapter seven

* * * * * * *

Tarot Journeys

"The little white dog pushed and prodded me up the hill, barking and nipping at my heels all the way. The higher we climbed, the lighter I felt. By the time we reached the summit, I was practically walking on air. Sadly, I had no idea what grave danger waited for us there."

—WRITING SAMPLE
BASED ON THE FOOL CARD

There's a remarkable correspondence between the two arts of writing and tarot reading. Writers often employ a literary model called the Hero's Journey, while tarot readers typically explore a course called the Fool's Journey. The two paths parallel each other almost completely.

The Fool's Journey

Arthur Edward Waite, the occult writer who helped design the classic Rider-Waite-Smith tarot deck, said the Fool is a spirit in search of experience. How does he go about gaining that experience? By traveling through the rest of the tarot deck, in an allegorical "Fool's Journey."

To see the Fool's Journey at a glance, divide the numbered Major Arcana cards into three rows of seven cards. The three rows depict three stages of life—youth, maturity, and mastery—and each card represents a milestone along the way.

First row. As children and young adults, most of us first learn the basics of our physical existence—and like the Magician, we learn how our movements and our will can change the world around us. We also learn to relate to our parents, the Empress and the Emperor, as well as teachers and other authority figures, like the Hierophant. As we reach adolescence, we start to think of ourselves as Lovers, and we steer a course for adulthood, like the Charioteer.

Second row. As young adults, we master other life lessons: we learn to find the courage and Strength to face our fears and insecurities. We learn to stand on our own two feet, like the Hermit. We experience the cyclical nature of luck and Fortune, as well as the inevitable struggle for equanimity and Justice. Most of us also learn that we will be expected to make sacrifices like the Hanged Man, face Death in its many forms, and find balance in Temperance.

Third row. The older we get, the more complex our lessons become. We learn that we must face our demons—the dark and shadowy world of the Devil—and we experience the dramatic, unexpected shakeups of the Tower. At the same time, however, we master the bright side: we learn to find guidance and support in the luminaries of the Star, the Moon, and the Sun. We learn to forgive and find new life, through Judgement. Ultimately, we learn that the cycles—and the lessons—repeat themselves, and that every ending leads to a World of new beginnings.

Writing Practice

When you're working with specific characters in mind, try to determine where they are on their own Fool's Journey. You can shuffle the deck and pull cards until you reach a Major Arcana card, or you can consciously relate events from your character's story to the cards.

Take, for example, a fictional character who's about to get his driver's license. He is literally—and metaphorically—stepping into the role of a Charioteer.

The Hero's Journey

The Fool's Journey closely parallels the Hero's Journey—the literary model that Joseph Campbell first outlined in *The Hero with a Thousand Faces*.* It's probably no coincidence: both the Fool's Journey and the Hero's Journey spring from the well of archetypal experience.

The Hero's Journey involves several rites of passage, all of which revolve around a basic storyline of separation, initiation, transformation, and return. The model dovetails with a number of popular epics, including Star Wars and the Harry Potter series. And even though the Hero's Journey dates back to the Iliad and the Odyssey, the storyline feels fresh and familiar to modern audiences, too.

It's easy to find the Hero's Journey in the cards. On the next page, you can even see it illustrated with some representative tarot cards.

---

*Joseph Campbell, *The Hero with a Thousand Faces* (Princeton University Press; Reprint edition, 1972)

16
Master of
the Two
Worlds

1
The
Ordinary
World

15
Rescue
from
Without

2
The Call to
Adventure

14
Flight

3
Refusal of
the Call

13 The Ultimate Boon

Allies, Mentors, and Helpers 4

12 The Abyss

The Crossing of the Threshold 5

Atonement
with the
Father
11

Guardians
and
Gatekeepers
6

Woman as
Temptress
10

The
Meeting
with the
Goddess
9

The
Supreme
Ordeal
8

The Road
of Trials
7

1. The Ordinary World. As the Hero's Journey begins, the protagonist is simply going about his everyday life. In the tarot, our hero is the "everyman" of the deck—the Fool.

2. The Call to Adventure. Without warning, a herald appears, and the hero learns that there's a whole other world beyond the place he calls home. The herald could be the angel of Judgement, trumpeting the awakening call to a new life.

3. Refusal of the Call. The hero typically tries to ignore the call to adventure—or even refuse it outright. He tries to remain in place, like the figure in the Four of Cups.

4. Allies, Mentors, and Helpers. Destiny and fate won't leave him alone, and the hero meets a wide range of characters who help him overcome his reluctance to proceed. The wise old Hermit, for example, might become the hero's best advisor, or a supernatural helper like the Magician could offer magical gifts and powers.

5. The Crossing of the Threshold. Ultimately, the hero has no choice but to proceed. Like the man in the Eight of Cups, he sets out on his quest.

6. Guardians and Gatekeepers, like the High Priestess, test the hero's commitment to his calling. He'll meet them coming and going, both as he embarks on his adventure and as he tries to make a return trip home.

7. The Road of Trials. As his story picks up speed, the hero undergoes a series of challenges—each one seemingly insurmountable, but all designed to help him reach his full potential. He finds the Strength to overcome his fears. He faces his demons, slays his dragons, and outsmarts the Devil himself.

8. The Supreme Ordeal. As the story reaches its climax, the hero finds himself in "the belly of the whale"—the final line between his old life and the new world that awaits him. Either literally or metaphorically, he'll face imprisonment in the Tower—until he's freed by a bolt of lightning that destroys all of his old preconceptions and ideas. The supreme ordeal can take several forms:

9. The Meeting with the Goddess. During his journey, the hero often meets the queen of the world—like the Empress, a symbol of Mother Earth.

10. Woman as Temptress. An irresistible woman, like the Star, could tempt him to abandon his pursuits.

11. Atonement with the Father. The hero could come up against a powerful father figure, like the Emperor. The hero will have to come to terms with him before he can complete his mission.

12. The Abyss. During his ordeal, the hero will probably meet Death face to face, too. A hard-fought victory at this stage will leave him feeling reborn, with a new awareness and a new appreciation for life.

13. The Ultimate Boon or the **Theft of the Elixir.** Once he passes through his ordeal, the hero wins his reward: the elixir of life, the Holy Grail, or his own personal Ace of Cups. At that point, the hero is practically home free. At last, he realizes his ultimate truth and discovers the meaning of life.

14. Flight. Unfortunately, the hero is probably still in danger; he'll need to plan a strategic Chariot-style escape with his prize.

15. Rescue from Without. The hero could get help from the outside world: one of the allies, mentors, or sidekicks he met along the way, like the Magician, could stage a rescue or an intervention.

16. Master of the Two Worlds. By the conclusion of the story, the hero has developed a sense of mastery over both of the worlds he's experienced. Like Temperance, he can bridge the gap between ordinary life and magical ability, along with the extremes of physical and spiritual existence, inner and outer realities, and human and divine interactions. Ultimately, the hero will discover the best prize of all: wisdom.

Writing Practice

Some of the correspondences between the Hero's Journey and the cards are obvious. The Magician card, for example, naturally corresponds to the magician archetype. Other associations, however, are more personal. You may want to decide for yourself which tarot cards you would connect to each step of the Hero's Journey.

The Hero's Journey Spread

This spread offers a simplified version of the Hero's Journey that brings a hero—and a story—full circle.

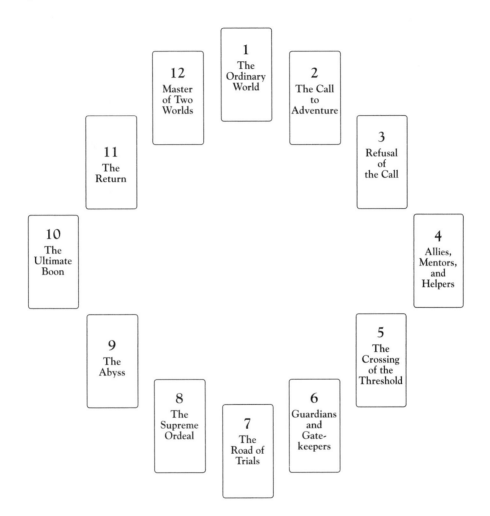

Writing Practice

Develop a story based on a random draw of the cards and the Hero's Journey spread. Here's an example inspired by the mythology of the first card, Justice.

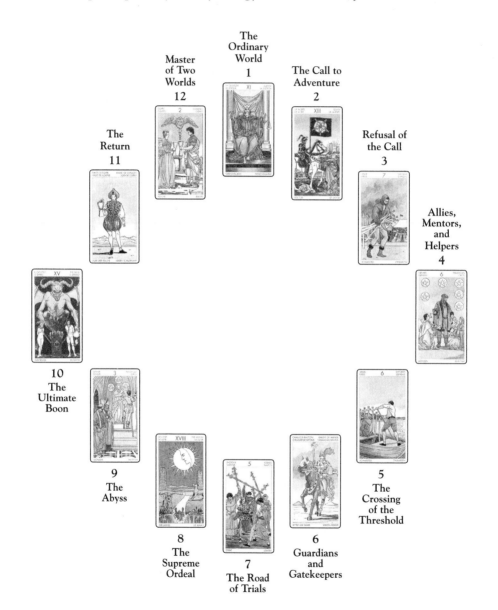

1. *The Ordinary World—Justice.* Our heroine, the goddess Themis, divides her time between her temple in Athens and her home on Mount Olympus.

2. *The Call to Adventure—Death.* As an immortal, Themis has been dispensing justice for centuries—but she's never experienced the human temptation to do wrong, or the desperation that a sense of mortality can impart. When Death passes by on his way to collect a condemned man, he invites Themis to visit his realm.

3. *Refusal of the Call—Seven of Swords.* Themis is intrigued, but she decides she's too busy to leave her post. The demands of the judicial system don't allow her any time to sneak away.

4. *Allies, Mentors, and Helpers—Six of Pentacles.* Themis happens to mention her decision to two of her assistants. They assure her that they can fill in during her absence.

5. *The Crossing of the Threshold—Six of Swords.* Themis, intrigued by the detailed account of her precepts, accepts Death's invitation, and she crosses the River Styx into the Underworld.

6. *Guardians and Gatekeepers—Knight of Wands.* A sentry at the gates of Hell blocks her entrance. It's his job to make sure that newcomers are truly dead—but as an immortal, Themis can't even prove that she has a soul. She must convince a sentry that is a friend of Death. It's such a bizarre claim that she's admitted through the door.

7. *The Road of Trials—Five of Wands.* The labyrinth passageways are not what Themis expected. All around her, a mob of confused and disoriented dead souls are elbowing their way to the various levels of Hell.

8. *The Supreme Ordeal—The Moon.* Themis breaks free of the crowd and turns into an overlooked stone doorway on her right. She finds herself in a moonlit field, where she's chased by wolves. At last she reaches a stone circle, which she recognizes as an ancient holy site.

9. *The Abyss—Three of Pentacles.* She enters the circle, and finds herself in a dark, smoky courtroom. It's packed with the souls of corrupt lawyers, judges, and jurors who now conduct meaningless mock trials in Hell. They're delighted to find themselves in a position of power over Themis; they quickly charge her with insensitivity to the human condition, and sentence her to death.

10. *The Ultimate Boon—The Devil. Themis is turned over to a demon, who mounts an iron collar around her neck and chains her to a dungeon wall. As he raises the chains, strangling her, Themis protests that she has only come to visit Death—not to experience it personally. Her pleas fall on deaf ears. As blackness surrounds her, the demon's maniacal laughter is the last thing she hears.*

11. *The Return—Page of Cups. When the darkness clears, Themis realizes with a start that she's been incarnated as a mortal, human child.*

12. *Master of Two Worlds—Two of Cups. She is thrilled to experience a lifetime of human events. When she dies again, she'll resume her throne, blessed with the experience of human existence.*

* * *

Characters and plot both need a place and time to call home—a scene for the action. The next chapter will help you explore a setting for your story.

chapter eight

Setting and Description

"After six days of rain, Jeff and Claudine feared they would find no escape from their own gloomy downpour of bitterness and resentment. They snapped at each other incessantly. They brooded in dark corners. Each blamed the other for the wet dog smell that permeated the house. At last, on the seventh day, the clouds broke and a glimmering rainbow arched across the sky. The children scampered outside, dancing for joy. As Jeff and Claudine followed, all of their troubles seemed to wash away."

— WRITING SAMPLE BASED ON THE TEN OF CUPS CARD

Every story is set in its own place and time. The setting helps establish atmosphere and mood— a mountaintop, after all, is a far different place than a coral reef. A well-chosen setting will also help your readers understand the characters, conflict, and theme of your story.

Location, Location, Location

You'll find a wide range of settings in the landscape of the cards: urban and rural, rich and poor, packed with people, or empty and barren. There's no shortage of sights and scenes to fill your story with realistic details and descriptions. Try pulling cards to represent the setting of your story, and fill in the details with imagery from other cards. It's okay to mix and match—in fact, that's an easy way to create a story world that's all your own. You can even create an entirely new universe for your characters to inhabit.

Once you've determined the overall setting for your story, you can also draw cards to illustrate

95

individual scenes. While your story might be set near the seashore, for example, your characters can move in and out of buildings, find themselves in a nearby forest, or take short trips to the city. If you're working with the Hero's Journey model, use tarot cards to distinguish between the character's ordinary world—the way things used to be—and the extraordinary, in which most of the drama takes place.

Writing Practice

Pull one card to represent the setting of your story, and then pull two more cards to add details and dimension to that setting; simply choose at least one image from each to incorporate in your story. Here are three sample cards that could help delineate the setting of a murder mystery:

Setting   **Detail 1**   **Detail 2**

Setting—Strength. The mystery will be set inside a hilltop castle.
Detail 1—Two of Swords. The castle has a moat; that's probably where the body will be discovered.
Detail 2—Ten of Pentacles. The castle also has walls with arched entryways; those are good places for suspects to linger in shadow and disappear.

Behind the Scenes

If you'd like to get a close-up view of the scenes and settings in your story, imagine yourself inside the cards, exploring the landscape and meeting personally with the characters you find there. You can use meditation and visualization as a gateway into the cards.

First, find a quiet spot where no one will interrupt you. Choose one card from the deck. Sit comfortably in a chair, with your feet firmly on the floor, and breathe deeply.

Relax and look at the card in front of you. Note every detail. As you study the card, imagine it growing larger and larger, until it stands before you like a doorway into another world. Picture yourself walking through that doorway and into the card. Look around, and describe what you see. What do you notice that you couldn't see from outside the card? What do you hear? What do you smell? What is the weather like? How does it feel to be inside the card?

You'll probably be surprised by what you'll experience. Many people who try this exercise report hearing background noise like wind, birds, and waves. You might feel the heat of the sun, or a cool breeze, or the grass underneath your feet. You might even smell flowers, grass, and salty sea air.

Writing Practice

Pull a single card, and think of it as a doorway into your story. Visualize yourself stepping through that entry point and into the scene pictured on each card. Write about the characters you meet there, along with the sounds, smells, tastes, and physical sensations you experience. Here's one example:

> *I'm in the Death card. I smell smoke, gunpowder, and blood. Death's white horse is sweating, and steam is rising from his back. The ground shakes a little when he stomps his hoof. It's dawn, and there's dew on the grass. Everything is strangely silent; there's no weeping or groaning, like I would have thought. There are no birds singing, either. The only noise I hear is the mumbled murmuring of the bishop; I think he's praying, but I can't be sure. He sounds very old and very tired. Far away in the distance, a child laughs.*

The Five Senses

You can expand your practice by collecting sensory information from a number of cards. Try pulling details and imagery from five cards—one for each of your senses. Take, for example, these impressions:

| Sight | Sound | Smell | Taste | Touch |

Sight—Knight of Swords. Clouds race across the sky, and trees bend in the wind.
Sound—Queen of Wands. A cat meows.
Smell—The Sun. The air smells hot, with a hint of dry, black dirt on the breeze.
Taste—Seven of Pentacles. The flavor of fresh tomatoes.
Touch—The Page of Wands. The ground is hard underfoot.

Description

A good description entails more than a rote account of the landscape or interior design. As you write, try to combine sensory details with emotional impact, by describing the surroundings' effects on your characters' emotions. Your settings might remind your protagonist of his childhood, or fill your antagonist with a sense of despair that dates back to a storm or a terrorist attack.

As you use tarot cards to develop your descriptions, look for symbols and motifs that can add telling information about a character's physical and psychological environments. Use strong nouns to describe those symbols, rather than weak adjectives and adverbs. Keep straight exposition to a minimum, and be judicious in your use of telling details. Let your readers connect some of the dots.

A Sense of Style

There's more to good storytelling than characters and plot, of course. The cards can also help you with pace, point of view, style, and voice.

Pace describes the rhythm and movement of a story. Whether you're working on a five-hundred word vignette or an epic novel, you'll want to maintain a comfortable pace throughout the course of your story. Think of it like running: people can sprint for short distances at a pretty good clip, but most of us don't have the endurance to maintain breakneck speed through a marathon story. Adjust the pace of your writing so readers can catch their breath occasionally. Tarot cards can help: if you shift between the Major and Minor Arcana, or cards that show a lot of action and cards that depict a more leisurely reaction to events, your story will naturally flow at a comfortable pace.

Point of View. When you choose to tell a story from your protagonist's point of view, you're telling a "first person" story. If you choose to use a first-person point of view, however, you'll need to develop a character with remarkable powers of observation—because he or she will be your reader's only source of information. If your protagonist doesn't see, hear, or know about an event, it won't have an avenue into the story. Happily, you can use tarot cards for insights and information about your first-person character's feelings, thoughts, and experiences.

Tarot cards are also a good tool if you'd like to reveal the thoughts and feelings of an entire cast, adopting a third-person point of view. You have two choices here. "Third person limited" describes stories that delve deeply into the thoughts and feelings of a single character; an outside narrator is able to reveal the details of the protagonist's personal experience, as well as report objectively about other events in the story. "Third person omniscient" puts the narrator in a godlike position; every character's most private thoughts are an open book, and they can play out in full view of the reader, too. No matter which type of third-person point of view you choose, you'll be free to reveal whatever you learn from your background tarot readings.

Style. Your subject will often determine the style you'll use in your writing. You might take a journalistic approach, or aim for a scholarly tone. Your style could be descriptive, conversational, humorous, or reserved. If you'd like to experiment with various styles, try writing from the perspectives of several cards in your deck: the Emperor tells a different story than the Hanged Man does.

Voice. Your voice should be as clear and distinct in your writing as it is in your everyday conversations. While you can obsess about vocabulary, grammar, punctuation, and syntax, the easiest way to develop your voice as a writer is simply to read your work out loud—just as you would read tarot cards for a friend or family member. If you stumble and stammer over some of the sentences, you've got some rewriting to do. If all the words flow as naturally from your lips as they did from your pen, you've found your own voice.

Figures of Speech

"To me," Truman Capote said, "the greatest pleasure of writing is not what it's about, but the music the words make." Tarot cards can help you make music with your writing, too. They can help you tap into your most artistic self, and they can help you access a universe of symbols, imagery, archetypes, and allegories.

Symbolism. Symbols come in many forms: visual images and descriptions, objects, situations, incidents, settings, speeches, and characters. The one thing that symbols have in common is that they all represent something greater than themselves. Almost everything associated with tarot is a symbol. The card images are symbolic. The numbers and words on the cards are symbolic; so are the colors. Even the structure of the deck is symbolic. A single card—and a single symbol—can actually represent several layers or dimensions of meaning. The Fool, for example, usually symbolizes youth, inexperience, and innocence. It also represents birth, rebirth, the descent of spirit into matter, and beginnings and endings.

Archetypes. Some of the most obvious symbols in tarot are the archetypal characters in every card. Archetypes are cosmic stereotypes that transcend the limits of time and place.

Allegories. Those symbols and archetypes can be arranged—and rearranged—into allegorical stories that illustrate the human experience. The Fool's Journey, for example, is an allegory.

Personification. You can also use tarot cards to personify symbols, so that plants, animals, and inanimate objects in the cards can assume human qualities. Think of the moon, for example, as a goddess. Picture a cloud as a fleeting thought. Play with the concept of water as emotion. You can breathe life into any image or symbol you spot in the cards.

Motifs. Some symbols appear throughout the deck. There are trees and birds throughout the deck, along with other topographical features like rivers, lakes, and streams. Man-made elements like pillars, walls, and castles are a common element in many cards.

Even the symbols of the four suits—wands, cups, swords, and pentacles—recur as a motif you can use in your writing. Repeated symbols, imagery, and concepts can unify your composition and help you develop your theme.

Similes and Metaphors. Occasionally, a tarot symbol can work its way into your text as figure of speech—like a simile. Your antagonist's hatred for small children, for example, could be like the three sharp lances that pierce the heart in the Three of Swords. Meanwhile, your protagonist could be experiencing life on a metaphoric level: you might spot the Two of Wands, and realize that your hero really does hold the whole world in his hands.

* * *

It's time for brainstorming. We've covered characters, storylines, setting, and description. Your head should be buzzing with story ideas and half-finished novels . . . but if you're still looking for something to write about, turn to the next chapter.

chapter nine

*

*

*

*

*

*

*

Breaking
Writer's Block

"I saw the white horse galloping across the field, and the grim-faced rider bearing down on me. The look of quiet desperation in his eyes mirrored my own. Quickly, I tried to assess my options. I could run. I could play dead. I could duck. In the end, I decided to fight back."

—WRITING SAMPLE
BASED ON THE DEATH CARD

Any blank page can be intimidating. When you have a tarot deck, however, inspiration is as close as the nearest card—and you'll be amazed at how quickly your ideas will flow.

At first, it might seem like magic. In tarot writing, the ideas seem to come from a mystical outside source and flow straight through you, from the cards on the table to the pages of your notebook. Don't be fooled, however. The real magic is happening inside your head. Tarot cards simply help you tap into your subconscious mind—the true source of archetypal images and symbolism.

Instant Inspiration

Here are some ways to use tarot cards to get words flowing onto a blank page.

Complete Description. Describe a single card in as much detail as you can muster. Start at the top and work your way down. Then describe the background and work your way toward the foreground. Notice the predominant colors as well as the mood and emotion in the card. Describe the scenery, characters, and action—and don't be surprised to find an entire story unfolding as you work.

The Language of Symbols. Choose a card and list every symbol you can see in it. Then write about what each one means to you, your characters, or your story. If you're unsure about meaning, consult a symbol dictionary.

Zoom Lens. Find one small detail in a card. Describe it completely, and then zoom out to incorporate that description in the larger picture.

Mix and Match. Pull characteristics from the figures in two or more cards and combine them to create an entirely new personality.

Timed Writing. This is a staple of many writing practices: simply set a timer for five or ten minutes, and begin. It doesn't matter what you write; your only goal is to start writing, and keep writing, until your time is up. Timed sessions force you to write without overanalyzing your efforts or doubting your talents. They also help unblock your communication skills and prime the pump for further work.

If you're doing a limited timed-writing session, you must stop when the timer goes off. If you're using the session simply as an icebreaker, however, you can keep writing for as long as you like.

You might like to start by writing,

"This card reminds me of _____."

"This image makes me feel _____."

"This card makes me think _____."

"This card makes me want _____."

Snapshot. Choose a single card, and write a one-page story that explains or describes what's happening. Try to add drama. Be imaginative.

What Happens Next. Draw a card and write about what you imagine might happen next.

Flash Fiction. Write a very short story—between 250 and 750 words—based on a single card. Try to include all the elements of a more traditional story: exposition, foreshadowing, inciting force, rising action, crisis, climax, falling action, resolution, denouement, and conclusion.

Alternate Point of View. Choose a card and write a story or poem from the point of view of any person in the card—or for that matter, any animal or even any *thing* in the illustration. Then write the same story or poem from the point of view of any other figure in the card.

Inanimate Object. Write a story from the point of view of an inanimate object in the card.

Outer Space. Write about the space that surrounds an object in the card.

Role Reversal. Write about a card that falls upright—and then turn it upside down, and write about it from a reversed perspective.

Personality Profiling. Observe strangers in public, and match them to cards that seem to suit their personalities. Alternately, find cards that remind you of people in your own life. Record your results.

Parts of Speech. Draw a card to represent a noun, an adjective, and a verb. Then write a story incorporating those three words into a story.

Patterns. Throw three, five, or seven cards onto the table in a random pattern. Then make sense of them. Explain their connections. Weave them into a story. What relationship do you see among the cards?

Seventy-eight-line Stories. Go through the tarot deck. For every card you turn up, write one sentence of a story.

House of Cards. Stack a few cards like the floors of an apartment building, and write about the tarot card characters who live on each level. Describe who they are, how they decorate, and how they get along with the neighbors.

Changing Rooms. Pull a character from one card and plop him into another card— possibly displacing the original inhabitant in the process. Or take a character from any card and put him in a completely new location: try a high school dance, a car dealership, or a grocery store. Send him into a pharmacy, a fitness club, a hotel bar, or a taxi. Experiment with your own favorite places.

Flashback. Pull a card, and write about a character as a young child.

Flash Forward. Pull a card, and write about a character as an old man or woman.

The Narrator. Choose a character from any card to narrate your story.

Keywords. Most tarot cards have titles printed on them; some even include keywords. Any words you spot on a card can free your imagination. Write an impromptu story based on a card's title or keyword. Feel free to play: you don't have to take them literally. Perhaps when you see "Stagnation," it's time to send your character to a bar called "Stag Nation." You can also develop your own keywords for each card, and use them for inspiration.

Book, Chapter, Verse. Use the title of a tarot card as the title of a story, a chapter, or a poem.

Little White Book. Almost every tarot deck comes with a little white book of abbreviated interpretations for the cards; tarot readers commonly refer to it as the "LWB." Close your eyes, open your little white book at random, and put your finger on the page. Use the phrase or sentence you land on as the opening line of a short story.

Headline News. Choose true stories from the day's news to diagram with the cards, and lay out additional cards to fictionalize the story. You might want to try a Celtic Cross spread to get an overview of the past, present, and future of a story.

Memory Game. Draw a card, and imagine that it represents a snippet of memory from your own childhood, or from the childhood of a fictional character. Embellish it, disguise it, and turn it into a story.

Aesop's Fables. Find an animal in the cards, personify it, and write a fable.

Sixth Sense. Describe a series of supernatural characters, each one stranger than the one before. Use all five senses in your descriptions.

Pros and Cons. Develop a debate between two characters—for and against an idea.

Point of View. Describe the same scene from the viewpoint of several characters.

Games for Writing Groups

As a creative tool, tarot cards truly come to life when they're used in the company of others. Any of the ideas in this guide will take on new dimensions when shared with other people, but the following ideas are designed specifically for writing groups.

Checking In. As your meeting begins, ask everyone to choose a card to describe his or her recent work. Invite participants to go through the deck and find their own cards—or draw cards at random to challenge everyone's symbolic awareness and storytelling ability.

Gifts and Talents. What specialties do your members bring to the writing table? Have everyone draw a card from the deck, facedown, and explain to the group how the card illustrates their gifts, talents, and abilities. Others in the group may add to each person's comments.

Instant Inspiration. Have each member of your group draw a card and use it as the inspiration for a paragraph, scene, or story.

Prompt Attention. On slips of paper, copy some "Writing Prompts" ideas from the card descriptions in Part III of this book—at least one for each member of the group. Pass them around, or have members pull them at random from a stack.

Assigned Writing. Ask everyone to draw a card, and then use it to develop a writing assignment for someone else. That way, a single card will get both people thinking about the elements of the story. If one writer draws the Page of Cups, for example, he could tell his partner to write about the fish jumping out of the cup.

Thirty-second Stories. You'll need a timekeeper for this game—someone with a good watch will do. Pass around a well-shuffled tarot deck and ask each player to draw a card. The first player starts telling a story based on the card in his or her hand. After exactly thirty seconds, the narrative immediately passes to the next player—mid-sentence, if necessary—who incorporates his own card into the storyline. Continue around the table until everyone has had two or three turns to add to the tale.

Casting Couch. Pick a popular movie or television show that everyone in the group has seen. Then recast it with characters from the tarot. Choose cards to represent the setting, the plot, key scenes, and important locations as well.

Reporter's Notebook. For straightforward story development, try a classic journalistic construction based on the five Ws (and an H): who, what, when, where, why, and how.

Groupthink. Shuffle the deck and deal one card to each person, then use them to write a story together. Assign one story element to each player, starting with the basics: a protagonist, antagonist, setting, and storyline. As you work together, pull additional cards to add color and details, including physical descriptions, personality quirks, secondary characters, unexpected crises, and subplots. Conclude with cards that represent the resolution of your story.

The Living Writer's Cross. If your group has at least eleven members, you can work together to create a living Writer's Cross—a life-size version of the storytelling spread pictured earlier in this guide. Draw one card to serve as the basis of a story, then shuffle the deck and deal one card each to eleven people. As the cards are dealt, have the players stand in the positions of cards in a Celtic Cross spread—and have them assume the roles and personas of the cards they hold. Each participant should offer his or her take on the story, in character, and in light of their position in the spread. Other players can ask for elaboration or choose more participants to stand in as clarification cards.

The "Castle of Crossed Destinies" Game. Novelist Italo Calvino based his book *The Castle of Crossed Destinies* on tarot cards. In his story, a group of travelers find themselves in an enchanted castle, mysteriously deprived of their ability to speak. They begin to share their life stories by laying tarot cards on a table. This game for writing groups is based on the spreads in Calvino's story:

- The first player should shuffle the deck, lay down a single card to represent the subject of the story, and then deal eight "storytelling" cards in two rows of eight cards each. As deftly as possible, that player should weave the cards into a story. The cards can be read up or down, forward or backward, or even diagonally.

- The second player follows suit. He should lay one new card to represent the subject of his story, and add two rows of new cards for the story itself.

- The design should play out like a crossword puzzle. Players can start their stories by building on the cards that are already on the table, or they can establish entirely new rows of their own. Either way, every player in the game should ultimately be working with two rows of eight cards.

- If there are a lot of players in your group, you can use fewer cards. There are no hard and fast rules in tarot—or in writing—so you can adapt the game to suit your needs.

The Castle of Crossed Destinies Spread

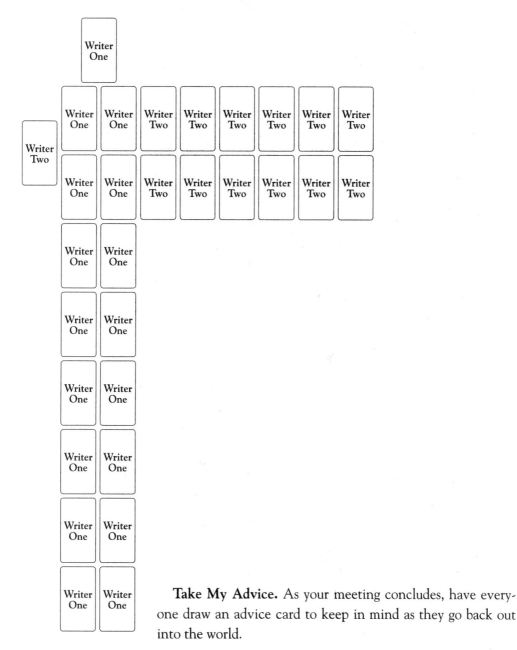

Take My Advice. As your meeting concludes, have everyone draw an advice card to keep in mind as they go back out into the world.

Poetic Inspiration

Tarot cards can inspire your poems. You can use the tarot for new ideas, or to add depth to a work in progress. You can go into a card to find symbols, metaphors, and motifs for your work. You can also use the cards to find vivid descriptions and concrete imagery. Here are some ideas for tarot-based poetry:

Swinging Singles. Base a poem on a single symbol, image, or card.

Mirror Image. Base the shape, structure, or framework of a poem on a physical image.

The Body Knows. Play with the physical impact or emotional experience of a card.

Say Again? Repeat the name of a symbol or image from a card.

Juxtaposition. Compare and contrast two cards, images, or symbols.

Set the Timer. Write for five, ten, or fifteen minutes without stopping, and then review what you've written and circle the parts you like. Turn those segments into a poem.

First Impressions. Write down the first thing you think of when you look at a card. Don't hold back; what comes to mind may or may not be directly related to the illustration.

Nonsense. Write a nonsense poem based on a card.

Mixed Metaphors. Use metaphors, and mix them any way you like.

A Little Alliteration. Use words that start with the same sound.

Be Sensible. Use all of your senses—sight, sound, smell, taste, touch—and write a poem based on the sensation in each card.

The Sound that Sounds the Sound. Imagine the sounds you would hear within a card, and use onomatopoeias—words like "pop" or "buzz"—that sound like the image they represent.

Abstract Art. Use the concrete imagery of the cards to describe an abstract concept.

Gone, but Not Forgotten. Write an *apostrophe*—a poem addressed to someone or something that is absent from your life, but might be present in the cards.

Thesis, Antithesis, Synthesis. Pull three cards, then play them against each other in a poem about opposition and unification.

Label Maker. Label objects in the card, and use those words in a poem.

Be Brief. Write a one-sentence poem based on a card, but spread that sentence out over several lines.

Write *Who* You Know. It's an old writer's maxim that you should write what you know. In this case, however, you can write about *who* you know. Pull a card to represent someone you know, then write a poem about that person based on the specific concrete imagery and symbols in the card.

Psychic Poetry. Turn a card facedown, and base a poem on your psychic impressions.

Narrative Poetry. Tell a story, in verse form, based on a card. Include the setting, characters, conflict, plot, and resolution.

Prose Poetry. Write a poem in the form of a paragraph, not lines.

Past Tense. Use a card to describe something that happened to you in the recent past.

From Bad to Verse. Write the worst poem you can muster, based on the card you dislike the most.

The Five Ws. Begin a poem with the words who, what, when, where, or why.

Big Picture. Use a Major Arcana card as the theme of a poem.

Twenty-two. Write a twenty-two-line poem about the twenty-two Major Arcana cards.

Mystery Date. Pull a card, write a poem about that card, but make the description vague, so the reader will have to guess what it's about.

Parts of Speech. Write a poem based on four cards: the first for the subject of your poem, the second for adjectives that describe your subject, a third for an action, and a fourth for the location of your subject.

It's Insignificant. Find what you believe is the least important symbol in a card, and write about it.

chapter ten

The Tarot Card Writing Coach

"Years ago, when I was young and foolish, I believed I already knew all the answers. I butted heads with everyone I met—especially my teachers. They were like tiresome old goats, bleating and blocking my path. As I advanced in years, however, something changed . . . and somewhere along the way, I turned into an old goat myself. Now I know better. These days, I don't want to block anyone's progress. I just want to show them a shortcut."

—Writing sample based on the Hermit card

Millions of people have turned to tarot cards for insights and advice into their personal lives. It probably won't surprise you to learn that the cards can serve as a source of wisdom and advice in your writing life, too.

Writing Coach

Some people call tarot cards the poor man's psychiatrist. They serve equally well as a poor man's writing coach. When you're in the process of editing and revising your story, you can consult the cards for suggestions and advice.

Try pulling cards to answer the following questions:

How does your story relate to other stories?

Are you retelling an ancient myth or legend?

What element of the story should you drop?

What early idea should you resurrect?

Which sections of your story should you delete?

Which sections should you expand?

Did you overlook any important plot points?

What details should you add?

What should be your writing goal for today?

Where can you look for additional insights, inspiration, and information?

What alternate route can you take through your story?

What are you underestimating?

What are you overemphasizing?

How can you be more comfortable as you write?

How can you be more productive?

Advisory Board. Separate the Major Arcana cards from the rest of the deck. Put them in order, from 0 through 21—the Fool to the World. Now, as quickly as you can, flip through all of the cards. Your goal should be to glean a single piece of advice from each one. Don't think too hard. Don't dwell on any one card for too long. Write down the first thing that comes to mind, even if it doesn't make sense. Alternatively, you can turn to the sixteen Court Cards for an ersatz advisory panel.

Personal Assistant. Tarot cards can help you stay on top of the routine tasks you face as a writer. For example, you ask the cards to give you friendly reminders.

What should you work on today?

Whom should you call?

Whom should you e-mail?

How should you approach that person?

What should you discuss?

What should you hold back?

Whom should you visit?

Whom should you remember?

What are you forgetting?

What should you remember?

Submissions. If you'd like to try your hand at divination, conduct a reading for your-self to:

Analyze the publication you're considering.

Assess the publisher.

Divine what type of material the publisher is looking for.

Determine how your submission will be received.

Predict how you'll feel when you hear from them.

Pitch. Use the cards to craft a thirty-second summary of your story that will interest readers, editors, and agents. Structure it like a program description from a television guide.

Critical Opinions. If you've ever put pen to paper, you've probably met your inner critic—the hissing little demon that stands behind you, always just out of sight, look-ing over your shoulder as you write. It's his voice that tries to keep you from writing, change what you write, and make you question and doubt your own experiences. With tarot cards, you can evade your inner critic—and you can even outsmart him. Choose a single card to represent your inner critic. If you choose the card on purpose, he might look like the Devil, the duplicitous Five of Swords, or the glowering Four of Pentacles. You might also choose a card at random. Consider the possibilities. What if your inner critic is the beatific Empress? Is she hiding a dark side? What might that say about you?

Now write back to your critic. Answer his criticisms, tell him where he's wrong—and let him know when he's right. After all, most critics just want someone to agree with them. You can also open a dialogue with your critic. Question, interview, and challenge him. If you like, find an advocate in the cards: simply choose a tarot card to represent your champion, and let that character duke it out with your inner critic. Imagine, for example, choosing the King of Swords as your advocate. Put them head to head, and watch the sparks fly.

Ultimately, you could decide to go all out and choose a card to represent your inner writer, struggling to achieve and accomplish. You could also choose a card to represent your most vocal critic—and a card to stand up for you as a fan and supporter. Eventu-ally, you could even find a card who would represent an inner editor, one who will come out for a gentle, supportive rewrite. The cards that play each role could change from day to day. Just watch the interaction and record the results.

Shelf Appeal. Start planning now for the day your story hits the bookstore shelves. Pull a few cards to get a sense of what the cover of your book should look like. Use the same techniques you used to develop your story to devise compelling back-cover copy for your book. And just for fun, ask a few characters from the cards to write endorsement blurbs for your cover.

Self-Determination

You might want to think of your story itself as a character in its own right, with wants, needs, goals, and objectives. Pull cards to divine the answers to the following questions:

- How do your characters feel about you as their creator?
- How do your characters want their stories to end?
- Which ending do your characters fear most?
- Why do your characters want *you* to tell their story?
- Why is this story worthwhile?
- What advice would each character give you?

Writing Practice

Human beings often spend much of their lives thinking about God, wondering about their creator, trying to visualize a god or a goddess, and imagining what their Higher Power was thinking when earth was created. When you write a story, you become the god of your own universe. All that power prompts the question: What do your creations think of you? Pull the cards to find out what your characters imagine your thought process to be. You might discover some holes in your descriptions, implausibility in your logic, or a lack of clarity in your thinking and descriptions.

> *Question (to the Seven of Cups): What do you think of the book I'm writing?*
>
> *Answer: I think there are a lot of hidden gems in your writing. There is some really good material in there. Organization seems to be a*

problem, though. Have you thought about consolidating some of the chapters? I think you could winnow it all down into seven main points.

*   *   *

In the next section, you'll learn more about individual cards, so every card in the deck can unleash a torrent of creative possibilities in your writing.

PART III

A Writer's Guide to Tarot Cards

THE FOLLOWING PAGES WILL TAKE you through all seventy-eight-cards in the deck. You'll find detailed written descriptions of the images and symbols in each card, as well as mythic, astrological, and literary correspondences that you can incorporate in your writing practice.

MAJOR ARCANA

0. The Fool

THE FOOL IS THE LEAD player in the drama of the deck. He represents every man, woman, and child fortunate enough to find themselves in the cards. He's the happy wanderer on the journey of life, and he knows that half the fun is getting there.

Some people think of the Fool as both the first and last card in the Major Arcana; like the Greek letters Alpha and Omega, the Fool represents both the beginning and the end. No matter how many times the Fool has run his course, he remains perpetually innocent and pure, unblemished and unspoiled by previous experience, untarnished by disappointment, and unscarred by experience. He's never concerned about his final destination.

In most versions of the card, the Fool is perched on the edge of a cliff—a not-so-subtle allusion to disaster and destruction. According to the mystical tradition that equates the Fool with the element of air, however, he won't fall when he steps off the cliff. Instead, he'll float, or fly, or soar on the wings of his imagination.

Of course, there's always a chance that he could be embarking on a fool's errand—a fruitless mission or an impossible task. Just to be on the safe side, he might want to look before he leaps.

In a story reading, the Fool may represent an explorer, adventurer, hero, or traveler—and in writing, almost every hero or protagonist can be represented by the Fool.

Key Symbols

Leap of Faith. Symbolically, the Fool is a metaphor for the soul, plunging from a heavenly spiritual existence into physical form on the earthly plane. In fact, Arthur Edward Waite—the original designer of the cards in this book—called the Fool "the soul in search of experience." In that sense, the Fool is willing and able to take a leap of faith, to put theory into practice, and dive headlong into a new life.

Cliffhanger. The cliff is a chasm, a void, a sharp, clear division between one world and the next.

Guard Dog. The little white dog in the card is a loyal companion, defender, and guide. He may represent instinct, a primal form of intuition; the Fool's conscience, a cautioning inner voice; or the social mores and expectations that keep our most outlandish behaviors in check.

Feathered Cap. A feather in one's cap is a sign of honor and accomplishment.

Patterns of Nature. The circles on the Fool's tunic represent spheres on the Kabbalistic Tree of Life.

Cinch It. The Fool's belt is made up of the seven planets of ancient astrology, which in turn correspond to the seven days of the week.

Red Rose. The red rose in the Fool's left hand symbolizes passion.

Walking Stick. The walking stick in his right hand represents balance.

Karmic Baggage. The bag tied to the end of the walking stick could hold memories, lessons, and souvenirs of a previous life—which makes it, in effect, karmic baggage. Some tarot readers suggest that it holds the breath of life, which the Fool uses to animate the world around him. Many say the bag contains tokens from the four suits of the Minor Arcana—a wand, a cup, a sword, and a pentacle—which will serve as the tools for his journey.

The Eye of God. The sun symbolizes light and energy from a higher power, and guidance from a consciousness that's greater than our own

A Range of Possibilities. Snow-capped mountains represent obstacles to be overcome, new heights to be scaled, new challenges, and the promise of accomplishment.

Numeric Significance. The Fool is the "zero" card. In everyday terms, most of us think of zero as a starting point, from which we count our way up—or down, into negative numbers. It's not, however, a "natural" number. We don't use zero for addition, subtraction, or any basic mathematical operations. Simply put, zero doesn't count for anything. Since zero falls outside the sequence of ordinary numbers, it is unbound by rules of order. It floats freely, outside of time and place. In fact, the concept of zero implies a sort of non-existence, a netherworld, a no man's land between presence and absence. It is the great divide, the vaporous border between two parallel universes. Zero can step into either world with equal grace and ease. It's not compelled to take its place in a lineup with other numbers. That concept dovetails nicely with the thought of the Fool, free to come and go throughout the rest of the cards at will.

Keywords

Upright: New beginnings, fresh starts, innocence, freedom, originality, eccentricity, adventure, idealism, youth, enthusiasm, excitement, daring, bravery, spontaneity, initiative, invention

Reversed: Folly, foolishness, mania, ineptitude, carelessness, stupidity, negligence, distraction, aimless, flighty, unfocused, unmotivated

Astrological Associations

The Fool is an original, a freethinker, and a rebel—which aligns him closely with the planet Uranus, the planet of innovation and revolution.

Uranus rules the eleventh house of the zodiac, where astrologers look for information about social causes and groups. Uranus also rules Aquarius, the sign of futuristic thinking.

On a related note, Aquarius is associated with the Star card.

Myth and Legend

Back during the time of kings and castles, the fool was the inverse counterpart to the king. While everything the king said was automatically the rule of law, everything the fool said was a joke. Fools had no social status, no respect, and no place in high society. They were simpletons, beggars, the objects of mockery and abuse. And yet, they were sometimes the only people who could speak truth to power, concealing their wisdom in the form of a jest. A fool could confront the king when his advisors couldn't speak freely.

The Fool has been compared to a wide range of figures from fables, myths, and stories, including Punch (of Punch and Judy fame), Renaud the Fox (a medieval European trickster), the Coyote and Raven tricksters of American Indians, the Green Man of spring, and Parsifal (or Percival), one of King Arthur's Knights of the Round Table.

The Fool could be a wise fool, a court jester, a carnival fool, the joker from a regular deck of playing cards, or a harlequin.

The Fool can also be compared to any mythic character who undertakes a mission or a quest, or a hero's journey.

Literary Archetypes

The Fool can embody any number of literary archetypes, including the divine child, the hero or the heroine, the innocent child, the jester, the outlaw, Jung's *puer aeternus* or eternal child, the seeker, the son, the wanderer, and the wise fool.

The Fool and Your Writing Practice

As a writer, you're the consummate Fool: you're always ready and willing to take a leap of faith and dive into a blank page. You're a soul in search of experience, and you're driven to discover new worlds of spirit and imagination.

You're in tune with the rebellious Uranus energy of the card, too. You're not content with the status quo. In fact, you're probably more forward thinking than most of the people you know; some of them might think you're eccentric or odd. Don't worry. Eventually, the world will catch up to you through the pages of your books.

Writing Prompts

Write about:
- the contents of a purse or a backpack
- a talking dog
- a leap of faith
- a fall from grace
- a fear of heights
- the bottom of a cliff
- an original invention
- a rebel who gets his wish
- a fool who rises to power
- the spirit of an unborn child

I. The Magician

WRITERS HAVE A SPECIAL CONNECTION to the Magician card because the archetypal figure is associated with Mercury, the messenger of the gods. He's a master communicator, and he represents all those who struggle to master the language arts of storytelling and self-expression.

The Magician never stammers; he has his patter down cold. He doesn't fumble with his props, either, because that would break the spell. His act is well rehearsed. It's so smooth, in fact, that it belies the countless hours of practice it's taken to perfect.

Like all magicians, he has also mastered the art of misdirection. The Magician always has a trick or two up his sleeve.

Generally speaking, the Magician card signifies willpower and communication. In a story reading, the Magician may represent a showman, performer, messenger, or sales person.

In some tarot decks, the Magician is sometimes called the Juggler, which hearkens back to the tradition of street performers.

Key Symbols

Roses and Lilies. The Magician stands in a garden of roses and lilies, which reminds most readers of the Old Testament's Song of Songs: "I am the Rose of Sharon, the lily of the valleys." The red roses symbolize passion, and white lilies symbolize purity.

Lemniscate. The figure eight shape above his head is a lemniscate, a symbol of infinity.

Costume Design. The Magician's white tunic represents a pure and innocent soul. That soul is shrouded in red robes, which symbolize the passionate physical nature of the human body.

Snakeskin Belt. In many versions of the card, the Magician belts his robe with an Ouroboros, a snake eating its own tail. Like the lemniscate, the Ouroboros is a symbol of eternity.

Magic Wand. The Magician's wand is pointed at both ends, to channel and refine energy along its length. Because a wand is an extension of the human body and an instrument of an individual's will, it should match his or her proportions. Some say a magician's wand should be as long as the distance from wrist to his elbow, or from elbow to fingertips.

Body Language. The Magician gathers cosmic energy with the wand in his right hand. That energy flows through him, and he uses his left hand to direct it back into the world. In the process, he uses willpower to reshape the physical world. His gesture embodies the philosophic principle "As above, so below"—the theory that our physical and material existence reflects a higher consciousness.

Tools of the Trade. The four props on the table are taken straight from the Minor Arcana—wand, cup, sword, and pentacle. They symbolize the four suits and the four realms of existence: spiritual, emotional, intellectual, and physical. Wands correspond to fire and spirit. Cups correspond to water and emotion. Swords correspond to air and intellect. Pentacles correspond to earth and physical existence.

Numeric Significance. The Magician is the first card in the Major Arcana. One is the first number, so it symbolizes leadership. It's an obvious symbol of unity and singularity. The number one can even be thought of as a thesis—an original statement of thought, belief, and perception, still unchallenged by other competing ideas. The number one also represents the source of all existence. It symbolizes fertility, and the potential and possibility of every new beginning. That symbolism is reinforced by the graphic nature of both the Arabic numeral 1 and the Roman numeral I; both shapes are phallic symbols.

Keywords

Upright: Skill, diplomacy, self-confidence, talent, will, power, mastery, cunning, showmanship

Reversed: Misuse of gifts and talents, trickery, sleight of hand

Myth and Legend

The Magician card is associated with Mercury, the Greek god of speed and communication. (In Rome, Mercury was known as Hermes.) Mercury was the messenger of the gods, the bringer of dreams, and a psychopomp—a spirit guide who would lead the souls of the dead into the Underworld. And thanks to his association with communication—and his gift for fast talking—Mercury was also the god of orators, merchants, liars, and salesmen. The Magician has also been compared to Merlin, as well as the mountebank of the European Carnival, and the trickster gods of American Indians.

Astrological Associations

The prattle of a stage magician is almost as entertaining as his tricks. The silver-tongued carnival barker is also an act unto itself. Even a telephone sales call can be amusing, given the right script and the right salesperson.

What do they all have in common? Mercury, the trickster god.

In our solar system, Mercury is the closest planet to the sun, so it has the smallest orbit: eighty-eight days. The planet's speed and agility mark it as the ruler of short, quick trips, neighborhood errands, and workday commutes. That same fleet-footedness is connected to Mercury's role as messenger of the gods.

Mercury rules two signs: Gemini, which is associated with the Lovers card, and Virgo, which is associated with the Hermit. Mercury also rules the third house of communication and sixth house of work and service to others.

Literary Archetypes

The Magician may embody any number of literary archetypes, including the alchemist, the magical helper, the magus, the mystic, the psychic, the psychopomp, the shaman, the sorcerer, the trickster, and the wizard.

The Magician and Your Writing Practice

Before the days of mass communication, there was a time when anyone who could write was considered a magical being. In fact, in a time when most people were illiterate, anyone who could commit thoughts and ideas to paper—anyone who could cast a "spell," in the literal sense of the word—was altering reality, transforming thought into substance, and performing one of the most amazing feats of all time. Even now, writers still have the power to attract an audience's attention with the power of their words, as well as to mystify and amaze their readers with their talent and dexterity.

When the Magician shows up in your writing practice, you might want to channel the Magician's magic into your writing practice by working with a real "magic wand"— a pen or pencil so smooth that it makes words flow through you, rather than from you.

Writing Prompts

Write about:

- a stage or street magician
- a performer who doesn't know when he's not on stage
- an act of stage magic that unexpectedly becomes real
- a magician's assistant, wife, or family member
- a wizard or sorcerer
- a sorcerer's apprentice
- someone in a magician's audience
- a traveling salesman
- a snake-oil salesman whose product actually works
- a mythological trickster

2. The High Priestess

THE HIGH PRIESTESS IS THE guardian of cosmic mystery. She keeps close watch over the doorway between this world and the next. If she chooses, she can pull back the curtain and reveal all the secrets of life—but first, you'll have to prove you're worthy of her knowledge and understanding.

Most tarot readers identify closely with the High Priestess. She is naturally intuitive, and she has honed her psychic gifts through patient study and observation. She can see past, present, and future at a glance; no detail goes unnoticed. She makes an excellent teacher and guide into the world of spiritual enlightenment—provided that the student is ready.

The High Priestess is the card of intuitive wisdom and understanding. In a story reading, the High Priestess may represent a wise woman, psychic, intuitive, counselor, therapist, psychologist, or psychiatrist.

In some tarot decks, the High Priestess is called the Papess or the Female Pope.

Key Symbols

A Knowing Glance. The High Priestess' Mona Lisa smile is mesmerizing, but it's perplexing, too. Is she amused, or is she annoyed? Will she speak, or will she maintain her code of silence? Her approval might seem to wax and wane like the crescent moon at her feet.

Pillars of Wisdom. The two columns on either side of the High Priestess represent the twin pillars of the Kabbalistic Tree of Life. One is black, and one is white; together, they symbolize the diametrically opposed concepts of mercy and severity, light and darkness, spirit and matter, and destruction and creation.

Initial Impressions. The columns are inscribed with a B and a J, which stand for two Old Testament figures: Boaz, who was King David's great-grandfather, and Joachim, a high priest in King Solomon's temple.

The Veil Between the Worlds. The curtain suspended between the two columns represents the curtain that hung in the Temple of Solomon—the veil between this world and the next.

Palms and Pomegranates. The curtain is covered with palms and pomegranates, symbols of male and female fertility. The pomegranates are laid out in the shape of the Kabbalistic tree of life, a model of creation.

Phases of the Moon. The High Priestess' crown is a representation of the waxing, full, and waning moon. Another crescent moon lies at her feet. The moon is reflective; it's connected with intuition and psychic ability, because it casts the light of the sun back toward its source. The symbolism of the moon can even suggest an irresistible attraction that ebbs and flows over time, like the moon's gravitational pull on the tides.

Feminine Wiles. The moon is also a powerful symbol of feminine energy. Because the moon waxes and wanes on a twenty-eight-day cycle, it represents the cyclical, changing nature of existence. The moon's phases also resemble the three phases of a woman's life: the maiden, waxing toward full; the mother, a woman in full bloom; and crone, still able to shed light in her waning days.

Pregnant Pause. The moon is a symbol of pregnancy and birth, because it reflects the changing shape of a woman's body as she moves through the stages of pregnancy, childbirth, and recovery. Each month, the moon opens as a slender wisp of light, grows round and full, and then returns to its previous form. Even when they're not pregnant, women undergo a monthly cycle of change and transformation.

Plus Sign. The cross on the front of the High Priestess' gown is a solar cross, a perfectly proportioned symbol of balance and equality.

Book of Secrets. The scroll in the High Priestess' lap is a Torah, the Hebrew book of the law. Only the first four letters of the word are visible; the rest of the scroll is shrouded in the folds of her cloak, like a closely guarded secret.

Tora, Tora, Tora. The word "tora" is an anagram for "rota"—the Latin word for "wheel." The letters can also be transposed to spell "tota," which means "all," and, of course, "tarot."

Numeric Significance. The High Priestess is the second card in the Major Arcana. Twos represent duality, like the black and white pillars behind the High Priestess. The number two suggests pairs and combinations, as well as relationships, partnerships, attraction, and opposition. Twos also represent conversation and debate—the point and counterpoint of two opposing ideas, or the antithesis that rises up in response to almost every thesis. The nature of the number two also signifies a wide range of concepts that come in pairs: heaven and earth, male and female, active and passive, conscious and unconscious, and day and night.

Written as a Roman numeral, the "II" on many renditions of the cards looks like the two pillars that stand behind the High Priestess. The Roman numeral II also resembles a gateway or a doorway, as well as female genitalia—the gateway to life when a child is born.

Keywords

Upright: Intuition, psychic ability, spirituality, wisdom, depth, tenacity, revelation, secrets, mystery, the unrevealed future, silence

Reversed: Conceit, superficiality, shallowness, surface knowledge

Myth and Legend

Some tarot readers believe that the High Priestess card depicts the fabled Pope Joan, who disguised herself as a man and rose through the ranks of the church during the ninth century. Using the name John Anglus, she ascended to the throne of St. Peter and served as pope for more than two years. No one realized that she was secretly a woman—until she collapsed during a procession and gave birth on the steps of St. Peter's cathedral. She reportedly died within hours. Some say she died of childbirth; others say she was torn apart by a vengeful crowd.

The story is usually discounted as myth or legend, and the church denies that Pope Joan ever existed. A related account, however, seems to have historical backing. At the end of the thirteenth century, a nun named Sister Manfreda Visconti was elected papess of her order. Her followers hoped she would serve to depose Pope Urban VIII and usher in a new, feminine age of the church. Her reign was short lived, because the orthodox papacy of Rome burned her at the stake in 1300. She was immortalized, however, in the Visconti-Sforza tarot deck that was painted as a wedding gift for her distant cousin, Bianca Maria Sforza.

In early decks, the High Priestess was sometimes depicted as Juno, complete with a peacock companion, to avoid offending the Catholic Church. In other decks, she is a priestess of Isis. The High Priestess is also connected to the vestal virgins of ancient Greece, the Sybil oracles, and all of the goddesses of the moon.

Astrological Associations

The High Priestess is inextricably linked with the moon—the ruler of the night, gardener of dreams, and guardian of the subconscious mind. She rules the dreamlike world of the unconscious mind, intuition, and imagination, and her moods ebb and flow like the tides.

The moon rules the fourth house of the zodiac, where astrologers look for information about motherhood and nurturing influences. The moon also rules Cancer, the sign of home and family.

On a related note, the sign of Cancer is associated with the Chariot card.

Literary Archetypes

The High Priestess may embody any number of literary archetypes, including the anima, the gatekeeper, the guardian, the guide, the love goddess, the magical helper, the medium, the mentor, the mystic, the poet, the writer or the scribe, the psychic, the shaman, the teacher, the virgin, the visionary, and the witch.

The High Priestess and Your Writing Practice

The High Priestess holds a sacred scroll in her lap—the Torah, the book of the word. She recognizes that words are sacred because they have the power to shape reality. In fact, much of our civilization was founded on an appreciation for words, which made it possible to pursue logic, philosophy, and science.

On a practical level, you can also identify with the High Priestess as a writer herself; she records her wisdom and observations in her secret book of life, and she guards and measures her words carefully. She has mastered the wise woman's maxim: to know, to will, to dare, and to keep silent.

Staying quiet can also help you keep your writing on track. When you pull the High Priestess card during the course of your work, it could suggest that your plans and ideas are like the seeds in the pomegranate. Expose them to the elements only when they're ready, and plant them in fertile soil that can help them take root and thrive. Don't show your work to others too soon, and don't open yourself up to criticism and critique before you're ready to bloom.

Writing Prompts

Write about:

- something—or someone—behind a curtain

- what it's like to eat a pomegranate

- a cloistered nun

- a vestal virgin

- a temple whore

- a librarian in the cosmic Hall of Akashic Records

- a witch

- a group of wise women who work in secret

- a fortuneteller

- a dream journal

3. The Empress

The Empress is a creative force—an archetypal mother who constantly generates new life. Perpetually pregnant, she's a symbol of fertility and growth.

Like the High Priestess before her, the Empress is a link between the physical and spiritual worlds. She doesn't station herself at a gateway, however: she *is* merely the gateway between spiritual and material existence. She glows with confidence and good health, and she's up to the physical demands of creation.

The Empress' creative energy is inspiring, and her enthusiasm can be contagious. She celebrates the excitement of new life—so much that she runs the risk of smothering her creations with love and affection.

Like every mother, however, the Empress has a dark and dangerous side: while she will fight to the death to protect her young, there are times when she can slip into the guise of the Dark Mother—the Creator-Destroyer, who can refuse her children passage into the world, or remove them from existence, even after birth.

Generally speaking, the Empress card signifies a period of creation, nurturing, and growth. In a story reading, the Empress may represent a pregnant woman, mother, artist, or gardener.

Key Symbols

Garden of Delights. The Empress' domain is a garden of earthly delights, where trees blossom with flowers and a clear blue stream ensures lush growth and a promising harvest. Her garden is a refuge and a paradise, where nature will tend to her young until they come to fruition.

Zodiac Sign. The Empress' heart-shaped shield is inscribed with the symbol of Venus, the planet of love and attraction. She sits on a cushioned throne, another symbol of Venus' love of beauty and comfort.

Crown of Wisdom. She wears a jeweled crown, a sign of her intellect and authority.

Global Authority. She holds a scepter with a globe, a symbol of her earthly realm. It's also a phallic symbol that represents her ability to cooperate (and sometimes control) a male partner.

Iconic Beauty. The Empress is young, blond, and beautiful—like Marilyn Monroe or Princess Diana. Like those lost icons, she'll never show signs of sickness or age; she is a perpetual symbol of youth and vitality.

Rushing Waters. The waterfall and clear blue stream in the background symbolizes her connection to life, fertility, and emotional well-being. Her flowing robes reinforce that symbolism.

Evergreens. The cypress trees are a symbol of eternal life, and the fruit-bearing trees represent fertility and growth.

Pregnant Pause. The Empress is closely connected to concepts of love, marriage, and motherhood. In a tarot reading, the Empress often relates to the relationship between mothers and children.

Wifely Duties. Because we can assume that the Empress is married to the Emperor (the next card in the Major Arcana), she symbolizes marriage, partnership, joint efforts, shared aspirations, and common goals, hopes, and dreams.

Numeric Significance. The Empress is the third card in the Major Arcana. Threes symbolize creation—the result of two separate forces combining to create a third entity. A mother and a father produce a child together. A thesis and an antithesis combine to produce a synthesis. The number three can also represent body, mind, and spirit, or past, present, and future. Many religions believe in a holy trinity, such as Father, Son, and Holy Spirit, or Maiden, Mother, and Crone, or the triple goddess of the New, Full, and Old Moon.

Keywords

Upright: Fertility, creativity, productivity, pregnancy, potential, growth, abundance, comfort, beauty, happiness, pleasure, success, artistic ability, nurturing, sensuality

Reversed: Stubbornness, laziness, infertility, chaos, disorder, smothering affection, overprotection

Myth and Legend

Among tarot readers, the Empress is generally considered to be Demeter, the goddess of the harvest and the mother of Persephone. When Persephone was kidnapped, Demeter's grief almost destroyed the world.

According to legend, Persephone leaves her mother's side to pick flowers. Alone in a meadow, she was fair game for Hades, Lord of the Underworld. He reached up, pulled her down into his realm, and forced her to become his bride.

As Demeter searched desperately for her lost daughter, life on earth came to a standstill. At that point, Zeus stepped in. He forced Hades to relinquish Persephone—but not before Hades had tricked her into eating four pomegranate seeds, which condemned her to remain in the Underworld forever. After some negotiation, the gods decided that Persephone would simply be compelled to return to Hades for four months a year—one month for each seed she had consumed. As a result, Persephone was allowed to spend eight months with her mother.

When Persephone is away each winter, in the dark and foreboding land of the dead, Demeter grieves and the earth grows cold. But when Persephone returns, Demeter—and the earth itself—springs back to life.

Astrological Associations

The Empress surrounds herself with beauty, graces her children with affection, and maintains a sense of passion for her husband. All told, she makes a home that reflects her romantic ideals—much like Venus, the planet of love and attraction.

Venus rules marriage, partnerships, and friendships, and its influence leads to strong attachments, both to people and property.

Venus represents stability and comfort, as does Taurus, the sign that falls under Venus' rule. Venus also rules the second house of the zodiac, where astrologers look for information about one's home and material possessions.

On a related note, Taurus is associated with the Hierophant card.

Literary Archetypes

The Empress may embody any number of literary archetypes, including the anima, the artist, the creator, the earth mother, the goddess, the matriarch, the mother, and the queen.

The Empress and Your Writing Practice

The Empress is the consummate card of creativity. She represents every writer who is open to inspiration and willing to serve as a vessel for new worlds to take shape. She is fearless and unbowed by labor and delivery, including the hard work that accompanies the birth of any writing project. She's willing to lose control of her rational ideals, and submit to the primal realities of the birthing process. It's a lot like writing a book.

When the Empress card falls in the course of your writing work, it could signify that you're in the process of gestating a concept or an idea. Great writing takes time, but the Empress demonstrates that you have both the energy and the inspiration to produce tangible works of art.

Writing Prompts

Write about:

- creativity

- fertility

- a pregnancy—planned or unplanned

- labor and delivery

- the birth of a miracle child

- Demeter and Persephone

- a comparison between birth and death

- a living person's visit to the afterlife

- a "dark mother" like Kali, the creator-destroyer

- a crone, with her days as maiden and mother behind her

4. The Emperor

Each day, the Emperor steps warily into the garden of the Empress, surveys the property, and creates order out of his wife's creative chaos. It's no easy task, but the Emperor is the ultimate authority figure. He is a visionary ruler, a fearless conqueror, and a tireless administrator. He is master and commander, protector and provider—the epitome of leadership. He is willful and stubborn, forceful, confident, courageous, and strong—and he rules through logic, reason, and will. His word is law.

The Emperor's job is also bigger than most of us can comprehend. While ordinary kings ruled nations, emperors commanded entire groups of nations. You might even say that the Emperor is the king of the world. As a result, the Emperor knows how to delegate his authority, form alliances, and measure allegiances.

Generally speaking, the Emperor card symbolizes leadership, order, and control. In a story reading, the Emperor may represent a father, administrator, disciplinarian, or authority figure.

Key Symbols

Cubic Throne. The Emperor's throne is an emblem of his power. It is a massive, rough-hewn throne of solid stone—the essence of structure and stability, and a tangible example of the solidity of a geometric cube.

Desert Landscape. While the Empress held court in a lush and fertile garden, the Emperor rules from a harsh desert landscape. The mountains in the background subtly reinforce the rock-solid stability of his rule. The Empress' influence is present, however, in the rivers and streams that wind their way through his realm.

Rams' Heads. The armrests and the back of his throne are carved with rams' heads, which are a direct reference to his Aries-style leadership and drive.

Crown. The Emperor wears a jeweled crown, a symbol of the divine right of kings, and a long white beard, like a figure in a child's drawing of God.

Scepter. His scepter, a symbol of his rulership and authority, is shaped like a crux ansata, a symbol of life that dates back to ancient Egypt.

Battle Armor. Underneath his red velvet robes, the Emperor wears a full suit of armor, which suggests that he's always ready to rise up, protect, and defend his empire.

Sex Appeal. The Emperor is clearly virile, and his masculinity is a suitable counterpart to the Empress' fertility. Symbolically, that makes the Emperor a seminal thinker, too.

Numeric Significance. The Emperor is the fourth card in the Major Arcana. Fours symbolize structure, stability, and security, because four points come together to form a solid. There are four walls in a room, and four corners to a house. There are four dimensions: width, length, height, and time. There are four cardinal directions: north, south, east, and west. There are four seasons, four winds, and four phases of the moon. There are four elements, and four corresponding suits in the Minor Arcana.

Keywords

Upright: Stability, power, control, dominion, authority, leadership, protection, reason, logic, confidence, ambition, civilization, order, control

Reversed: Tyranny, abuse or misuse of power, war, conquest, strife, poor leadership

Myth and Legend

The Emperor is sometimes compared to the Greek god Zeus or the Roman god Jupiter. Zeus was the celestial ruler of all the gods on Mount Olympus—many of whom he fathered himself. Zeus' pantheon is also scattered through the myth and legend of the tarot, where you'll find his offspring referenced in many cards.

While Zeus was married to Hera, he was a notorious adulterer who carried on with a wide range of goddesses and mortal women. His wife gave birth to his children Aries, the god of war, and Hebe, the goddess of youth. Zeus' affair with Leto, a daughter of the Titans, led to the birth of Apollo, the sun god, and Artemis, goddess of the hunt. His affair with Themis, the goddess of justice, created the three Fates. And Athena, the goddess of wisdom, sprang full-grown from his head. You could cast an entire series based on this single card.

Historically, the Emperor is related to other, real-life emperors, like Charlemagne, Jason, Alexander the Great, Napoleon, and Julius Caesar.

Astrological Associations

The Emperor is ready to protect and defend his realm at a moment's notice—like Aries, the god of war for whom the sign was named.

Aries is the first sign of the zodiac, which makes it a symbol of leadership. In fact, the Emperor typifies the Aries personality: a natural-born leader, commanding, forceful, bold, courageous, and confident.

Aries rules the first house of the zodiac, where astrologers look for information about self-image, public image, physical descriptions, and first impressions. Aries is ruled in turn by Mars, the planet of energy and aggression.

On a related note, Mars is associated with the Tower card.

Aries is a fire sign.

Literary Archetypes

The Emperor can embody any number of literary archetypes, including the animus, the dictator, the father, the god, the judge, the king, the Midas, the patriarch, the ruler, and the visionary.

The Emperor and Your Writing Practice

While the creative energy of the Empress may inspire great writing, you're at your best when you take charge of your work—like the Emperor. Your confidence and self-discipline make the difference between a scattered, surface-level approach, and a carefully planned and organized piece of writing. You know how to go beyond brainstorming and into logic and analysis, structure and organization.

When the Emperor card shows up in the course of a writing project, it's a sign that you can be daring in your approach. Pick your battles—and your conquests. You're in command, and you can take control.

Writing Prompts

Write about:

- a father or a grandfather

- a dictator, tyrant, or a benevolent despot

- an absent father

- a single parent

- a throne

- a square

- a ram

- a desert

- the weight of responsibility

- armor and self-defense

5. The Hierophant

LIKE THE HIGH PRIESTESS, THE Hierophant is a spiritual leader and teacher. His wisdom, however, is rooted in the formal precepts of organized religion. While the High Priestess encourages seekers to find intuitive sources of wisdom, the Hierophant expects his followers to pursue a more traditional course of discipline and study.

The Hierophant's hard-line position is understandable. He's worked long and hard to master a religious tradition that took centuries to develop. He's found a system that works, and he can simplify the great mysteries of life—as long as his followers are willing to take his word as gospel. He's also committed to preserving a system of beliefs, to make it available to future generations.

The word hierophant shares the same origin as the word hierarchy, an organization with varying levels of authority—and a hierophant is the final authority on matters of faith. He has the power to speak on behalf of God, to explain the teachings of divine wisdom, and to serve as a bridge between this world and the next.

In a story reading, the Hierophant may represent a licensed teacher, professor, psychiatrist, or priest.

Key Symbols

Seat of Power. The back of the Hierophant's throne is arched like a doorway, and he sits before two columns—pillars of the church. The Hierophant is a gatekeeper of the first order.

Papal Authority. Traditionally, ordained ministers and priests like the Hierophant have the power to perform sacraments of baptism, communion, forgiveness and reconciliation, confirmation, marriage, holy orders, and last rites.

Bless You. The Hierophant's right hand is raised in blessing—a simple but powerful gesture of benevolence and compassion.

Power of Three. His left hand holds a triple cross, symbolizing the past, present, and future, as well as tripartite gods—particularly the Father, Son, and Holy Spirit, although the same symbolism could also apply to god as youth, father, and sage, or maiden, mother, and crone.

Keys to the Kingdom. The two crossed keys on the floor in front of the Hierophant are the keys to wisdom, as well as the keys to heaven. The keys could also suggest that a study of organized religion is also one way to understand the foundation of western civilization, the elements of western thought and philosophy, and an appreciation for classic art and literature. The keys also have a strong tarot connection: many tarot readers refer to the cards themselves as "keys."

Student Teachers. Two acolytes, or students, kneel at the Hierophant's feet. They are tonsured monks, and their heads are shaven as a sign of their vows. The acolyte on the left wears a robe embellished with the red rose of passions; the one on the right has a robe embellished with the white lilies of purity. Both bow in reverence—a reminder of the value of learning and teaching.

Creatures of Earth. The columns behind the Hierophant feature carvings that look like the Taurus glyph.

Numeric Significance. The Hierophant is the fifth card in the Major Arcana. Fives symbolize the five senses, the five points on a star, and the five vowels in the English alphabet. Some metaphysicians suggest that five is important because it symbolizes a fifth element—Spirit.

Keywords

Upright: Education, knowledge, theology, organized religion, structure, discipline, culture, values, social and religious institutions, social conventions, tradition, formality, conformity, orthodoxy, obedience, blessing, marriage, alliances, mercy, goodness, inspiration

Reversed: Dogma, repression, judgmentalism, intolerance, servitude, criticism, fear, and guilt

Myth and Legend

In ancient Greece, a hierophant was a high priest who guided his followers through the sacred rites of the Eleusinian Mysteries, a ritual celebration of death and rebirth. Each year, the hierophant would lead a re-enactment of the goddess Persephone's kidnapping by Hades, god of the underworld, as well as her eventual return. Some followers believed that participation in the ritual would guarantee a life after death in the Eleusinian Fields. As Christianity began to spread, church leaders condemned the mysteries, but the rites continued for hundreds of years and greatly influenced early Christian teachings and practices.

Today, the role of the Hierophant lives on in every spiritual teacher who guides his followers through the mysteries of ancient ritual and tradition.

Astrological Associations

The Hierophant is associated with the astrological sign of Taurus. It's a good fit: like many churchgoers, people with a strong Taurus influence are traditionalists who value faithfulness, monogamy, and procreation.

Taurus rules the second house of the zodiac, where astrologers look for information about an individual's home and material possessions. Taurus is ruled, in turn, by Venus, the planet of love and romance.

On a related note, Venus is associated with the Empress card.

Taurus is an earth sign.

Literary Archetypes

The Hierophant can embody any number of literary archetypes, including the father, the gatekeeper, the god, the guardian, the guide, the herald, the high priest, the judge, the mentor, the mystic, the patriarch, the priest, the psychopomp, the ruler, the seeker, the shaman, the sorcerer, the teacher, the visionary, the wise old man, and the wounded healer.

The Hierophant and Your Writing Practice

Some writers love the Hierophant; others avoid him. Your regard for the man could well depend on how you feel about the grammar police.

The Hierophant will insist that you know the place of a transitive verb, that you can diagram your sentences, that you understand the rules of writing—but once you have mastered the basics, the Hierophant will also grant you the permission to break the rules and forgive your split infinitives. If you are a careful and thoughtful writer, the Hierophant will also help assure your place in a long line of saintly poets, bards, and storytellers.

Writing Prompts

Write about:

- a set of keys
- a holy book
- a priest with a secret life
- a religious service that takes an unexpected turn
- a sin of omission
- a blessing or a curse
- a sacred promise, obligation, or vow
- a religious souvenir
- something hidden under an altar
- a set of ceremonial robes

6. The Lovers

EVERYONE RECOGNIZES THIS HAPPY COUPLE: they are the beguiling Eve and her handsome husband Adam, the progenitors of the human race.

While the card usually suggests love and marriage to the uninitiated, it actually illustrates the complexities of relationships—especially between people with opposing world views. The image of the two Lovers hints at the constant give-and-take of attraction and opposition, and it implies an ongoing cycle of conflict and reconciliation. As a writer, you'll see those issues unfold in your own creations.

The Lovers card is also a symbol of choice. After all, Adam and Eve's entire storyline hinges on a single monumental decision, with repercussions that will affect all of their descendents.

Generally speaking, the Lovers card symbolizes relationships and communication. In a story reading, the Lovers may represent a newly engaged couple, a married couple, close-knit siblings, twins, or people in a close, committed relationship.

Key Symbols

Opposition and Attraction. Obviously, the Lovers card can symbolize love, romance, and marriage, as well as peace, happiness, friendship, and cooperation. But the card also illustrates the twin principles of opposition and attraction. In fact, the card symbolizes dualities on every level: male and female, yin and yang, dark and light, thesis and antithesis. Fundamentally speaking, the card illustrates the fact that opposites attract.

Nude Pictures. In most versions of the card, Adam and Eve stand naked and unashamed. They haven't yet been corrupted by the real world. In fact, they're still under the watchful guardianship and protection of Raphael, one of four archangels in the tarot.

The Archangels of Tarot. Raphael is one of seven archangels—and one of just three mentioned specifically by name in the Bible. (The other two, Michael and Gabriel, also appear on tarot cards: Michael is the angel of Temperance, and Gabriel blows his horn on the Judgement card. One of the four "unnamed" archangels, Uriel, is on the Devil card.). Raphael's name means "God has healed," and he is the archangel of marriage, healing, joy, happy meetings, and travel.

Sun Protection. Raphael is shielding the unclothed lovers from the overwhelming radiance of the sun—a symbol of God, as well as the burning rays of reality and conscious awareness.

Higher Consciousness. The clouds underneath Raphael represent a higher consciousness, and the veil between heaven and earth.

The Garden of Eden. Walled enclosures represent safety and protection, and gardens symbolize rest and reflection, order over chaos, and refuge.

Philosophical Branches. The Tree of Life is on the right, and the Tree of Knowledge of Good and Evil is on the left.

Whispered Secrets. A serpent—often a symbol of female wisdom and feminine wiles—is winding its way up the Tree of Knowledge, whispering seductively in Eve's ear.

Forbidden Fruit. The apples on the Tree of Knowledge are the forbidden fruit—the wisdom that comes with experience.

Peaks and Valleys. Distant mountains represent obstacles to be overcome, new heights to be scaled, new challenges, and the promise of accomplishment.

Numeric Significance. The Lovers card is the sixth card in the Major Arcana. The number six historically symbolizes the human being, because man was said to be created on the sixth day. Six also symbolizes the sixth sense—psychic ability—as well as the six directions of space: left, right, forward, backward, up, and down.

Keywords

Upright: Love, romance, attraction, desirability, flirtation, communication, wise choices, partnerships, balance, duality

Reversed: Infidelity, suspicion, jealousy, obsession, abuse

Myth and Legend

The story of Adam and Eve is one of the world's oldest dramas. Some people might see the story as a tragedy: a seemingly a perfect couple, living in a perfect world, succumbs to a momentary temptation—and in the process, they lose everything they once held dear.

In many respects, however, Adam and Eve's experience is a coming-of-age story. Until they took a risk and tempted fate, they were living like children. Once they were out of the garden, they could take responsibility for themselves. It was only in the real world that Adam and Eve could make their own decisions, and rise or fall on their own merits. Ultimately, they didn't fall from grace; they took a leap to another level of reality, and another plane of existence and experience.

Astrological Associations

Astrologically, the Lovers card is associated with Gemini, the sign of the Twins. While most of us associate the sign with sibling relationships, it can also describe any spiritual or soul mate connection between two people.

Gemini rules the third house of the zodiac, where astrologers look for information about communication, neighborhoods, and sibling relationships. Gemini is ruled in turn by Mercury, the planet of speed and communication.

On a related note, Mercury is associated with the Magician card.

Gemini is an air sign.

Literary Archetypes

The Lovers can embody any number of literary archetypes, including the love goddess, the lover, and Jung's *syzygy*, or divine couple.

The Lovers and Your Writing Practice

Actors, singers, public speakers, and radio personalities typically communicate with thousands—even millions—of people at once. The most successful ones, however, typically don't think of their entire audience when they're performing. Instead, they imagine themselves addressing one person—one friend, one relative, or one smiling face in the crowd.

That's a technique that works for writers, too. When you sit down to write, direct your energy toward just one person—your ideal reader. That way, you'll be one of two people in communication with each other, like the Lovers in the card. In the process, you'll be relating personally to all of your fans, admirers, and readers who will choose your work over all the other books on the shelf—and eagerly await your next release.

Writing Prompts

Write about:

- a doomed relationship
- an ancient tree
- a garden
- a talking serpent
- an angelic messenger
- a healer
- twins: identical, fraternal, conjoined, or separated at birth
- adultery
- a nudist colony
- a woman who knows too much

7. The Chariot

THE CHARIOTEER IS A MAN on the move, and he's in the driver's seat—both literally and metaphorically. He knows where he wants to go, and he doesn't need to ask for directions.

The Chariot is a card of forward motion and change. It depicts the timeless quest for exploration and conquest. It also embodies a certain contradiction: while the charioteer stands in place, he moves ahead. He can also see the world from the comfort of a home on wheels.

Generally speaking, the Chariot card symbolizes travel and adventure. It hints at an unstoppable chain of events that have been set into motion, and a destiny that can't be avoided. In a story reading, the Chariot card may represent a traveler, soldier, warrior, driver, explorer, or a person on a mission.

Key Symbols

Get in the Car. Chariots were developed as weapons of war, but also as tools of exploration and a pathway for trade and international relations. They symbolize both the positive and the negatives that result from travel and exchange with other groups of people. Historically, triumphant warriors would parade upon their return from battle, often displaying the spoils of war.

Buckle Up. The belt around the charioteer's waist is the zodiac belt—the circle of constellations and signs that embrace the sun.

All-Steel Construction. The charioteer's armor signifies that he is both prepared for battle and protected from harm.

The Riddle of the Sphinx. The chariot isn't pulled by horses—it's pulled by a mysterious team of Sphinxes, who pose riddles for travelers before they are permitted to pass into new territory. The Sphinxes are both a combination of four creatures—a human's head, a bull's body, lion's feet, and eagle's wings—that represents all four elements.

Opposition Party. The Sphinxes have little in common: one is black, while the other is white. The colors symbolize the opposition and duality of light and dark, male and female, and action and reaction. The Sphinxes may seem to be at odds with each other, but the charioteer can control his team even when they seem headed in two different directions.

Power Steering. One symbol is noticeable for its absence: there are no harnesses to tie the Sphinx to the chariot, and no reins to connect them to the charioteer. Instead, the young man guides his team with the power of his words and the tone of his voice.

Moon Roof. A canopy of stars serves as the chariot's roof. It's blue and dotted with a map of the constellations, to symbolize the protection of heaven and the guidance of the universe.

GPS Navigation. The canopy is held up by four posts that represent the four Hebrew letters in the name of God (Yod, Heh, Vau, Heh), as well as the four elements, the four seasons, the four directions, and the four suits of the Minor Arcana.

Hood Ornament. The shield on the front of the chariot depicts a yoni and a lingam, two Hindu symbols that represent the union of male and female. The shield is topped with a winged solar disc, which represents Horus, the Egyptian god of the midday sun.

Off-Road Ability. The walled city behind the charioteer symbolizes civilization. The fact that the charioteer is leaving the city indicates that he is willing to leave the safety of a fortress in order to protect and defend those he leaves behind.

Numeric Significance. The Chariot is the seventh card in the Major Arcana. Seven is a mystical, magical number. Classically, there were seven days of creation. There are seven gifts of the Holy Spirit: wisdom, understanding, counsel, fortitude, knowledge, piety, and fear. There are seven deadly sins: envy, sloth, gluttony, wrath, pride, lust, and greed. There are seven virtues: faith, hope, charity, fortitude, justice, temperance, and prudence. (You can see most of them in the Major Arcana.) Alchemists had seven metals: gold, silver, iron, mercury, tin, copper, and lead. There are seven visible planets: the sun, the moon, Mars, Mercury, Jupiter, Venus, and Saturn. There are seven days of the week, seven notes in a musical scale, seven colors of the rainbow, and seven chakras. Because the seventh day is a day of rest, seven is the number of self-reflection and philosophy. To fully randomize your tarot deck before a reading, shuffle it seven times.

Keywords

Upright: Movement, forward motion, travel, speed, war, warriors, battle, conquest, triumph, victory, parades, will, control, direction, independence, drive, spirit
Reversed: Delays, opposition, stasis, entropy, parking and traffic violations

Myth and Legend

The charioteer is sometimes compared to the Greek god Apollo, who drove the chariot of the sun, or the prophet Elijah, who was carried to heaven in a chariot of fire. In many versions of the card, the charioteer wears the two faces of Janus as emblems on his uniform. Janus was the Roman god of gates and doors, beginnings and endings, and transitions—particularly the transition of the past to the future, youth to adulthood, and between peace and war.

The charioteer closely resembles Oedipus Rex, the hero of the classic Greek tragedy written in 430 B.C. When Oedipus was born, his father—King Laius—went to the Oracle of Delphi to inquire about the baby's fate. The Oracle told him that Oedipus was destined to kill his father and marry his mother. As a result, King Laius left the baby in the wilderness to die. Happily, a shepherd discovered the abandoned infant and brought him to the childless King Polybus to raise.

Oedipus grew. Eventually, he learned that he had been adopted, and he headed off in his chariot to find his biological father. Along the road, he met King Laius. The two men didn't recognize each other, of course—and after an ugly confrontation, Oedipus killed the traveling king.

Oedipus continued on his way, completely unaware that he had just murdered the man he was looking for. Before long, Oedipus happened to encounter a Sphinx, who refused to let him pass unless he could answer a riddle: What is it that goes on four legs in the morning, two legs in the afternoon, and three legs in the evening? The answer, of course, was man, who crawls on four legs as an infant, walks on two legs as an adult, and walks with a cane in his old age. Enraged at Oedipus' cleverness, the Sphinx turned to stone.

The illustration on most versions of the Chariot card depicts Oedipus at that point—young, smart, strong, and in search of his heritage and his birthright. He doesn't yet realize that he has already begun to fulfill his monumental destiny.

Astrological Associations

The Chariot card corresponds to Cancer, the sign of home and family. At first glance, it's an odd combination, because the warlike charioteer is clearly not a homebody. However, the charioteer does travel in a home away from home—much like the Cancerian crab, who travels with his home on his back. And while he may be a world-weary veteran on the outside, he's an old softie on the inside—also like the crab, whose tough shell conceals a soft, tender creature.

Cancer rules the fourth house of the zodiac, where astrologers look for clues about home and family life, as well as maternal influences. Cancer, in turn, is ruled by the moon, the planet of reflection, intuition, and inspiration.

On a related note, the moon is assigned to the High Priestess card.

Cancer is a water sign.

Literary Archetypes

The Chariot card can embody any number of literary archetypes, including the animus, the herald, the hero, the messenger, the outlaw, the prince, the psychopomp, the rebel, the rescuer, the son, the übermensch, the wanderer, and the warrior.

The Chariot and Your Writing Practice

To an observer, a writer at work doesn't seem to be doing much—but when you're sitting in your chair, chewing on your pen, and gazing motionless out your window, the wheels are spinning in your head. The writer's journey is marked by flights of fancy and voyages of imagination.

Like you, the charioteer in the Chariot card is a driving force—and he's determined to move forward. He'll follow his dreams, no matter how far they lead. Girded in armor, ready for battle, he is a warrior and adventurer, king of the open road. He's ready to help you blaze new trails across a blank page, too.

Writing Prompts

Write about:

- a traveler

- a road trip

- a mobile home

- the contents of a glove compartment

- a traffic accident

- an armchair tourist

- a journey to a foreign land

- a soldier

- a conqueror

- a homecoming or victory parade

8. Strength

Everyone likes the Strength card's depiction of courage, willpower, and self-control, as a young woman demonstrates the patience and presence of mind it takes to tame a lion.

In the earliest tarot decks, the card was called Fortitude—a word that describes the willpower and spiritual strength we need to endure long periods of adversity. That's probably the real reason people like the card so much. On some level, we can all identify with the woman in the card, and we all aspire to have the courage of our convictions.

Fortitude is one of the four cardinal virtues. Two others, Justice and Temperance, make an appearance in the tarot, but their sister Prudence is missing from the deck.

In some tarot decks, Strength switches places with Justice, which makes it card 11 instead of card 8. The change does not affect the meaning of the card.

Generally speaking, the Strength card signifies bravery, self-discipline, determination, and force. In a story reading, Strength may represent a pet owner, animal lover, animal trainer, veterinarian, or middle-school teachers.

Key Symbols

Work Clothes. The young woman wears servants' clothes, to demonstrate that she's not a member of royalty or high society: she is an ordinary person with courage and self-control, and she stands for confidence and liberation from fear.

Control Freak. Your impressions of the woman's gesture will probably change, depending on your mood and attitude. Is she closing the lion's mouth, or forcing it open?

Wild Child. The lion symbolizes humanity's animal nature—our wild, untamed instincts and desires. In fact, the lion could suggest humanity's most primal needs, for food, sleep, procreation, and self-preservation. Of course, the image could be a metaphor. The two figures in each image may actually be two separate aspects of a single personality. One is civilized; the other, an example of the most primal creatures on earth.

Lemniscate. Those animal drives are perpetual and ongoing, symbolized by the lemniscate—a symbol shaped like a figure eight, which symbolizes infinity. The lemniscate seems to float just above the woman's head, constantly in range of her consciousness.

Leader of the Pack. Lions have a social hierarchy of their own that rivals many human societies.

Castle Walls. In the background, the fortressed castle walls symbolize watchfulness, refuge, royal sovereignty, and divine guidance. The young woman in the card, however, is strong and self-assured, daring enough to stand outside the safety and protection of the castle in the background.

Numeric Significance. The Strength card is the eighth card in the Major Arcana. Eights represent infinity, because they resemble the lemniscate, the sideways symbol of infinity. There are also eight points on the wheel of the year. To Christians, eight is a symbol of baptism and spiritual rebirth; many baptisteries and baptismal fonts have eight sides. Eight also represents the eternal spiral of regeneration.

Keywords

Upright: Strength, power, energy, force, fortitude, heart, lust, life force, will, self-control, self-esteem, self-preservation, animal nature, instinct, heroism, ability, mastery, courage, self-control

Reversed: Weakness, cowardice, fear, embarrassment, self-criticism, shyness, reluctance

Myth and Legend

The Strength card could remind you of a number of myths, legends, and stories about lions. It could suggest the fable of Androcles, the runaway Roman slave who pulled a thorn from a lion's paw. Years later, he was captured and condemned—but when he was thrown to the lions, the animal he saved spared his life, too.

The Strength card mind reminds you of the legend of Hercules, who killed the Nemean lion—despite the fact that its skin could not be penetrated by spears or arrows. After he strangled the lion with his bare hands, Hercules wore its skin as a protective cloak.

The Strength card could relate to New Testament stories of the Christians who were fed to the lions, or Daniel, who was rescued from the lion's den.

It might even remind you of the fairy tale of Beauty and the Beast, or Frank Stockton's short story, "The Lady or the Tiger?"

Astrological Associations

The Strength card is associated with Leo, the sign of lionesque courage and showmanship. Leos love the limelight; they are brave and courageous performers.

Leo rules the fifth house of the zodiac, where astrologers look for information about fatherhood and creativity—procreation and recreation. Leo, in turn, is ruled by the sun.

On a related note, the astrological sun corresponds to the Sun card in tarot.

Leo is a fire sign.

Literary Archetypes

Strength can embody any number of literary archetypes, including the Amazon, the anima, the heroine, the innocent child, the maiden, the martyr, the virgin, and the visionary.

The Strength Card and Your Writing Practice

Writing takes courage. In fact, writing takes more fortitude and strength than most people can muster. Writing is an act of revelation that invites readers into your head and your heart—and that's a process that can leave you feeling bruised and bloodied.

The Strength card suggests that writing isn't much different from lion taming. First, you'll have to subdue the wild, misplaced words that leap from your pen to your throat, choking and blocking what you really want to say. Then you'll have to tame your syntax and grammar, civilize your sentences, and train your paragraphs to lie nicely on the page.

It's a process of self-discipline, and the reward is huge: with any luck, you'll wind up with a poem, story, or screenplay on your lap, purring like a kitten.

Writing Prompts

Write about:

- a lion tamer
- a virgin
- animal passion
- a pet
- wildlife
- self-control
- cages
- restraints
- an urban jungle
- courage and fear

9. The Hermit

YOU MIGHT NOT RECOGNIZE HIM at first, but you've already met the Hermit. He's the Fool who leaped out of the first card in the deck. In this depiction, he's simply older and wiser. He has climbed the mountain of time and experience, and he's ready to serve as a guide for anyone who wants to follow in his footsteps.

The Hermit isn't part of ordinary civilization, but he does keep watch over the world from his post on the mountaintop. He's reclusive, but he's not exclusive; his followers know where to find him. He even holds a lamp of wisdom to serve as a beacon and a guide.

The Hermit card usually represents wisdom, prudence, and illumination, as well as philosophy, introspection, and meditation. The card illustrates the concepts of solitude, silence, and leadership by example.

In a story reading, the Hermit may represent a librarian, philosopher, researcher, or scientist.

Key Symbols

Lamp of Wisdom. The Hermit holds a lantern high in his right hand, a symbol of light and leadership.

Light of Time. The earliest renditions of the card were known as "Time," and they depicted Saturn—also known as Father Time—holding an hourglass.

Solomon's Seal. The light in the Hermit's lantern is a six-pointed star, like the Star of David and Solomon's Seal. Historically, the shape symbolized the union of opposites, such as male and female, heaven and earth, and fire and water.

Stability and Structure. In his left hand, the Hermit leans on a tall walking stick for support; it's basically a third leg, which makes him more stable when he stands. The walking stick is also reminiscent of the Fool's staff and the Magician's wand.

Vantage Points. The Hermit stands at the summit of one mountain, and the distant peak in the background could be the place where we first met the Fool.

A Hooded Robe. The Hermit dresses like a Capuchin friar, a member of an order that takes a vow of poverty and ascetic living. His robes suggest austerity and asceticism; he's living proof that a simple lifestyle can enhance spiritual development.

Cloak of Invisibility. The Hermit's cloak protects him from the elements and from prying eyes.

Numeric Significance. The Hermit is the ninth card in the Major Arcana. Because there are nine months of pregnancy, the number nine symbolizes selflessness, compassion, universality, humanitarianism, and spirituality.

Keywords

Upright: Solitude, isolation, introspection, introversion, meditation, withdrawal, wisdom, philosophy, mysticism, prudence, deliberation, disguise, experience, guidance

Reversed: Paranoia, introversion, agoraphobia

Myth and Legend

Some tarot readers compare the Hermit to the ancient Greek Diogenes, who practiced the philosophy of cynicism. He was a radical, offbeat character who roamed the streets and courtyards of ancient Greece like a dog: Plato described him as a "Socrates gone mad."

Diogenes believed in leading—and living—by example, as he attempted to expose vice, conceit, and the errors of conventional thought. He was a master of self-control and abstinence who weathered extremes of heat and cold with only a coarse cloak to protect him from the elements. He carried a walking stick—and according to legend, he also carried a lantern through the marketplace during the daylight, searching in vain for an honest man.

The Hermit also seems to embody the legend of Merlin the Magician, and even the wounded healer, Chiron.

Astrological Associations

The Hermit is associated with Virgo, the sign of mental and physical health consciousness. While Virgo is the sign of the virgin, most Virgos aren't always virginal in the usual sense of the word. In Latin, Virgo means "unmarried" or "self-possessed." Virgos give of themselves by choice, not out of a sense of obligation. They have integrity, and they always stay true to themselves.

Virgo rules the sixth house of the zodiac, where astrologers look for information about work and service to others. Virgo, in turn, is ruled by Mercury, the planet of speed and communication.

On a related note, Mercury corresponds to the Magician card.

Virgo is an earth sign.

Literary Archetypes

The Hermit can embody any number of literary archetypes, including the gatekeeper, the guide, the magical helper, the magus, the mentor, the messenger, the miser, the mystic, the outlaw, the poet, the writer, or the scribe, the psychic, the self, the shaman, the sorcerer, the teacher, the visionary, the wanderer, the wise old man, the wizard, and the wounded healer.

The Hermit and Your Writing Practice

In many ways, the Hermit has a lot in common with writers. In fact, writers usually are hermits. When they work, writers close themselves off from the rest of society—but that's so they can ultimately contribute something of substance to the world.

Traditionally, hermits chose a life of solitude and prayer away from the distractions and temptations of the world. Most hermits, however, would tell you that a life away from humanity isn't a life *apart* from humanity. In fact, the very act of leaving civilization behind tends to draw followers who want to do the same—just as your words will draw readers into the solitude and contemplation of your thoughts.

Writing Prompts

Write about:

- a magic lantern

- a crutch

- a walking stick

- a pair of sandals

- a cloak of invisibility

- a hooded monk

- a hermit

- a philosopher

- a cave

- a retreat

IO. The Wheel of Fortune

THE WHEEL OF FORTUNE IS the spinning wheel of destiny and fate. It moves through time and space, constantly cycling and recycling energy and matter. It serves as a measure of existence, and implies that there's an element of chance in everybody's life.

Traditionally, the Wheel of Fortune suggests that events are in motion, and that change is on its way. It's a vivid reminder that what goes up, must come down—and that what goes around, comes around.

The Roman poet Juvenal described that spin during the first century: "Fortune can, for her pleasure, fools advance, and toss them on the wheels of Chance."

Generally speaking, the Wheel of Fortune symbolizes luck and good fortune. In a story reading, the Wheel of Fortune may represent a gambler, investor, real-estate speculator, or risk takers.

Key Symbols

Target Practice. The wheel itself is the main focus of the card. It's orange, a fiery color that suggests energy and heat.

Spelling Practice. The four Arabic letters in the disc's outer rim—T, A, R, and O—are the same four letters also appeared on the High Priestess' scroll. Read them clockwise, and they spell "Tarot." Counterclockwise, they spell tora, like the Hebrew holy book. If you start at the bottom and read clockwise, the letters spell rota, which is Latin for wheel. There are Hebrew letters on the wheel, too. The four letters, Yod, Heh, Vau, Heh, make up the name of God—pronounced "Jehovah" in English. They suggest that God is at the center of everything.

Alchemical Symbols. The symbols inside the wheel are alchemical symbols: sulphur is the triangle, salt is the circle, mercury is the circle with horns, and dissolution is the wavy lines. The three alchemical elements were once thought to be the three basic forms of matter.

Riders on the Storm. The riddling Sphinx at the top of the wheel is actually a combination of four creatures—he has a human head, a bull's body, a lion's feet and tail, and tucked behind his back, eagle's wings. The serpent Typhon, on the left, is an ancient monster who attempted to overthrow Zeus as the king of gods and men. He was cast underground, where he remained to cause volcanic eruptions and windstorms. The Anubis, a jackal-headed god who represented the Egyptian priesthood, is on the right.

Apocalypse Now. The same four creatures that constitute the Sphinx's body—an angel, an eagle, a lion, and a bull—appear in the corners of the card, too. They are the four beasts of the Apocalypse the prophet Ezekiel saw in his vision of "Ezekiel's Wheel." They're also the four fixed creatures of the zodiac: Aquarius the Water Bearer, Scorpio the Eagle, Leo the Lion, and Taurus the Bull. The four creatures symbolize the four dimensions: width, length, height, and time. They represent the four cardinal directions: north, south, east, and west. They are reminders of the four seasons, the four winds, the four phases of the moon, and the four ages of man: infancy, youth, adulthood, and old age. The four creatures also symbolize the four elements and the four suits of the Minor Arcana.

Pieces of Eight. The Wheel itself is divided into eight sections. The divisions symbolize the four cardinal directions—North, South, East, and West—along with the midway points, Northeast, Southeast, Southwest, and Northwest. The divisions are also a graphical representation of the wheel of the year, with the spring, summer, winter, and fall equinoxes, as well as the cross quarter midpoints of the year.

Numeric Significance. The Wheel of Fortune is the tenth card in the Major Arcana. The number ten has primal, deep-seated significance for all of us. When babies are born, parents immediately do a quick tally of fingers and toes. When we learn to count as children, we use our ten fingers as tools. Ten is the number of culmination, completion, and perfection. There are also ten spheres on the Kabbalistic Tree of Life, and ten numbered cards in each suit of the Minor Arcana.

Keywords

Upright: Good fortune, good karma, good luck, destiny, chance, success, expansion, perpetual motion, cycles, wheel of life, wheel of the year

Reversed: Reversal of fortune, bad luck, instant karma, standstills, and delays

Myth and Legend

In myth and legend, three female goddesses—the fates—are responsible for spinning the wheel of life and weaving the fabric of every individual's life. The Greeks called them the Moirae, or "apportioners." Clotho spun the thread, Lachesis measured it, and Atropos snipped it with her shears.

They didn't operate in silence: Lachesis was said to sing of things that were, Clothos of things that are, and Atropos of things that were still to be. You could do the same, with a simple past, present, and future spread for your favorite character.)

The fates were supporting characters in a number of Greek myths: they fought with Olympians in a war against the Giants. They weakened Typhon when he challenged Zeus. They condemned the newborn hero Meleager to an early death, by declaring that his life would last only as long as a burning log on the hearth. His mother outwitted the fates, for a time, by pulling the log from the fire and hiding it until her child was grown.

Astrological Associations

Astrologers call Jupiter the Great Benefic, the bringer of luck and good fortune. The expansive planet is the perfect match for the Wheel of Fortune. As the largest planet in our solar system, Jupiter symbolizes growth—especially on a philosophical level. Jupiter represents the process of expanding your worldview through travel to distant lands, friendships with foreign people, and higher education.

Jupiter rules the ninth house of the zodiac, where astrologers look for information about higher education and long-distance travel. Jupiter also rules Sagittarius, the sign of philosophy and adventure.

On a related note, Sagittarius is associated with the Temperance card.

Literary Archetypes

The Wheel of Fortune, as well as the characters on the card, can embody any number of literary archetypes, including the creator, the destroyer, the fates, the god, the goddess, the teacher, the thief, and the trickster.

The Wheel of Fortune and Your Writing Practice

According to legend, the three Fates spin the wheel of fortune for everyone—just as a writer spins tales and determines the lifespan of fictional characters. It's no small feat to master your own universe, or to give life and take it away—even if your power is only on paper.

It's also interesting to note that one of the animals on the card, the jackal-headed Anubis, was a variant of Thoth, the ancient Egyptian god of language and writing.

When the Wheel of Fortune appears in the course of your writing practice, it can remind you of your unique position as a writer. You have the power of creation in your hands: all you have to do is spin the wheel.

Writing Prompts

Write about:

- an unexpected stroke of luck

- a sudden reversal of fortune

- a winning lottery ticket

- a Ferris wheel

- a fortuneteller

- a prophet

- animals with the power of speech

- alchemical symbols

- a change of seasons

- a change of heart

II. Justice

AT FIRST GLANCE, THE JUSTICE card seems simple and self-evident. It's clearly a depiction of balance and fairness. It's also a metaphor for peace: when disputes threaten orderly civilization, a quick appeal to Justice should be able to restore domestic tranquility.

In real life, however, questions of justice are complex and thought provoking. While most people think of themselves as reasonable and fair-minded, there's no end to the debate about the meaning of true justice—or the best way to secure it.

Generally speaking, the Justice card represents balance, fairness, reason, and equity. It could indicate an involvement in legal issues, such as contract and license issues, lawsuits, and arbitration. In a story reading, Justice may represent a lawyer, judge, litigant, criminal, police officer, or a member of the courtroom staff.

Key Symbols

Karmic Justice. Most of us have seen depictions of Justice in courtrooms and attorney's offices. This version, however, is missing the blindfold we've come to expect. Her eyes are wide open: she sees the whole truth, and she's not forced to rule based on technicalities. As a result, she dispenses spiritual and karmic justice, which is more reliable and fair than legal justice.

Double-Edged Sword. Justice holds a double-edged sword—a reminder that fairness cuts both ways. She holds the sword of justice in her dominant right hand, ready to cut through distractions and delays. She knows how to get right to the point.

Scales of Justice. There are two sides to any argument, and Justice is ready to weigh both in her perpetually balanced scales.

Perfect Balance. Her pose is balanced, too: her arms are steady, and she is the picture of equilibrium.

Holding Court. Justice sits between pillars, like her predecessors the High Priestess and the Hierophant. According to the deck's designer, however, she inhabits another realm of spirituality. "The pillars of justice," Waite wrote, "open into one world and the pillars of the High Priestess into another." The pillars probably symbolize the twin Kabbalistic pillars of Mercy and Severity; she sits between them, in a position of balance.

Crown of Wisdom. The crown on her head symbolizes a keen intellect, a command of logic, and a well-deserved position of authority.

Robe. Traditionally, judges wear robes to emphasize the neutrality, uniformity, and dignity of justice.

Numeric Significance. Justice is the eleventh card in the Major Arcana. Numerologists consider eleven a master number, because it amplifies the power of a single "one."

Keywords

Upright: Justice, karma, equality, equilibrium, equanimity, equity, legal action, contracts, lawsuits, trials and judgments, fairness, balance

Reversed: Injustice, delayed justice, bias, judicial misconduct, abuse of power, bribery, payoffs, red tape, complications

Myth and Legend

The Justice card is sometimes associated with Themis, the Greek goddess of Justice who helped keep the infant Zeus safe from his father Cronos, or Time. She was also a gifted prophet who served for a time at the Oracle of Delphi. Themis had the gift of prophecy, but she resigned from the shrine of Delphi to become the Greek goddess of Justice.

The Justice card is also associated with Ma'at, the Egyptian who weighed the hearts of the dead for honesty, truth, and goodness. On her scales, a pure heart would weigh no more than a feather. While Ma'at was the Egyptian goddess of truth, she was also the embodiment of cosmic order: she was responsible for ensuring that the universe followed a consistent, predictable set of rules. She was also the wife of Thoth, the Egyptian god of language.

Astrological Associations

The goddess of Justice holds the scales of balance—the emblem of the sign of Libra. The iconographic imagery links the card to Libran concepts of balance, equanimity, and grace, both personal and political.

Libra rules the seventh house of the zodiac wheel, where astrologers look for information about marriages and partnerships. Libra is ruled by Venus, the planet of love and beauty.

On a related note, Venus is associated with the Empress card.

Libra is an air sign.

Literary Archetypes

Justice can embody any number of literary archetypes, including the Amazon, the anima, the gatekeeper, the goddess, the guardian, the judge, the ruler, and the teacher.

Justice and Your Writing Practice

As a writer, you know that the pen is mightier than the sword. When the Justice card appears in one of your readings, you might be called upon to use the power of words to fight for truth and justice, and defend those who have no voice.

On a more practical level, the Justice card might suggest that you need to use a double-edged sword to cut through confusion, eliminate excess verbiage, or get straight to the point.

Writing Prompts

Write about:

- balance and equilibrium

- a courtroom

- a legal case, lawsuit, or trial

- a lawyer, judge, or jury

- one of the less recognized people in the legal system, such as a file clerk or a stenographer

- a whistle-blower
- a bail bondsman
- karma
- a goddess in modern times
- the view from the top of a courthouse

I2. The Hanged Man

THE HANGED MAN MIGHT BE the world's first writer. According to one interpretation of the card, he's the Norse god Odin, who hung himself on the World Tree for nine days. The Norns of destiny rewarded his sacrifice with the gift of written language; they gave him the runes, an ancient alphabet that now dates back more than 3,000 years.

For centuries, Odin's runes were carved on stone, etched into metal, and burned into wood. The crudely shaped letters of the runic alphabet had literal meanings, like "ice" or "cattle." More importantly, the runes had symbolic significance. In fact, a rune master who knew the secrets of the written word could invoke the power of the Norse gods. (In the wrong hands, that power could be deadly.) Some rune masters carved stories, poetry, and descriptions that have lasted for centuries, guaranteeing them the immortality that most writers can only dream of.

Generally speaking, the Hanged Man card symbolizes contemplation and self-sacrifice. In a story reading, the Hanged Man may represent a student, writer, political prisoner, philosopher, or mystic.

Key Symbols

A New Worldview. The Hanged Man card certainly offers a new perspective. He sees the world from a viewpoint that is radically different from the norm. From his unorthodox position, he can think of new solutions to old problems.

Time Out. Suspended in midair, the Hanged Man is able to suspend the ordinary cares and concerns of everyday life. When he lands on his feet, normal life can resume.

Altered Reality. Even though he's hanging upside down, the Hanged Man doesn't seem to be suffering. He looks peaceful, even happy; there's a halo around his head, signifying divinity, and he's in a mystic trance. He seems to be entering an altered state of being, and possibly even a state of enlightenment.

A Symbolic Death. Ultimately, the Hanged Man is a mystic. He won't suffer a physical death as a result of his time in the tree, but he will undergo a spiritual initiation through a symbolic death and resurrection. Once he's back on his feet, he'll experience a resurrection of sorts.

Going Down. The position of the Hanged Man's head sometimes represents a descent into the underworld. Lucifer, the dark angel, was said to have been cast out of heaven headfirst, straight into hell. The upside-down posture might also remind you of an unborn child, suspended in the womb. In fact, the card occasionally symbolizes rebirth and transitions from one life to another—and in initiation ceremonies, new members of mystical groups are sometimes suspended upside down.

"T" Time. The leafy branches of the tree form a T-shaped cross, like the Greek letter Tau—an ancient symbol of eternal life that's sometimes connected to a symbolic death.

Cross Your Legs. The Hanged Man's legs are often crossed in the shape of the numeral 4, just like many versions of the Emperor. The pose is designed to suggest stability, even though the ground is swept away.

Numeric Significance. The Hanged Man is the twelfth card in the Major Arcana. The number twelve is a reminder of other significant "dozens," such as the twelve tribes of Israel, the twelve apostles, the twelve months in a year, and the twelve signs of the zodiac.

Keywords

Upright: Sacrifice, withdrawal, restraint, foresight, wisdom, meditation, rebirth, transition, initiation, isolation, separation, patience, enlightenment, perspective, alternate reality, reversal

Reversed: Unwilling sacrifice, martyrdom, punishment, imprisonment, treason

Myth and Legend

The most famous hanged man in history is Jesus Christ. In a bizarre twist on the crucifixion story, however, the Hanged Man is sometimes compared to Judas Iscariot, who betrayed Christ for thirty pieces of silver. In fact, some versions of the card actually depict Judas, hanging upside down, with coins falling out of his pocket or purse. The

Hanged Man has also been compared to Saint Peter, who insisted on being crucified upside down to avoid being compared to Jesus.

Historically, the card was sometimes called "The Traitor," because traitors like Judas were hung upside down. The practice isn't dead, either: as recently as World War II, the Italian leader Mussolini was hanged upside down for his corrupt rule.

Astrological Associations

The Hanged Man spends hours—or even days—in a trancelike state of suspended animation. He is in perfect synch with Neptune, the planet of spiritual and psychic enlightenment.

The Hanged Man's consciousness transcends the physical, just as Neptune itself seems to escape the ordinary bounds of physics. After all, the planet is composed mostly of ethereal mist and gasses. It's a planet of dreamlike illusion, and existence removed from the limitations of physical concerns.

Neptune rules the twelfth house of the zodiac, where astrologers look for mystic secrets. Neptune also rules Pisces, the sign of psychic ability.

On a related note, Pisces is assigned to the Moon card.

Literary Archetypes

The Hanged Man can embody any number of literary archetypes, including the divine child, the martyr, the messiah, the mystic, the outlaw, the poet, the writer, or the scribe, the psychic, the rebel, the seeker, the shaman, the visionary, the wanderer, and the wounded healer.

The Hanged Man and Your Writing Practice

Written language truly is a gift. It takes patience, perseverance, and sacrifice to master. As Odin discovered, writing also calls you to see the world from new and unusual perspectives.

Writing is magic in its purest form. The ancient rune masters knew that written language gives form to abstract concepts. The simple act of writing makes ideas become real; it gives them physical existence.

It's practical magic, too. Think about the spellbinding possibilities you can manifest the next time you write a grocery list, and then stand back in amazement later, when you find your refrigerator full of food.

Writing Prompts

Write about:

- a mystic
- a traitor
- a hangman's noose
- a man frozen in time
- a woman in a trance
- an out-of-body experience
- a 180-degree change in perspective
- a landmark tree
- an alternate reality
- a mysterious alphabet

I3. Death

BELIEVE IT OR NOT, THE Death card isn't a bad omen. It's not a portent of doom or imminent destruction. Instead, it's a card of transition; it heralds the completion of one chapter of life, and the exciting new start of another.

The Death card almost never refers to an actual, physical death. In practical terms, it's more likely to suggest a release, a change of form, a transformation, or the little deaths of sex and sleep.

When the Death card rears its ugly head in a tarot reading, it could also refer to a death that's already transpired—especially if that passing has gone unnoticed or unacknowledged. It may call for the release of old habits, old patterns, and old relationships that have served their purpose and now should be relegated to the pages of history.

In a story reading, Death may represent a dead person, grieving survivor, health worker, hospice aide, medical examiner, mortician, or spiritual guide.

Key Symbols

Grim Reaper. Death is the proverbial pale rider on a white horse. He marches across the battlefield of life, mowing down all those in his path. He is the ultimate equalizer, a democratizing force, and he will eventually conquer the king, the bishop, the maiden, and the child alike.

Thermodynamics. According to the first law of thermodynamics, energy is never created or destroyed—it's simply converted from one form to another. While the Death card does suggest an ending, it also promises a new beginning.

Don't Pollute. Death has been this way before: the field is littered with body parts on their way to the recycling bin.

Dry Bones. The skeleton has always represented the bare bones of the matter.

Farm Tools. A scythe can only mean harvest, even if it refers to the harvest of souls.

Armored for Battle. Death wears armor of black steel, the familiar battle wear of a king's knight. This warrior, however, has nothing to lose. He knows that his victory is inevitable.

Mystic Rose. Death carries a black banner emblazoned with a mystic white rose, a symbol of life and resurrection.

River Crossing. The small ship in the background is sailing on what seems to be the River Styx, the mythic landmark that separated the land of the living from the land of the dead.

Sunrise, Sunset. The rising and setting sun has symbolized death and resurrection since the time of ancient Egypt.

Passageways. The sun is stationed between two pillars that are reminiscent of the pillars behind the High Priestess, Justice, and the Moon. In every case, the pillars represent a gateway, or a passage to another world.

Numeric Significance. There are thirteen lunar months, or thirteen full moons, in every calendar year. Thirteen is sometimes thought to be an unlucky number, because there were thirteen diners at Jesus' last supper. In the tarot, the Death card is number thirteen. Thirteen can also be positive; there are thirteen items in a baker's dozen, for example.

Keywords

Upright: Transition, transformation, rebirth, recreation, regeneration, change, alteration, mortality

Reversed: Destruction, corruption, loss, failure, annihilation, inertia, sleep, lethargy, loss of hope

Myth and Legend

The Death card, like all of the cards in the tarot deck, is an allegorical image. It's probably based on similar images that were developed during the fourteenth century, when the Black Death swept across Europe. It suggests the danse macabre, the allegorical images of dancing skeletons that were generated as a result.

Even now, the black-robed figure reminds some people of the priests who perform last rites at the bedsides of those who are very ill. The Grim Reaper is also a variant on the ancient psychopomp, a conductor of souls.

The card also hints at the myth of the Phoenix, the mythical bird that burns and then is reborn from its own ashes. The bird is a symbol of destruction and purification by fire and subsequent rebirth from the ashes. It's a metaphor for transformation and change, metamorphosis and rebirth. It doesn't represent the loss of energy; instead, it symbolizes a conversion.

Astrological Associations

While most people fear death, those who are born under Scorpio's influence are unafraid of darkness. In fact, they're fascinated by the interconnected mysteries of death and sex.

Scorpio rules the eighth house of the zodiac chart, where astrologers look for information about sex, death, and other people's money. Scorpio, in turn, is ruled by Pluto, the planet of death, regeneration, and unavoidable change. And on a related note, Pluto is assigned to the Judgement card.

Scorpio is a water sign.

Literary Archetypes

Death can embody any number of literary archetypes, including the destroyer, the fates, the gatekeeper, the guardian angel, the guide, the judge, the psychopomp, the shadow, the shaman, the sorcerer, the thief, and the trickster.

Death and Your Writing Practice

While most people dread the sight of the Death card in a tarot reading, writers tend to celebrate its appearance. That's because the Death card can portend a dramatic shift in a story. It can introduce an element of danger: it's dramatic and life altering.

As a writer, also keep in mind that you are a type of psychopomp—a conductor of souls, and a guide to hidden worlds. No land is too dark or too frightening for you to explore.

On a practical note, the Death card can also remind you to eliminate words, phrases, scenes, and chapters that don't move your story along. "To be a good writer," Iris Murdoch said, "you have to kill your babies." When the Death card falls in the course of your writing practice, it might be time to cull the herd.

Writing Prompts

Write about:

- someone who is on his deathbed
- someone who has died
- someone coming back from the dead
- a killer
- a psychopomp
- the Grim Reaper
- life after death
- communication with the dead
- a ghost
- how your characters will die, even if their deaths have nothing to do with the story you're developing

I4. Temperance

THE TEMPERANCE CARD DEPICTS MICHAEL, the archangel of healing. He straddles the divide between two worlds—water and earth—and demonstrates the curative powers of balance and moderation.

Temperance was one of the five cardinal virtues in ancient Greece, and it's one of the four cardinal virtues of the Catholic Church. While the word describes the process of cutting wine with water, its most current interpretation usually implies a total abstinence from alcohol. The word also refers to a mechanical process: just as steel is tempered by fire and ice, people are tempered—made harder and more durable—by time and experience.

Generally speaking, the Temperance card symbolizes harmony and grace. In a story reading, Temperance may represent a winemaker, pharmacist, nutritionist, cook, doctor, nurse, or holistic healer.

Key Symbols

Mix and Match. The Temperance card could be a literal depiction of the temperance process: the archangel Michael might be watering the wine, an ancient practice designed to keep drunkenness to a minimum. On a more symbolic level, Michael is actually pouring the essence of life from one chalice into another—and in the process, he's blending the elements of fire, water, earth, and air.

When Worlds Collide. While most tarot cards depict extremes—between black and white, day and night, hot and cold—Temperance symbolizes the importance of merging and combining two conflicting forces. He is a unifying presence in a world of opposition and duality.

Alchemical Magic. To some degree, the card also illustrates the principle of alchemy, a magical philosophy concerned with the transmutation of base metals into gold. The two chalices in Michael's hands may symbolize the sun and the moon, or a man and a woman. The water flowing between them represents a shared bond and an exchange of energy. According to tarot tradition, the water is rising from the lower cup up to the top, violating gravity and laws of nature.

Shore-Footed. Michael divides his time between two worlds, with his left foot on the dry land of logic, and his right foot submerged in the water of emotion. His pose harmonizes the spiritual and physical realms of our existence.

The Long and Winding Road. In the distance, a winding path leads to a mountain range. The image suggests bridges and pathways to other worlds of mind and spirit.

Body Adornment. In many versions of the card, Michael wears the astrological glyph of the sun on his forehead, and the square and triangle of the septenary on his chest. The septenary represents the seven theosophical principles of man: higher self, spirit, mind, animal nature, life force, etheric body, and physical form.

Flower Power. Two yellow irises are blooming on the shore near his feet. Iris was the goddess of rainbows, and rainbows were thought to be a bridge between this world and the next.

Immortality. The mountain path leads to a peak where the sun is rising, crowned in the glory of eternal life.

Keywords

Upright: Temperance, economy, moderation, frugality, management, combinations, unification, balance

Reversed: Intemperance, imbalance, mismanagement, irreconcilable differences, enablers

Myth and Legend

The iris flowers growing along the shoreline symbolize Iris, the Greek goddess of rainbows. Rainbows symbolized a bridge between heaven and earth, which probably inspired Iris' role as a messenger of the gods.

Whenever the gods argued, Zeus would also send Iris to the Underworld to fill a golden jug with water from the River Styx. Each god was required to drink from the jug. If he or she had lied, they would immediately fall over breathless for a year, and subsequently be cut off from councils and feasts for the next nine years.

Astrological Associations

The archer of Sagittarius is a wily creature, a restless adventurer and ersatz philosopher. Half man, half horse, he's a seamless blend of man and beast—which makes the sign a good fit for the Temperance card. Both concepts embody a skillful blend of opposites. The analogy even extends to the bow and arrow that represent the centaur: the symbol is a combination of motion and stillness, an arrow propelled by a stationary bow.

Sagittarius rules the ninth house of the zodiac, where astrologers look for information about higher education, philosophy, and long-distance travel. In turn, Sagittarius is ruled by Jupiter, the planet of luck and expansion.

On a related note, Jupiter is assigned to the Wheel of Fortune card.

Sagittarius is a fire sign.

Literary Archetypes

Temperance can embody any number of literary archetypes, including the alchemist, the artist, the creator, the destroyer, the enchantress, the guardian angel, the magical helper, the magician, the magus, the sorcerer, the witch, the wizard, and the wounded healer.

Temperance and Your Writing Practice

A writer's art is all about balance. Good writers, for example, constantly balance the elements of plot, including action, dialogue, and description. They balance their characters, meting out good qualities with bad, and carefully measuring the dynamics between their protagonists and antagonists. They even balance their use of long words and short words.

A writer's life also demands balance. Most writers must juggle their creative work with another career to put food on the table. Most writers also have family responsibilities, relationships, and friendships to maintain.

When the Temperance card appears in your writing practice, you might want to reflect on how you find balance in your work as a writer.

Writing Prompts

Write about:

- alcohol: you can focus on its use, misuse, or abuse

- the Prohibition movement

- a drunk driver

- an alcoholism and drug addiction counselor

- the boundary between the conscious and unconscious

- the dividing line between thought and intuition

- a guardian angel

- a sign language interpreter

- a marshy shore

- stepping stones

15. The Devil

IF YOU'RE LOOKING FOR THE consummate antagonist, you've come to the right place. The Devil is the perfect anti-hero. He's rude, he's crude, and he'll get what he wants or die trying. Nothing can stand in his way—not even hellfire and damnation pose a threat to the master of the Underworld.

The Devil also knows how to make the most of first impressions; he knows how to intimidate his opposition. In fact, the Devil's image is so exaggerated that it borders on parody. Start with the gnarled horns on the top of his head: he's not someone most of us want to butt heads with. His pointed ears, bat wings, and talons suggest that he maneuvers well in the darkness, but he's blinded by the light. And his goat-like legs, covered in matted fur, are a convincing touch that he's more animal than human.

While the Devil is the personification of all evil, he also offers a secret glimpse at every person's dark side. He's obviously connected to sin and temptation, as well as the pitfalls of human existence, like lust, gluttony, greed, sloth, wrath, envy, and pride.

In a story reading, the Devil may represent a drug addict, alcoholic, gambler, enabler, abuser, or victim. The card could also indicate that someone is feeling devilish, bedeviled, or is playing the devil's advocate.

Key Symbols

Angels and Demons. Believe it or not, the Devil is actually one of the four archangels in the tarot deck. He is Uriel, and his name means "Flame of God." Most people, however, know the Devil as Lucifer, a name that means "Bearer of Light." Both names are oddly reassuring: they suggest that darkness defines light, and makes it possible to discern the difference between good and evil.

The Horned God. The Devil's horns connect him to Capricorn, the sign of the goat. People with a strong Capricorn influence usually feel driven to prove themselves in business and society. In this case, however, the Devil demonstrates that an obsession with outward appearance can imprison the spirit in the material world.

Misplaced Priorities. The inverted pentagram on the Devil's forehead symbolizes a perversion of all that is holy and good. Upright, a pentagram symbolizes the human form, living in balance and health. Reversed, it represents a disdain and disrespect for human existence. In fact, the word devil is "lived," spelled backward.

Bat Wings. The Devil's bat wings suggest that he is a creature of darkness, a frightening specter who can spread panic, disease, and fear.

Self-Aggrandizement. The Devil has put himself on a pedestal, which he grips with the horrid talons of a vulture, a carnivorous bird that feasts on the dead.

Mirror Images. Oddly enough, many versions of the Devil card are actually a grotesque mirror image of the Lovers card, in which the pair has been trapped and enslaved by their own misplaced priorities. The Devil clearly demonstrates the shadow side of a dysfunctional or abusive relationship. The Devil also mocks the Hierophant by raising his right hand in a demonic blessing over the young couple in his keep.

The Devil's Minions. The young couple in the card is naked, like Adam and Eve—but they're not in the Garden of Eden anymore. In fact, the Devil has cursed them with horns and tails, so they more closely resemble their dark master. Their tails are burning, and the flames seem eerily reminiscent of the trees that stood behind them in the Lovers card.

Chain of Fools. The chains represent the wickedness of sin, and entrapment in a web of evil or illusion. They symbolize slavery, entrapment, violence, fraud, trickery, and schemes that cause harm to others. Even so, it's interesting to note that the couple in the card isn't chained tightly. They could free themselves if they wanted to.

The Devil You Know. At times, the Devil card symbolizes the many repercussions of sin, including guilt, shame, denial, and inhibitions. The Devil card might also represent someone who is repressing their emotion, passion, and ambition.

Keywords

Upright: Materiality, material force, material temptation, obsession, the dark or shadow side of an issue, weakness, abuse, addiction, violence, evil, sexuality, sensuality, devil's play, devil's advocate, devil-may-care

Reversed: Sin, temptation, obsession, addiction, materialism, scapegoating, weakness, abuse, violence, evil

Myth and Legend

The Devil is a Christian invention—but many of his characteristics happen to be derived from Pan, the mythic god of music, nature, sheep, and shepherds. Pan's head and torso looked human, but from the waist down, he was a goat, with fur-covered legs and animal hooves.

Pan was a god of physical pleasures, including sexuality, food, and drink. He was wild: he could even inspire panic. Because of his association with Pan, the Devil has come to symbolize erotic pleasure, wild behavior, and unbridled desire.

Pan was a close associate of Dionysus, the god of wine. As a result, the Devil card occasionally symbolizes alcohol and drug abuse.

The Devil card can also be connected to Cernnunos, the horned nature and fertility god of the Celts, and Baphomet, the creature that's usually depicted as a goat's head superimposed on an inverted pyramid.

Occasionally, the Devil card relates to Pluto or Hades, the lord of the underworld and the king of the dead.

Astrological Associations

The Devil card corresponds to Capricorn, the sign of business success and social standing. Most Capricorns are keenly aware of both. Like their symbol, the goat, they are constantly climbing.

Capricorn rules the tenth house of the zodiac, where astrologers look for information about business and career. Capricorn is ruled, in turn, by Saturn, the ringed planet of boundaries and limitations.

On a related note, Saturn is assigned to the World card.

Capricorn is an earth sign.

Literary Archetypes

The Devil can embody any number of literary archetypes, including the destroyer, the dictator, the king, the outlaw, the rebel, the shadow, the shaman, the sorcerer, the thief, and the trickster.

The Devil and Your Writing Practice

When the Devil appears in your writing practice, you can take a cue from Pan, and be playful in your writing. You might also focus on the physical senses he proscribed. If you're in a darker mood, the Devil card could suggest that it's time to kick your story up a notch: it might be time to take your characters to hell and back again.

The card's connection to Capricorn could also be a sign that it's time to focus on the business aspects of your writing practice, and pay some attention to your bottom line..

Writing Prompts

Write about:

- sin

- temptation

- sex

- drunkenness

- addiction

- entrapment

- chains

- blasphemy

- hell

- a creature of the night

16. The Tower

EVERY STORYLINE HINGES ON A moment of crisis—and no card illustrates that moment more clearly than the Tower card. It's a dramatic image: in the middle of a dark and stormy night, lightning strikes. Sparks fly, a tower crumbles, and two people are forced to dive headfirst into a new reality.

In most tarot readings, the Tower symbolizes a dramatic change. It can represent a move to a new location, a breakup, or a release. The Tower can also symbolize the destruction of false ideas and beliefs, a purge, or an intervention. Ultimately, the Tower experience is one of purification, as an old structure is torn down so that renovation can begin.

The Tower card sometimes refers to breakups or breakdowns, and the disintegration or collapse of a structure you thought was stable—like a relationship, a home, or a career. Just as frequently, however, the Tower represents enlightenment, inspiration, and release; for anyone trapped inside, it's a "Get Out of Jail Free" card.

In some tarot decks, the Tower card is sometimes called La Maison Dieu, which means the House of God. It's a term that used to refer to hospitals.

In a story reading, the Tower card may refer to prisoners, guards, revolutionaries, rebels, liberators, and people who are moving from one home to another.

Key Symbols

Visionary Architecture. A tower is a symbol of achievement. It's the physical manifestation of a reach for the sky. Normally, the construction of a tower represents vision and the discipline to achieve high ideals and lofty goals. A tower also serves as a lookout station: it's a platform for a long-range view.

Phallic Symbol. The Tower is also a distinctly masculine image, one that suggests potency and sexual energy.

A Bolt from the Blue. In the Tower card, the top of the structure—its metaphoric head—is struck by a bolt from the blue. The lightning strike represents a forceful clearing of pent-up energy and overbuilt ideas.

Path of Fire. The lightning's jagged path through the sky roughly follows the path that energy takes as it flows down the Kabbalistic tree of life, zig-zagging from sphere to sphere.

Get Out of Jail Free. The tower catches fire—a symbol of destruction—and two people plunge or leap to the rocky ground below. The woman on the right is a queen, but her relationship to the man beside her is for you to determine. He could be her servant, son, brother, adviser, consort, or prisoner.

Precipitation. In the background, raindrops are shaped like yods, the smallest letter in the Hebrew alphabet. Every other letter in Hebrew incorporates the shape of a yod, so it symbolizes the premise that the divine is present in everything.

Keywords

Upright: Insight, illumination, enlightenment, inspiration, epiphany, awakening, freedom, escape, liberation, and release

Reversed: Disaster, catastrophe, destruction, upheaval, fall, ruin, alarm, adversity, calamity, misery, oppression, imprisonment

Myth and Legend

The Tower has been compared to the biblical Tower of Babel, Rapunzel's tower, and the ivory towers of academia. Some have compared the image to Saint Paul's miraculous escape from prison.

On rare occasions, the Tower even symbolizes punishment on a Biblical scale, like the retribution God inflicted on the builders of the Tower of Babel. As a writer, you'll be interested to note that God used the confusion of language as a curse.

The story is shorter than you probably remember. Here's the King James version:

> And the whole earth was of one language, and of one speech. And it came to pass, as they journeyed from the east, that they found a plain in the land of Shinar; and they dwelt there. And they said one to another, Go to, let us make brick, and burn them thoroughly. And they had brick for stone, and slime had they for mortar. And they said, Go to, let us build us a city and a tower, whose top may reach unto

heaven; and let us make us a name, lest we be scattered abroad upon the face of the whole earth. And the Lord came down to see the city and the tower, which the children of men builded. And the Lord said, Behold, the people is one, and they have all one language; and this they begin to do: and now nothing will be restrained from them, which they have imagined to do. Go to, let us go down, and there confound their language, that they may not understand one another's speech. So the Lord scattered them abroad from thence upon the face of all the earth: and they left off to build the city. Therefore is the name of it called Babel; because the Lord did there confound the language of all the earth: and from thence did the Lord scatter them abroad upon the face of all the earth. (Genesis 11: 1-9)

Astrological Associations

The Tower is associated with Mars, the red planet of energy, aggression, and self-defense. Both the card and the planet are intense, masculine symbols.

Mars rules the first house of the zodiac, where astrologers look for information about leadership. Mars also rules Aries, the sign of leadership.

On a related note, Aries is associated with the Emperor card.

Literary Archetypes

The Tower can embody any number of literary archetypes, including the destroyer, the martyr, the miser, the outlaw, the rebel, the shadow, and the sorcerer.

The Tower and Your Writing Practice

For writers, the Tower illustrates a common creative phenomenon: the flash of inspiration that strikes in the middle of the night. It depicts the sudden insight, the shock of recognition, and the story that demands to be written. It suggests the rush of energy that propels pen across paper, and the liberation that comes from telling a story to completion.

Are you ready for inspiration to strike? If you're not, get ready: once you start thinking about the creative process, you become a lightning rod for ideas. You won't be able to imprison them for long.

Writing Prompts

Write about:

- a storm
- a blackout
- a natural disaster
- a prison
- a dungeon
- an attack
- an inspiration
- a move
- the ivory tower of academia
- the Tower of Babel

17. The Star

THE STARS HAVE INSPIRED MYTHS and legends for thousands of years. Throughout history, storytellers gathered around campfires at night. As their eyes followed trailing wisps of smoke toward heaven, they'd take turns unfolding dramatic tales of heroism and adventure—many based on the constellations themselves.

We still tell stories around the occasional campfire, and we still look to the stars for inspiration. We also look toward the sky to convey our stories: late at night, you can see satellites circling the earth, twinkling like stars, and beaming information and ideas around the world.

In a story reading, the Star may refer to an astronomer, astrologer, conservationist, ecologist, environmentalist, waiter, or waitress.

Key Symbols

Guiding Light. All stars symbolize inspiration, hope, and guidance. Small children make wishes on the evening star. Young lovers always watch for shooting stars, so they can make wishes for their happiness. And sailors, in sea and in space, navigate by the stars. The golden star in the center of the card, however, symbolizes focus. That's because every star in the night sky is in itself a sun, the center of its own solar system. The central star might also symbolize a nova or supernova of understanding, the creation of new solar systems, and galaxies, far, far away from our experience and understanding.

Seven Sisters. The seven smaller white stars in the card symbolize the days of the week.

Celestial Symbolism. Stars sometimes represent immortality. According to some traditions, each star in the night sky is an unborn or departed soul.

Time Travel. When you admire the stars, you are literally looking into the past. Every glimmer of starlight has traveled thousands of years, across lifetimes and centuries, to meet us in the dark. In a tarot reading, the Star card could refer to past lifetimes and experiences. The Star card could also refer to astral travel, out-of-body experiences, or dreams.

Famous Stars. The star in this design is Sirius, the Dog Star, but it might also be compared to the Star of Bethlehem, the Star of the Magi, Venus, the morning and evening star, or the North Star that guides sailors through the night.

Mythic Figures. The woman, who looks distinctly like a goddess of eternal youth and beauty, is kneeling. In *The Pictorial Key to the Tarot*, Arthur Edward Waite said the woman was the goddess of truth unveiled.

A Bridge of Light. The star goddess' left knee is on the solid ground of logic and reason, but her right foot is submerged in the watery world of emotions.

Magic Elixir. She holds two earthenware jugs filled with the water of life, and she leans forward to pour one of them into the lake. Beside her, the other empties on the shore, where it finds its way back to its source.

Talking Bird. A silver ibis, nesting in a tree, stretches its wings in the background. The ibis was a symbol of Thoth, the Egyptian god of language.

Keywords

Upright: Hope, faith, wishes, dreams, promises, expectations, confidence, guidance, inspiration, wish fulfillment

Reversed: Broken dreams, dashed hopes, disappointments, unfulfilled wishes, darkness, obscurity

Myth and Legend

The goddess in the Star card might be Nut or Nuit, the Egyptian goddess of the night sky. Her name itself means night: she arched protectively over the earth, covered in stars, where she served as a barrier between chaos and the orderly workings of the cosmos. Each night she would swallow the sun, so that she could give birth to the morning. The Egyptians identified with Nut: they used to say that every woman was a Nutrit, a little goddess.

Western mystics associate Aquarius with the Star card, and connect it to Ganymede, the handsome young cupbearer of the gods. Ganymede lived alongside the gods on Mount Olympus, where he kept their cups filled with ambrosia—the water of life, the nectar of the gods, and the drink of immortality.

The Star itself could be a depiction of Phospheros and Hesperos—two names for the rising and setting morning and evening star. The Star could be Venus, the brightest star-like light in the sky. The Star might also be Sirius, the Dog Star, the Star of Bethlehem, the Star of the Magi, or the North Star that guides sailors through the night.

Astrological Associations

What could be more astrological than the stars? The stars and the signs of the zodiac have helped shape our very understanding of the human psyche. In tarot, the Star card is also associated with Aquarius, the sign of social consciousness and futuristic thinking.

Aquarius rules the eleventh house of the zodiac, where astrologers look for information about social groups, social causes, and technology. Aquarius is ruled, in turn, by Uranus, the planet of freedom and rebellion.

On a related note, Uranus is assigned to the Fool.

Aquarius is an air sign.

Literary Archetypes

The Star can embody any number of literary archetypes, including the Amazon, the anima, the enchantress, the goddess, the innocent child, the magical helper, the maiden, the mystic, the poet, the writer, or the scribe, the priestess, the virgin, and the visionary.

The Star and Your Writing Practice

Since the dawn of time, storytellers have used the stars as launching pads to describe their most secret hopes and dreams. Every constellation in the night sky is associated with a corresponding myth or legend.

The ancient Greeks transformed the musings of a few sky-gazing shepherds into legends that would last for centuries. Their stories, like the light of the stars, traveled through time and space to reach us. Each one is a twinkling reminder of our shared history.

Now it's your turn to carry on the tradition.

Writing Prompts

Write about:

- a shooting star

- a fleeting wish

- time travel

- a naked woman

- a tree on a hill

- a sacred bird

- an ancient myth, recast in modern terms

- a servant girl—or boy

- holy water

- wine

18. The Moon

THE MOON IS THE EARTH'S companion, a partner in time and space. Symbolically female, she reveals herself in bits and pieces—and she hides the dark side of her nature.

The image of the card itself is hauntingly familiar. The moon, large and low on the horizon, casts its rays over an ancient stone gateway. Two dogs—one wild, one domestic—stand guard nearby. In the foreground, a crayfish crawls out of a primordial sea; it's taking the first step on an evolutionary path that leads as far as the eye can see.

Generally speaking, the Moon symbolizes the dreamlike world of intuition, and the shadows of mystery and illusion. In a story reading, the Moon may represent a psychic, dreamer, spy, femme fatale, hidden enemy, or traitor.

Key Symbols

Dance Partners. For eons, the golden sun has pursued the silver moon endlessly around the globe. Some cultures consider the two luminaries brother and sister, while others refer to them as husband and wife. In either case, the sun and the moon are a primordial couple, and their heavenly partnership symbolizes the constant give and take between light and dark, action and reaction, masculine and feminine, radiance and reflection, and the conscious and subconscious mind.

Reflective Properties. Just as the moon reflects the sun's light, it also reflects our unconscious needs and desires.

Dark Mysteries. Because the Moon is shrouded in shadows and darkness, it represents secrets and mysteries that may not be understood—or even recognized.

Night Vision. The moon also symbolizes the intuition and the unconscious, because most people sleep when the moon is out.

Phases of the Moon. The moon symbolizes fertility and creativity, because its twenty-eight-day cycles so clearly match the monthly menstrual cycle, as well as the pregnant female form: slim, then round and full, then slim again. The moon's phases also resemble the three phases of a woman's life: maiden, mother, and the crone.

Gravitational Pull. Tides rise and fall in answer to the beckoning call of the moon; the pull of gravity is almost impossible to resist.

Evolution in Action. The Moon is a card of evolution, because it depicts a crab crawling out of the primordial sea onto the dry land of civilization. The evolutionary motif is reinforced by the tamed, domesticated dog, accompanied by his wild cousin, the wolf. The pairing of the two creatures hints at terrors both wild and domestic.

Howl at the Moon. The dogs in the card also remind us of the monsters that haunt our nightmares—the werewolves and other wild beasts who symbolize our tenuous hold on civilization. Both suggest that we're all just one bite away from madness.

Shadowy Behavior. The full moon has always been linked to lunacy—wild and erratic behavior. Historically, the Moon card was linked to deception and subterfuge, as truth could be hidden in the shadows. It's a telling reminder of Jung's shadow archetype, too.

Keywords

Upright: Reflection, dreams, romance, femininity, intuition, the unconscious, the subconscious, cycles

Reversed: Deception, darkness, danger, shadows, secrets, hidden enemies

Myth and Legend

Throughout myth and history, the moon has usually been a feminine symbol; the luminary is traditionally perceived as a mate or companion to the sun.

In tarot, the Moon card is associated with the Greek goddess Artemis, the goddess of the hunt. (The Romans knew her as Diana.) Her hounds accompanied her as she chased playfully through the skies with her twin brother Apollo, god of the sun.

In her role as hunter, Artemis could take life, cleanly and without reservation. She wasn't a goddess of death, however. In fact, she was the goddess of childbirth, and she was dedicated to shepherding new life into the world. Immediately after she was born, she helped deliver her own twin brother. In ancient Greece, women in labor would cry out to Artemis for relief; they believed that she could either kill their pain, or kill them to end their suffering.

Astrological Associations

Oddly enough, the Moon card is not traditionally associated with the moon in our sky. Instead, the Moon card is associated with Pisces, the sign of intuition and psychic ability.

Pisces rules the twelfth house of the zodiac, where astrologers look for information about our deepest, darkest secrets and desires. Pisces, in turn, is ruled by Neptune, the planet of mystery and illusion.

On a related note, Neptune is assigned to the Hanged Man.

Pisces is a water sign.

Literary Archetypes

The Moon can embody any number of literary archetypes, including the anima, the goddess, the guardian, the guide, the magical helper, the maiden, the mother, or the crone, the mystic, the priestess, the psychic, the psychopomp, the queen, the shadow, the shaman, the virgin, the visionary, and the wanderer.

The Moon and Your Writing Practice

Some people plan their work around the phases of the moon, beginning new projects when the moon is new, rounding them out as the moon waxes toward full, and concluding them as the moon wanes into the night. Before the next cycle, when the moon is still dark, they plan their next projects.

When you see the Moon card in your work, you might want to cast an eye toward the night sky, and begin or wrap up a writing project accordingly.

Writing Prompts

Write about:
- a span of twenty-eight days
- something that happens after midnight, in moonlight, or in shadow
- the phases of the moon
- a rising tide

- the cycles of nature
- an eclipse
- a crab
- a pack of dogs
- a werewolf
- a hunter

19. The Sun

THE SUN IS A JOYFUL, optimistic card. It depicts the very center of our solar system—as well as a fair-haired child who personifies its radiance in human form.

The sun is the source of heat and light and life on earth, which makes it a symbol of energy and health. It also represents consciousness, enlightenment, and illumination.

The Sun is also the ultimate card of self-awareness. In astrology, the Sun symbolizes the ego and the self, because it represents the central focus of every individual's life—himself. No matter how perceptive or empathetic we are, it's impossible to see the world from someone else's point of view. We can only see the world from our own perspective, at the center of our own existence.

In a story reading, the Sun may refer to a child, a farmer, a horseman, a musician, or a poet.

Key Symbols

Action! The sun isn't reflective, like the moon, but active. The sun radiates the energy and heat that the moon later reflects. Symbolically, it embodies masculine principles of energy and action, as opposed to feminine qualities of receptivity and reaction.

Visible Light. While almost nothing can hide from the bright light of day, the sun does conceal its own secrets; some of the rays the sun emits are visible, while others fall into the ultraviolet end of the spectrum.

Special Events. The sun is the marker of annual events like birthdays and anniversaries, as well as solar holidays like solstices and cross-quarter days.

Golden Child. The child in the card is naked, because his enthusiasm is unbridled and pure. His nudity also symbolizes his innocence, and hints at cosmic safeguards and protection that can help shield him from corrupting influences. He's the original fair-haired child, chubby and cherubic, with a mass of golden curls.

Free Ride. The child's white horse is a hero's mount. It elevates him, empowers him, and propels him along a path to victory. Horses also represent mobility, partnership, and social status.

Standard Bearer. As he rides, the child waves a red banner, signaling the joy and exuberance of youth. The banner—technically, a standard, or a symbolic flag mounted on a pole—also represents a rallying point and an inspiration to victory.

Flower Garden. The child is riding past a garden wall, a symbol of safety and protection. Beyond the wall, there's a field of sunflowers—each one a symbol of hope and aspiration, as they reach for the sky. During the course of the day, sunflowers keep their faces turned toward the sun as it moves across the sky.

Sunrise, Sunset. Historically, the rising and setting sun has always been a symbol of life and death.

Keywords

Upright: Consciousness, optimism, happiness, contentment, enthusiasm, joy, light, enlightenment, clarity, glory, heat, passion, radiance, action, celebration, the ego, eclipses

Reversed: Sunburn, overexposure, blindness, drought, global warming

Myth and Legend

For thousands of years, humankind believed that the sun traveled around the world. Because the sun was reborn with every dawn, it became the god of rebirth. Even today, we worship the sun—at least from our favorite spot on the beach.

The sun symbolizes the light of the world—and in myth and religion alike, the sun represents the gods who die and are reborn.

The Sun card is closely related to Apollo, the god of the sun, whose sister Diana was goddess of the moon. Apollo pulled the sun through the sky in his golden chariot. His travels were emulated by Roman charioteers, who pursued a course based on the cosmic cycle of the sun.

Astrological Associations

Astrologically, the Sun card corresponds to its namesake, the sun.

The sun rules Leo, the sign of fatherhood and play, procreation and recreation. The sun also rules the fifth house of the zodiac, where astrologers look for information about creativity.

On a related note, Leo is associated with the Strength card.

Leo is a fire sign.

Literary Archetypes

The Sun can embody any number of literary archetypes, including the animus, the creator, the divine child, the father, the god, the messiah, the ruler, the self, the son, the *ubermensch*, and the visionary.

The Sun and Your Writing Practice

When the Sun card shows up in your writing practice, it may be time to send your work out into the bright light of day—so you can shine like the sun, be the center of attention, and enlighten others with the power of your words.

Writing Prompts

Write about:
- a birthday
- a banner
- a field of sunflowers
- a walled garden
- a white horse
- a red flag
- a golden child
- heat
- sunburn
- something hidden in plain sight

20. Judgement

THE JUDGEMENT CARD IS THE card of forgiveness and release. It's also a card of celebration, as the Archangel Gabriel heralds the start of a new life and a new world.

All of the figures in the card seem to be expressing wonder
and amazement. They've heard a higher calling, and they've
responded. Now, as they rise from their graves, they're literally undergoing the transformation of their lives.

Generally speaking, the Judgement card symbolizes a
willingness to be judged on one's own merits. In a story
reading, Judgement may refer to a herald, a messenger, or
a family.

Key Symbols

Wake Up Call. The Archangel Gabriel blows his horn
and, awakened by the sound, a cemetery full of the dead and buried rise and face the
music.

Pop Tops. The open caskets indicate that the people in the card are starting to
think outside the box.

Nuclear Family. The key figures in the foreground are a man, a woman, and a
child—a small, nuclear family—but they're not the only ones who thrill at the sound
of the trumpet. Other figures are rising in the background, too. This is a worldwide
phenomenon.

Full Exposure. All the people in the card are naked: they have no secrets.

Second Chance. They reach out to embrace a second chance at life, restored to
youthful health and vigor.

Banner of Life. The equilateral solar cross on the banner is a symbol of the union
of male and female, and positive and negative. A red cross is a universally understood
symbol of rescue, health, and healing.

Blue Sky. The clouds are a symbol of higher thought, as well as a veil between heaven
and earth.

Guardian Angel. The angel is larger than life. His outstretched wings fill the sky, symbolizing earthly protection from the elements of sun, wind, and rain—or fire, air, and water.

Spread the Word. Angels are heralds and messengers.

Natural World. The cypress trees in the background symbolize eternal life, and the bare brown earth suggests the promise of a newly cultivated field.

Keywords

Upright: Change, renewal, rebirth, resurrection, reawakening, consciousness, compassion, forgiveness, karma, destiny, responsibility

Reversed: Stasis, weakness, indecision, delay, an unwillingness to forgive and move on

Myth and Legend

Arthur Edward Waite, the man who designed the images in this deck, was a Christian mystic. His training and beliefs permeate most of the cards.

Anyone who's familiar with Christianity will recognize the story behind the Judgement card: it depicts the moment promised in Revelations, when the dead will rise, the gates of heaven will open, and there will be no further separation of heaven and earth.

The Judgement card, however, embodies much more than the simple story of judgment and resurrection on the last day—although that, in itself, would be enough. The card is also a symbol of a new lease on life, and a calling loud enough to wake the dead.

The angel of Judgement is the Archangel Gabriel, who first revealed that Elizabeth and her cousin, the Virgin Mary, would bear children. Elizabeth would give birth to John the Baptist, who in turn would herald the arrival of Jesus Christ. According to the Bible, Gabriel will also be the angel who blows the horn announcing Judgment Day.

Astrological Associations

The Judgement card is assigned to Pluto, the planet of transformation, death, regeneration, and unavoidable change.

Pluto rules the eighth house, where astrologers look for information about sex, death, and inheritance. Pluto also rules Scorpio, the sign of mystery.

On a related note, Scorpio corresponds to the Death card.

Literary Archetypes

The Judgement card can embody any number of literary archetypes, including the gatekeeper, the guardian angel, the herald, the judge, the king, the magical helper, the medium, the messenger, the messiah, the mystic, the psychopomp, the rescuer, and the visionary.

Judgement and Your Writing Practice

As every horror writer knows, the dead don't always stay that way. Even in everyday life, old ideas that we thought were dead and buried have a way of rising up to haunt us; some stories and characters simply refuse to lie quietly in their vaults.

When the Judgement card makes an appearance in your writing practice, it may be time to breathe new life into an old idea—one you thought was dead and gone. Visit your story graveyard, and resurrect the people and the plots you buried there. Forgive your own mistakes, and give them a second chance.

Writing Prompts

Write about:

- someone presumed to be dead
- a resurrection
- a call
- family togetherness
- forgiveness
- the end times
- a new life
- a trumpet
- a casket maker
- a prophet

2I. The World

THE WORLD DEPICTS A COSMIC dancer in the center of an expanding universe. As she completes each round of her spiral dance, a new revolution begins; she's a key player in a never-ending story.

The World is the last card in the Major Arcana—but it's not the final word. Every ending, after all, leads to a new beginning. This stage of the Fool's journey might draw to a close, but in a moment, the cards will be reshuffled and a whole new series of events will play out on the universe's table.

Generally speaking, the World card symbolizes completion and success. In a story reading, the World card may refer to a dancer, a champion, a nudist, a baby, or a reincarnated soul.

Key Symbols

Circle of Life. With the World card, all of the cards in the Major Arcana have come full circle. A circle is a symbol of eternity, because it has no beginning and no end.

Symbols of Infinity. The dancer's wreath is held together by ribbons in the shape of a lemniscate, the figure-eight symbol of infinity. Wreaths themselves are intertwined with concepts of death, resurrection, and immortality. We hang evergreen wreaths at Christmastime, as a symbol of everlasting life. We send floral wreaths to funerals. Historically, people even crowned their heroes with laurel wreaths, whenever they defeated an opponent in battle or in an athletic event—both of which represented victory over death.

Dance Costume. The dancer's scarf is another powerful symbol of beginnings and ends. Historically, newborn infants were wrapped in swaddling clothes, while the dead were wrapped in shrouds. Both were naked underneath. Look closely, and you'll notice that the shape of the scarf also resembles a lemniscate.

Magic Wands. The dancer holds a wand in each hand, like her counterpart in the first card of the Major Arcana, the Magician.

Talk to the Animals. The four winged creatures in the corners of the card are the four living creatures the prophet Ezekiel saw in his vision—an angel, an eagle, a lion, and a bull. They are the four fixed creatures of the zodiac: Aquarius the Water Bearer, Scorpio the Eagle, Leo the Lion, and Taurus the Bull—the four beasts of the Apocalypse. The four creatures also symbolize the four dimensions: width, length, height, and time. They represent the four cardinal directions: north, south, east, and west. They are reminders of the four seasons, the four winds, the four phases of the moon, and the four ages of man: infancy, youth, adulthood, and old age. In addition, the four creatures symbolize the four elements and the four suits of the Minor Arcana.

Begin Again. The World card is the last card in the Major Arcana, but it's also a starting point for a whole new cycle of adventures and experience in the everyday cards of the Minor Arcana.

Keywords

Upright: Completion, conclusion, perfection, success, celebration, reward, unity, universality, oneness, wholeness, synthesis, coming full circle, center stage, endings and beginnings

Reversed: Delays, hesitations, false starts

Myth and Legend

While she doesn't look particularly masculine in most renditions of the card, the dancer in the World card is often said to be a hermaphrodite—a person who is neither male nor female, but who exhibits characteristics of both sexes.

According to Greek myth, Hermaphroditos was the son of Hermes, the messenger of the gods, and Aphrodite, the goddess of love. A young fountain nymph named Salmacis fell in love with Hermaphroditos, but he ignored her. She turned to the gods for help, and prayed that she would be united with him forever. Her prayers were answered: when Hermaphroditos took a bath, they became one person.

Given that background, you might even think of the dancer as the embodiment of Jung's syzegy archetype—the divine couple, literally united as one.

Astrological Associations

The World card is assigned to Saturn, a ringed planet with clearly defined boundaries. While some see boundaries as limitations, they're more than an obstacle or a dead end. That's because borders do more than confine us: they define us.

Saturn rules the tenth house of the zodiac, where astrologers look for information about career and social standing. Saturn also rules Capricorn, the sign associated with work, achievement, responsibility, and drive.

On a related note, Capricorn corresponds to the Devil card.

Capricorn is an earth sign.

Literary Archetypes

The World card can embody any number of literary archetypes, including the Amazon, the anima, the animus, the artist, the creator, the destroyer, the divine child, the Fates, the self, the shaman, and the visionary.

The World and Your Writing Practice

The World card is the final stop on the Fool's Journey—and perhaps, the writer's journey, too. It's a card of accomplishment and success. It clearly delineates a world of endings and conclusions, as events come full circle, and crises and conflicts are resolved.

In most cases, the World card concludes one chapter, and lays the groundwork for a whole new cycle of adventures and experience. The World card might even conclude a story—but it also lays the groundwork for a sequel.

When the World card appears in your writing practice, take time to assess your progress—and to plan for a book tour.

Writing Prompts

Write about:
- a celebration
- a graduation
- a baby blanket
- a baptismal gown

- a bridal veil
- a burial shroud
- a traffic circle
- a last call
- a last dance
- a journey to the four corners of the world

MINOR ARCANA

Ace of Wands

The Ace of Wands is the first card in the suit of wands, the suit that corresponds to the ancient element of fire. It's the card of creative inspiration, and it's the spark that starts the fire.

Key Symbols

Fresh Start. All of the aces represent new beginnings. Because the suit of wands corresponds to spiritual life, the Ace of Wands symbolizes a new beginning on a spiritual level. The aces also symbolize gifts. In this case, spiritual growth is yours for the taking.

Signs of Life. The Ace of Wands is a single, massive branch, with budding leaves sprouting in a promising sign of life.

Creative Drive. It's no coincidence that the Ace of Wands is phallic in nature. It reflects the powerful drive for creation (and subsequent recreation) inherent in the human species. In fact, the Ace of Wands embodies the power to generate—and regenerate—countless generations. It represents potential in its purest form: raw, unbridled possibility, ready, willing, and able to be unleashed.

Higher Thought. The wand is emerging from a swirling silver cloud, a symbol of higher thought, as well as the separation between the worlds.

Hand of God. Most people think the hand in the card is the hand of God—or the hand of the Magician picking up one of the tools from his table.

Magic Wand. The Ace of Wands looks like a primitive magic wand.

Speak Softly. The clublike wand could double as a weapon, either for defensive or aggressive use. It may be a reminder to speak softly and carry a big stick.

Safe Haven. The castle in the distance symbolizes refuge, watchfulness, royal sovereignty, and divine guidance.

Astrological Symbolism. Astrologically, the Ace of Wands is associated with all of the powers of fire—the element associated with Aries, Leo, and Sagittarius.

Historical significance. A century ago, the Ace of Wands was said to herald money, fortune, and inheritance.

Keywords

Upright: Primal fire, energy, spark, creativity, virility, vitality, potency, desire, invention, enterprise, excitement, enthusiasm, force, strength, vigor, ignition, confidence, willpower, drive

Reversed: Impotence, delays, frustration, dissatisfaction, violence, cruelty, tyranny, decadence, destruction

Writing Prompts

Write about:
- a tree branch
- a wooden club
- a torch
- a match
- a magic wand

Two of Wands

The Two of Wands is a card of influence, authority, control, and dominion. It depicts a man with the will—and the power—to move beyond the initial stages of creation.

Key Symbols

Dominion. Traditionally, the Two of Wands is known as the card of dominion. The well-dressed man in the card has the power to master all that he surveys. Look at the card: he literally holds the whole world in his hands.

Boundaries. In most versions of the card, a regal-looking figure—presumably a nobleman or a businessman—stands behind a battlement. The low wall represents a protective boundary.

St. Andrew's Cross. The battlement is embossed with a banner of the red rose of passion and the white lily of purity. The two crossed staffs, in the shape of a St. Andrew's Cross, symbolize the harmony of rule and justice.

Geographic Features. The man stands above a protected bay or inlet rimmed by cliffs and mountains in the distance. The site's geography makes it easier to defend. It's also a convenient base of operations; he's in a position to trade.

The Sadness of Alexander. While the figure is apparently well off, Arthur Edward Waite suggested that it also hints at the "sadness of Alexander amidst the grandeur of this world's wealth." In antiquity, Alexander the Great reportedly was at a loss once he had no more worlds to conquer.

Keywords

Upright: Dominion and domination, strength, stronghold, ambition, resolution, courage, pride, vision

Reversed: Tyranny, weakness, revenge, restlessness, obstinacy, shamelessness, pride, subjugation, hesitation

Writing Prompts

Write about:

- a merchant marine
- a globe
- a long wait
- a low wall
- a vision of the future

Three of Wands

THE THREE OF WANDS IS a card of strong leadership ability, wealth, and power. It depicts a nobleman waiting and watching for his ships to come in. In a reading, the card symbolizes the strength of a well-run, well-funded business organization dedicated to enterprise, trade, and commerce.

Key Symbols

Established Strength. Traditionally, the Three of Wands is the card of established strength. The figure in the card has clearly established his stronghold.

Walled In. The man in the card is looking out over a low stone wall—a symbol of protection and boundaries.

Hidden Emotions. This is one of the few cards in the deck that doesn't reveal the character's face; it's impossible to know what he's thinking or feeling.

A Rock on a Sandy Shore. He's standing on a sandy surface with one foot resting on a small boulder. It's a position of strength.

Sailing Ships. Three ships sail across a bay, which suggest that he is involved in trade and exploration. Those pursuits suggest a sense of adventure and discovery—not only of markets and customers, but also of new lands, new sources of goods and services, and new opportunities for partnerships and alliances.

Growth Venture. The three saplings would suggest that the seeds of a promising partnership have not only been planted, but have also sprouted and taken root.

A Calculated Investment. The trader puts something of value out into the world—at some risk—in the hope that it will generate profit and wealth. He's willing to take a risk.

Color Symbolism. The businessman in the card wears yellow, red, and blue—the three primary colors, which also represent air, fire, and water.

Keywords

Upright: Established strength, business leadership and acumen, trade, commerce, cooperation, discovery

Reversed: Adversity, toil, disappointment

Writing Prompts

Write about:

- a risky investment

- a surprising business partnership

- a fleet of ships with unexpected cargo

- a storm at sea

- body language

Four of Wands

THE FOUR OF WANDS IS a card of family life and domestic tranquility, as a young couple prepares to celebrate their marriage in the courtyard of a medieval castle.

Key Symbols

Throw Rice. In many tarot decks, the card depicts a wedding couple. They're outdoors, which symbolizes a connection to nature and fertility.

Castle Architecture. They're pictured in a courtyard, with the walls and turrets of a medieval citadel behind them. The buildings symbolize civilization; the walls represent boundaries and protection, and the turrets symbolize a heightened outlook.

Divine Design. The couple is putting together a garland for a *chuppa*, a Jewish wedding canopy. It's a simple structure designed to represent a couple's first home together. The four wands that support the canopy symbolize the structure and stability of a house with four corners. The canopy itself represents protection from the elements as well as blessings from heaven.

Color Symbolism. The two people are dressed in complimentary colors of blue and red—one water, one fire. Their marriage is a partnership.

Good Fortune. Historically, the Four of Wands was said to symbolize unexpected good fortune—both upright and in its reversed position. It also symbolized the haven of country life.

Practice Makes Perfect. In *The Pictorial Key to the Tarot*, Arthur Edward Waite called this card "Perfected Work."

Keywords

Upright: Perfection, completion, stability, prosperity, peace, good fortune, harmony, success, happiness, marriage, union

Reversed: Instability, shakeups, conflict

Writing Prompts

Write about:

- a wedding

- a celebration

- a marriage

- your first home

- your parents

Five of Wands

THE FIVE OF WANDS IS a card of strife, struggle, competition, and chaos. Five young men are trying to work together, to coordinate their efforts. They're either on the verge of creating a five-pointed star design, or they're on the brink of anarchy.

Key Symbols

Sense and Sensibility. The five figures in the Five of Wands represent the five senses—sight, sound, touch, taste, and smell—which must work together to make sense of the outside world.

Organized Chaos. Each member of the group is struggling to find his place with the others. They're just a few steps away from forming a star-shaped design with their wands—a pentagram, a symbol of perfection and wholeness.

Spirit of Cooperation. The card has a disjointed quality. Part of the problem is the sheer number of participants in the card. Four young men with four pieces of timber would have no problem joining forces to devise a square. The introduction of that fifth element, however, offers a challenge to builders.

Invisible Glue. That fifth element may be a metaphor for the fifth element of the ancient philosophers. In addition to fire, water, air, and earth, many believed in an ether or spirit that would bind all four elements.

Color Symbolism. The figures are dressed in tunics of red, blue, yellow, green, and purple—the elemental colors of fire, water, air, earth, and spirit.

Higher Guidance. Clearly, the young men in the card could use the guidance and direction of an outside observer—someone who could see the big picture and help them work together to construct a form of beauty and symmetry.

Day Trading. Historically, the Five of Wands was said to be a good sign for anyone who wanted to engage in financial speculation.

Keywords

Upright: Group efforts, teamwork, conversations, games, sporting events, participation
Reversed: Quarrels, fights, clashes, strife, power struggles, disputes, litigation, legal proceedings, issues stalled in committee

Writing Prompts

Write about:

- an argument or a misunderstanding
- chaos and confusion
- committee work
- a construction project
- a political rally

Six of Wands

The Six of Wands is a card of victory, in which we see a conquering hero riding through a cheering crowd. He's probably leading a triumphal parade, returning from battle with the spoils of war.

Key Symbols

Soldier of Fortune. The hero has saved the day. His success in battle has made it possible for the rest of his community to live in peace and prosperity—at least for the time being.

Laurel Wreath. One of his rewards is the laurel wreath of victory. The wreath indicates that he has won the support of the people, along with their respect, recognition, and honor. Will he rest on his laurels? That remains to be seen.

Crowd Scene. The crowd is happy for his success—and their good fortune. It's not an outmoded concept: even now, we celebrate winning Super Bowl and World Series teams with ticker-tape parades.

High Horse. The rider's elevated mount separates him from the ordinary people on the street.

Riding partners. The horse is a long-standing symbol of freedom, power, independence, and movement. Throughout much of history, horses were also a sign of honor and nobility; they elevated their riders not only physically, but socially.

Dressed for Success. The hero and his horse are dressed in royal robes, a sign of their power, status, and prestige.

Keywords

Upright: Victory, triumph, success, acclaim, validation, vindication, messages and messengers, parades

Reversed: Defeat, infidelity, treachery, disloyalty, disrespect, apprehension, fear, an enemy at the gate

Writing Prompts

Write about:

- a victory parade

- the movement of a crowd

- the pounding of horses' hooves

- a hero's return

- a street scene

Seven of Wands

THE SEVEN OF WANDS IS a card of valor, bravery, and strength, even in the face of strong opposition At first glance, it seems like a simple battle scene—but every element is a metaphor for conflict.

Key Symbols

King of the Hill. At the edge of a steep cliff—a risky, dangerous setting—a young man stands his ground.

Defensive Posture. The embattled warrior is protecting his turf.

Strategic Advantage. Even though he's outnumbered, he's fighting from a position of power.

Solid Footing. Both of his feet are firmly on the ground.

Uphill Battle. His adversaries are fighting an uphill battle. We can't see the opponents, so we're left to imagine who they are and what they're fighting for.

Primitive Weapons. The warriors in this card are fighting with primitive clubs, rather than the more sophisticated swords of the tarot deck. This is not a high-tech battle; instead, it's a primitive struggle for land, dominance, and position. It's a spiritual battle, too—if swords were the weapon of choice here, they would imply a more intellectual, logic-driven battle.

Keywords

Upright: Valor, courage, persistence, advantage, negotiation, bartering, competition, success, gain, profit, victory

Reversed: Vulnerability, confusion, embarrassment, anxiety, indecision, hesitation, vacillation, strife

Writing Prompts

Write about:

- encroachment
- self-defense
- a slippery slope
- power mongers
- hand-to-hand combat

Eight of Wands

THE EIGHT OF WANDS IS a card of speed and communication. Historically, the Eight of Wands was associated with long-distance travel and messages from faraway places—and the card has kept up with the times. It's now associated with news and messages dispatched across long distances, electronically or by overnight express.

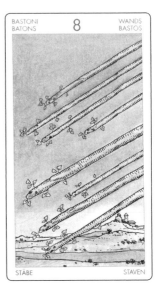

Key Symbols

Incoming messages. Eight leafy branches soar through the air like arrows, all flying parallel to each other at a 45-degree angle. They normally symbolize messages and communication.

Each wand could represent a separate message coming across the transom. Each one might also symbolize a separate mode of communication, such as phone calls, faxes, e-mail, text messages, conference calls, video conferences, radio and television broadcasts.

Slings and Arrows. Sometimes the Eight of Wands is associated with the slings and arrows of outrageous fortune. Some tarot readers view the eight wands as Cupid's arrows.

Fighting Words. Historically, the Eight of Wands was said to predict domestic disputes for married couples.

Moving Water. The river in the background symbolizes a flow of information or emotion; for centuries, river routes were a main avenue of travel and communication.

Safe Haven. The castle in the distance represents watchfulness, refuge, royal sovereignty, and divine guidance.

Landing Strip. In *The Pictorial Key to the Tarot*, Arthur Edward Waite said the wands are descending, not taking off. In other words, they'll land soon, and whatever they prophesize will soon manifest.

Keywords

Upright: Long-distance communication, instant messages, electronics, speed, swiftness, action

Reversed: Miscommunication, misinterpretation, delays, disruptions

Writing Prompts

Write about:

- a romance in the form of e-mail correspondence
- a poem in the guise of a fax cover sheet
- dialogue in the form of text messages
- interaction via video conference
- a new, yet-undiscovered technology

Nine of Wands

THE NINE OF WANDS IS the card of the wounded warrior—
the embattled hero who lives to fight another day. He is
battle-hardened, wary, and on edge. His back is stooped and
his posture guarded. His eyes are open and alert as though
he is expecting—and dreading—his enemy's approach.

Key Symbols

Last Stand. A weary man stands with a row of eight
wands behind him. Symbolically, his back is up against a
wall.

On Guard. He seems to stand defensively, as though
he's anticipating another attack.

A Pause in the Action. Despite the threat, he has found
a place where he can fall back, regroup his thoughts, gather
his strength, and prepare for whatever may come.

Die Another Day. The Nine of Wands is also a card of some hope; despite his physical condition, the wounded warrior has lived to fight another day.

Scenic Backdrop. Some tarot readers point out that the landscape in this card is flat
and one-dimensional. It may be an illusionary device, like a scenic backdrop or curtain
that hides the real action backstage.

Keywords

Upright: Resistance, courage, self-defense, discipline, willpower
Reversed: Obstacles, adversity, calamity, weakness, character flaws, fearfulness

Writing Prompts

Write about:

- a pause in the action
- a battle cry
- a security guard
- a night watchman
- an escape route

Ten of Wands

THE TEN OF WANDS IS a card of oppression. An overburdened laborer struggles under the weight of a heavy load of timbers—the ten wands that give the card its name.

Key Symbols

Beast of Burden. The ten wands in the worker's arms are a heavy load.

Disorganization. Not only are they a burden, but they're also an organizational nightmare. The wands are entangled, like good intentions gone awry. The general impression is one of inefficiency.

Not My Department. The tangled wands might symbolize red tape and overgrown bureaucracy.

Misalignment. The worker is stooped and unbalanced. The strain on his arms, back, neck and shoulders is probably excruciating. He seems almost certainly headed for a fall.

Close to Home. The only consolation may be that his destination isn't far away.

Keywords

Upright: Oppression, burden, cruelty, malice, revenge, injustice, overbearing force, failure, opposition, ill will, slander, envy, obstinacy, generosity, self-sacrifice, fortune, gain, treachery, subterfuge, duplicity, treason, trickery, deception, cunning, disguise, hypocrisy, disloyalty, hindrance, inconvenience

Reversed: Perseverance, dedication

Writing Prompts

Write about:

- a laborer

- a burden

- a mission

- a delivery

- a stumble or a fall

Page of Wands

THE PAGE OF WANDS IS a real fireball. In fact, according to tarot theory, he *is* fire—in human form. That's because all of the pages are said to physically embody the elements of their suit.

The Page of Wands is daring and courageous, filled with energy, ambition, and drive. He is impulsive—quick to react to any stimulus or provocation and quick to jump to conclusions. He's quick to fall in love and equally quick to lash out in anger.

Like fire itself, he can be warm and passionate. Without a safe place to burn, however, he can also rage out of control—and he could become unstable, violent, and destructive.

Key Symbols

Youthful Outlook. Like all pages, the Page of Wands is youthful, with childlike enthusiasm and an unbounded capacity to learn.

Messenger Service. During the Renaissance, pages were the youngest members of the royal court. It was their job to take news from one person to another. Because the suit of Wands is concerned with spiritual life, the fiery Page of Wands specializes in delivering spiritual messages.

Student Worker. Pages were also students, learning their future roles through apprenticeships. The Page of Wands focuses on spiritual lessons.

Confidence. The Page of Wands is confident and self-assured. Both of his feet are firmly planted on the ground, and he holds his wand with both hands.

Dry Heat. He stands alone in an arid desert. Because he is the personification of fire, he is comfortable in the heat. His face is even turned to the sun; he bathes in its light.

Keywords

Upright: A youthful person—fiery, spirited, creative, and outspoken—or a messenger with news about your career

Reversed: A rash, immature, thoughtless young person who speaks without thinking; a superficial, theatrical, cruel, and unstable young woman

Writing Prompts

Write about:

- a fiery young person

- a moment of passion

- a burning desire

- a spiritual message

- a spiritual lesson

Knight of Wands

THE KNIGHT OF WANDS, LIKE all of the court cards in his suit, is fiery and energetic. He's the proverbial tall, dark stranger of tarot—witty, flirtatious, and romantic. He can also be fierce, short-tempered, impulsive, and impetuous. He is a spiritual wanderer, traveler, and adventurer.

Key Symbols

Pyramid Power. Like the great crusaders of old, the Knight of Wands is on a journey, skillfully riding a cantering horse. He's traveling past several pyramids, a sign that he's in the hot, arid desert that fiery personalities enjoy.

A Knight's Quest. During medieval times, knights were adventurers and rescuers, sworn to defend the weak and helpless while they journeyed to fulfill a quest. Most stories about knights are actually stories about transformation. In most renditions, a knight is on a quest for a mystical object such as the Holy Grail. As he pursues his mission, he encounters—and overcomes—a series of obstacles, which have all been deliberately contrived to test and challenge him. By the end of his quest, the knight has learned that the mystical object he sought was never really the true goal of his adventure. Rather, the mission was one of self-transformation and change.

Astrological Symbolism. Astrologically, the four knights of the tarot are associated with the four mutable signs of the zodiac. The Knight of Wands represents the mutable fire sign of Sagittarius, which makes him outgoing and adventurous.

Elemental Symbolism. Elementally speaking, the four knights of the tarot are all fiery. They simply combine the element of fire with the element of their own suit. In this case, the Knight of Wands is a uniform blend of fire and fire.

Historic Significance. Historically, the Knight of Wands was connected with departures, absences, long journeys, and even emigration to a foreign land. It was also believed to foretell a frustrating marriage for a woman.

Keywords

Upright: A dark young man; spiritual rescue or adventure; departure, absence, flight, emigration, a move to a new home

Reversed: Rupture, division, interruption, discord, alienation, a break in a relationship

Writing Prompts

Write about:

- an excitable young man

- a pyromaniac

- a mysterious tablet with hieroglyphic figures

- a spiritual adventure

- a spiritual rescue

Queen of Wands

THE QUEEN OF WANDS IS a fiery redhead—and she's also one of the most charismatic figures in the tarot deck. She's the person every woman wants as a friend, and every man wants as a lover . . . or at least as a dance partner.

She's the life of the party, and she's used to being the center of attention. Friendly and outgoing, she's also a notorious flirt. Sometimes, those flirtations take her all the way into a one-night stand or an affair—even if she's married or in a committed relationship.

Her passion and enthusiasm know no bounds. She's physically fit, energetic, and strong. She can run marathons—spiritually, emotionally, and physically. She's also a smart, savvy businesswoman who loves money and success.

Key Symbols

Queen of Fire. Like all of the tarot's queens, the Queen of Wands is a mature woman, gracious and wise in the ways of the world. Queens, of course, are rulers—but their rule is based on the feminine principles of safeguarding and nurturing their realms. The Queen of Wands is charged with safeguarding and nurturing the suit of Wands, which corresponds to the fiery world of spirit.

Sunflowers. Almost every symbol in the card reinforces the Queen's connection with fire. The Queen of Wands is surrounded by sunflowers—symbols of fire and the heat of summer. They grow around her, and they're carved into the back of her throne. She even holds a sunflower in her left hand as a counterpart to the wand in her right hand.

Regal Lions. The lions on her throne represent the astrological sign of Leo, which is ruled by the sun. The queen herself is a lionesque personality. Technically, of course, she's a lioness—smaller, lighter, and more agile than the male of her species. Lion society is matriarchal, and the females are in charge of the hunt, too.

Black Cat. Her black cat, like a witch's familiar, sits knowingly at her feet.

Astrological Symbolism. Astrologically, the four queens of the tarot are associated with the four cardinal signs of the zodiac. The Queen of Wands represents the cardinal fire sign of Aries, which makes her a natural leader.

Elemental Symbolism. Elementally speaking, the four queens are all watery. Each one combines the element of water with the element of her suit. As a result, the queen of the fiery suit of wands embodies the steamy combination of water with fire.

Keywords

Upright: Fiery, energetic, passionate, powerful, dynamic, generous, willful, confident, friendly, kind, outgoing, dramatic, enthusiastic, optimistic

Reversed: Fierce, domineering, jealous, deceitful, potentially unfaithful, disorganized

Writing Prompts

Write about:

- a fiery redheaded woman
- a not-so-innocent flirtation
- a witch's familiar
- a black cat
- steam

King of Wands

THE KING OF WANDS IS a visionary entrepreneur. He's a mentor, a businessman, and an enthusiastic captain of industry. He never rests—as you can tell by his inability to sit still, even in the card. He is honest, courageous, and strong. He's a tireless defender of the persecuted and oppressed. And he is generous, almost to a fault.

The King of Wands is swift, strong, and impulsive. While he would normally be slow to form an opinion—and he's sometimes prone to indecision—he's also the type of person who likes to argue simply for argument's sake. Once he forms an opinion, he doesn't change it easily. He's fair, noble, just, courageous, and romantic. He also has a good sense of humor; he appreciates a well-executed practical joke.

Key Symbols

A Spiritual Leader. Kings are active rulers and protectors, willing to defend their realms and dispense justice on behalf of their countrymen. Wands cards all relate to spiritual and career issues. As a result, the King of Wands focuses his fiery energy on the spiritual realm.

A Man of Action. The King of Wands leans forward, legs apart, as though he could leap to his feet at any moment.

High IQ. Like all of the tarot's kings, he wears a ceremonial cap of maintenance beneath his crown. Head coverings symbolize intellect and thought.

Creatures of Fire. A lion, his royal emblem, is carved into the back of his throne. A small salamander, the elemental creature of fire, scurries past his feet.

Sorry, Girls, He's Taken. Historically, the King of Wands was thought to be a happily married man. It's interesting to note, however, that his wife—the Queen of Wands—is a notorious flirt.

Astrological Symbolism. Astrologically, the four kings of the tarot are associated with the four fixed signs of the zodiac. The King of Wands represents the fixed fire sign of Leo, which makes him a confident, courageous monarch.

Elemental Symbolism. Elementally, the four kings of the tarot are all airy intellectuals. They simply combine the element of air with the corresponding element of their own suit. In that regard, the King of Wands embodies the heady combination of air with fire.

Keywords

Upright: A strong, spiritual man; a business leader; a mentor; ambition, leadership ability, enthusiasm, optimism, entrepreneurial spirit, a self-made man

Reversed: Selfishness, severity, austerity, hunger for power, impulsivity, impatience

Writing Prompts

Write about:

- an entrepreneur
- a charismatic leader
- a revivalist
- a power monger
- a lion king

Ace of Cups

THE ACE OF CUPS IS the first card in the suit of cups, the suit that corresponds to the ancient element of water. It's the card of limitless emotion. It looks like a cup flowing over with happiness—but it could suggest a measure of tears, too.

Key Symbols

New Beginnings. All of the aces represent new beginnings; the Ace of Cups symbolizes a fresh start on an emotional level. The aces also symbolize gifts: in this case, love and friendship are yours for the taking.

Hand of God. An open hand, larger than life, holds a golden chalice balanced on its outstretched palm—like a gift or an offering.

My Cup Runneth Over. Cups correspond to the watery world of emotion, and in this case, there seems to be an abundance of emotion. In fact, the cup is overflowing.

Fountains of Desire. As the waters of love and friendship spill over the rim, they separate into clearly defined streams. Those streams, in turn, feed a tranquil body of water filled with lily pads—a symbol of fertility.

Holy Spirit. The white dove above the cup symbolizes spirit, and the communion wafer in its beak represents matter. While the image reflects the Christian rite of the Eucharist, it also suggests an unborn soul entering into physical form.

New Life. In fact, the Ace of Cups can sometimes indicate a pregnancy. The cup is a feminine symbol that represents the womb, while the dove and the host suggest the joining of a spirit and a physical body. Whether the pregnancy is literal or symbolic is a matter of interpretation: the Ace might refer to the birth of a new person or a creative pursuit.

Astrological Symbolism. Astrologically, the Ace of Cups is associated with all of the powers of water—the element associated with Cancer, Scorpio, and Pisces.

Keywords

Upright: New relationships, overflowing emotions, fertility, creativity, joy, contentment, nourishment, abundance—and in the case of pregnancy, the birth of a girl

Reversed: The end of a relationship, infidelity, selfishness, infertility, failed projects. Turned upside down, the Ace of Cups will soon be drained, nothing will be held in reserve.

Writing Prompts

Write about:

- someone who has forgotten how to feel

- the conception of a child

- the elixir of life

- a drink that would endow magical powers

- a peace offering

Two of Cups

THE TWO OF CUPS IS a card of love and partnership. It normally describes a romantic relationship, but it can describe a platonic friendship, too. The card depicts the synergy and productivity that occur when two kindred spirits work together toward a shared goal, dream, or vision. Together, they become more than the sum of their parts.

Key Symbols

Drink to Me Only with Thine Eyes. Two lovers gaze into each other's eyes, where they swim, oblivious to the sights and sounds of the outside world. Each holds a cup, and they're raising their glasses in a toast to each other.

Mercury's Caduceus. Above them, a lion's head—with wings—perches on a caduceus, the staff of the Roman god Mercury. According to legend, Mercury saw two serpents entwined in mortal combat. He separated them with his wand in a gesture that came to be recognized as a sign of peace.

Waiting in the Wings. The classic caduceus doesn't have a lion's head. The lion, however, is a symbol of recreation and procreation. It could represent a soul, waiting for a vehicle into which he can be born; a few glasses of wine could hasten his arrival.

Keywords

Upright: Love, attraction, romance, passion, desire, marriage, union, affinity, friendship, compatibility, affection, faithfulness, harmony, pleasure

Reversed: Infidelity, jealousy, longing, loneliness, isolation, misunderstanding, unrequited love

Writing Prompts

Write about:

- a first date

- a first kiss

- a new romance

- a love song

- the sound of corks popping and glasses clinking

Three of Cups

THE THREE OF CUPS is a card of friendship and celebration. Under the leafy branches of a vineyard in full bloom, three young women scamper, frolic, and dance, each raising a goblet high over her head. They celebrate the coming harvest, the richness of the fruit of the vine, and the transformation of grape into celebratory wine. At times, the Three of Cups could also depict the jealousies, backstabbing, gossip, and resentments that often flare up among groups of women.

Key Symbols

The Three Graces. Most versions of the Three of Cups look like classical artist's depictions of the three Graces. These were the mythic Greek sisters Aglaia, Euphrosyne, and Thalia—also known as Splendor, Mirth, and Good Cheer; or Beauty, Gentleness, and Friendship.

The Three Fates. The trio could also be seen as the three sister goddesses who wove each person's destiny. Plato described these three Fates: Clotho, the spinner, Lachesis, the allotter, who measured the thread; and Atropos, the inevitable, who cut the thread.

The Three Norns. Similar to the Fates, the three Norns were the Scandinavian goddesses of destiny. They lived beneath the World Tree Yggdrasil, where they wove the tapestry of fate. The first sister, Urd spun the thread. Verdani, the second sister, wove it in her loom. Skuld, the third sister, cut the final string.

The Triple Goddess. Some tarot readers see the three women as the three faces of the goddess—maiden, mother, and crone. The triple goddess embodies women at different stages of life.

The Three Virtues. The three young women could also represent the three theological virtues of faith, hope, and charity.

The Three Elements. The three women could even symbolize the three elements of water, air, and fire, dancing on the surface of the earth—uniting all four elements.

Harvest Dance. The bountiful crops that surround the three women suggests that there will be even more celebration to come.

Keywords

Upright: Parties, celebrations, dancing, drinking, girls' night out, pleasure, sensuality, happiness, conviviality, hospitality, good fortune, kindness, and merriment

Reversed: Excesses, physical exhaustion, hangovers, unplanned pregnancy

Writing Prompts

Write about:

- the three goddesses of fate

- three sisters

- three generations of women

- a bachelorette party

- a women's book club

Four of Cups

THE FOUR OF CUPS IS a card of disappointment. At first glance, the figure in the Four of Cups seems drained, listless, and uninspired. He sits under the branches of an ancient tree, staring at three cups. He doesn't seem to notice that a cloud has formed to his right. A strange, ghostly hand emerges from a vaporous mist, and a fourth golden chalice materializes right before his eyes. It's as though he's getting a close-up view of the image from the Ace of Cups. Even so, his expression seems more disenchanted than amazed.

Key Symbols

A Blind Eye. The figure in the Four of Cups might not realize that there is more to life than the things of this world; he has drunk from the cups of the material sphere, but he is blinded to the gifts of the spiritual realm.

Blended Pleasure. Traditionally, the Four of Cups is known as the card of "blended pleasure." It depicts the boredom, weariness, and discontent that sometimes follow a period of excitement or exuberance. It's the low that follows a high, or the depression that succeeds a period of mania.

Buddhist Meditation. The figure in the card could be Buddha, meditating under the Bodhi tree.

The Law of Gravity. Alternatively, he might be Sir Isaac Newton, who was said to have discovered gravity while he sat under an apple tree.

Odin's Experience. He might also be the Norse god Odin, just before he climbed up the World Tree—or right after he climbed down. At one point, Odin lost his eye under the World Tree; that might explain the blindness.

Keywords

Upright: Weariness, disgust, displeasure, discontent, dissatisfaction, boredom, dejection
Reversed: New friends, new adventures, regeneration, refreshment

Writing Prompts

Write about:

- a miraculous apparition that materializes in an unlikely place
- a peace offering
- disillusionment
- disappointment
- a holograph

Five of Cups

THE FIVE OF CUPS IS a card of loss and desolation. Head bowed, a young man stands on the dusty bank of a river under a cloudy gray sky. Three cups lie beside him, all on their sides, with their contents spilling and streaming away. The two cups behind him stand upright. An arched bridge in the distance spans a flowing river, leading to a fortress on the other side of its banks.

Key Symbols

Riverbanks. The dark-robed figure in the card is standing on the bank of a river, a symbol of the constantly moving and changing waters of life.

Bridge over Troubled Water. The bridge is a symbol of connection between two worlds.

Safekeeping. The building in the background is actually a keep—the fortified stronghold of a castle or a jail.

Spilled Milk. The cups, obviously, are the key symbols in the card. What did they hold—water, wine, or blood? And how did they spill? Was there an accident, or were they a libation, poured out upon the ground as an offering to the gods?

Cloak of Invisibility. The person in the card seems stooped with grief or regret. Sadness seems wrapped around him like a cloak. It could even serve as a cloak of invisibility; others can't see past it.

Loss. The Five of Cups could signify the loss of a loved one through death. The card can also refer to the loss of a friendship or a relationship—perhaps as a result of treachery or deceit.

Five Stages of Grief. The Five of Cups is also a vivid reminder of the five stages of grief defined by Elisabeth Kübler-Ross: denial, anger, bargaining, depression, and acceptance.

Historical Significance. Historically, the Five of Cups reversed was said to herald the return of a long-lost relative.

Keywords

Upright: Disappointment, disillusionment, dissatisfaction, sorrow, loss, bitterness, frustration

Reversed: A short-lived period of mourning, soon forgotten; acceptance, recovery, hope

Writing Prompts

Write about:

- a cloak of invisibility

- a bridge

- a spill

- a bankruptcy

- grief

Six of Cups

The Six of Cups is a card of nostalgia and longing for the happiness of days gone by. In most versions of the card, a small boy offers a little girl a gift—a nosegay of flowers. The sun is shining. It's a beautiful late spring or early summer's day.

Key Symbols

Childhood Innocence. The winsome young pair in the Six of Cups represent the innocence of childhood.

Fenced Backyard. The children are safe within a garden—a symbol of rest and reflection, order over chaos, and refuge.

Family Ties. The card often describes time spent with brothers and sisters or with childhood friends.

Childhood Sweethearts. The card could herald a reunion with someone from the past. It could even portend a reunion with a childhood sweetheart.

Historic Significance. One historic interpretation of the Six of Cups suggested that an inheritance was on the way.

Keywords

Upright: Memories, nostalgia, sentimentality, sweetness, innocence, childhood, affection, reunions

Reversed: Homesickness, longing, excessive attachment to the past, false memories, unrequited love

Writing Prompts

Write about:

- someone who can travel back in time

- someone who has lost his or her memory

- the children in the card as though they are senior citizens

- the children as though they're aging in reverse—so while they look like children, they have already lived for eighty years

- living in the past

Seven of Cups

THE SEVEN OF CUPS IS a card of wonder, amazement, and desire. A lone figure stands with his back turned toward us. He seems to be looking in amazement at a swirling bank of clouds, where seven golden cups hover in midair. Each one holds an offering.

Key Symbols

The Possibilities are Endless. The seven images hold choices and possibilities that flicker in and out of view. They may be temptations, daydreams, vices, or virtues.

Déjà vu. Believe it or not, you've seen the contents of each cup before, in the cards of the Major Arcana—which in turn correspond to the seven visible planets.

The woman is the Empress, which corresponds to Venus.

The veiled figure is the High Priestess, which corresponds to the Moon.

The serpent relates to the Magician, who traditionally wears a serpent belt. It corresponds to the planet Mercury.

The castle on the hill is the Tower, which corresponds to Mars.

The shimmering jewels are the good fortune promised by the Wheel of Fortune, which corresponds to Jupiter.

The wreath is the oval garland that surrounds the dancer in the World card; it corresponds to Saturn.

And the fire-breathing dragon is an alternate manifestation of the horse from the Sun card.

Keywords

Upright: Daydreams, fantasies, visions, illusions, imagination, reflection, meditation, contemplation, memories, dreams.

Reversed: Indecisiveness, error, ambivalence

Writing Prompts

Write about:

- a daydream

- images you see in clouds

- trophies and awards

- "all that glitters is not gold"

- a "choose-your-own-adventure" story

Eight of Cups

THE EIGHT OF CUPS is the card of success abandoned in pursuit of a larger dream. It depicts someone who seems to have it all. There's a void, however, and the absence is enough to compel him to turn his back on everything he owns and begin a quest for completion.

Key Symbols

A Missing Piece. The eight cups, neatly stacked, represent an orderly, prosperous existence. The void in the collection, however, symbolizes a want or need that is unfulfilled.

A Spiritual Quest. The solitary figure in the card is a seeker, a wanderer, an individual in search of meaning and completion. The Eight of Cups raises questions about material wealth and accumulation, as well as spiritual treasures, intellectual accomplishments, and emotional relationships.

The Mountain Pass. He seems to be headed toward a crevasse in a nearby mountain range, which is always a symbol of distance to travel, obstacles to be overcome, and new heights to be scaled.

Lost Lamb. He's reminiscent of the Biblical shepherd who left an entire flock in order to find a lost lamb.

Historic Significance. One archaic interpretation of the Eight of Cups said that it heralded marriage with a fair woman.

Keywords

Upright: Temporary success, waning interest, troubled relationships, abandonment, fear of commitment, non-commitment

Reversed: Delay, refusal to move on, unanticipated complications

Writing Prompts

Write about:

- a pilgrimage

- a return from a hunt

- a shepherd

- a scavenger hunt

- . . . or take a break from writing and go for a walk

Nine of Cups

THE NINE OF CUPS IS a card of material and physical happiness. It depicts a smiling innkeeper, sitting comfortably. He's the picture of contentment: he wears a satisfied smile and leans comfortably with his back against a bar. As they say in the United Kingdom, he looks like he might be in his cups—as though he's already had a few drinks himself—and he's ready and willing to share his good fortune.

Key Symbols

A Classic Character. The figure in the Nine of Cups might be one of the world's oldest stock characters. The bartender's role doesn't need explanation or development.

What are You Drinking? Most bartenders have the gift of gab; they can banter with anyone who might wander in. They're fully stocked with an array of conversation-starters—sports, politics, books, movies, and news of the day—as well as the social skills they need to talk to customers without alienating or antagonizing them. Every writer knows that introducing a bartender is a good way to get the main characters to open up.

Poor Man's Psychiatrist. In that way, bartenders are a lot like counselors and advisors. Bartenders hear a lot of confessions. Part of the job is offering advice and comfort in liquid form. A bartender is the poor man's psychiatrist, after all. For that matter, tarot readers have been called the same thing. You might even think of the bartender as a low-rent High Priestess, stationed before a curtain of drink that divides this world from the world of inebriation, where "spirits" trump material concerns.

Timeless Setting. Bars make good settings, too, because they're universal. Walk into a dimly lit tavern on a Saturday night, and without too much effort you could probably imagine yourself anywhere in the world, at any time in history.

Set 'em Up. The bartender in the card has all of his cups in a row, and he's ready to share the wealth. Just don't tease him about having ninety-nine bottles of beer on the wall.

Keywords

Upright: Social events, parties, gatherings, a comfortable mix of business and pleasure
Reversed: Drunkenness, overindulgence, hangovers, indiscretion, candor, faults, mistakes, imperfections, deprivation

Writing Prompts

Write about:

- a bar scene. You can write a fictional bar scene, or you can take a notebook to your favorite watering hole and record your observations. If you're not a drinker, head to a coffee bar.

- a cocktail party

- a dialogue between a bartender and one of your characters

- a hangover

- a mythic ally or helper who seems like an ordinary person

Ten of Cups

THE TEN OF CUPS IS the card of a happy home and family life. A husband and wife stand side by side. The man wraps one arm around the woman's waist, and they both raise their arms in a gesture of wonder and salute while the children hold hands and dance for joy. The whole family is standing on the bank of a lake or a stream, not far from their cozy cottage. Overhead, ten golden cups seem to shimmer in the arc of a colorful rainbow.

Key Symbols

Historic Significance. Historically, the Ten of Cups represented a good marriage—one that turned out to be even better than expected.

Productivity. The children in the card symbolize the productivity that can result from a successful partnership. It doesn't matter whether the children are literally the couple's offspring, or simply the tangible results of their relationship. In an ideal marriage, husband and wife enhance each other's creativity.

A Family of Four. The family in this card symbolizes a quaternary—a grouping of four that combines to form a whole, like the four Court Cards in each suit. They complement and complete each other. The number is also a nod to the four elements and the four suits of the Minor Arcana.

Home Sweet Home. The cozy cottage in the background obviously illustrates a happy home, a warm and comfortable refuge from the outside world.

Water. The stream in the background is the river of life that runs from one card to another, connecting all of the cards in the tarot. It symbolizes the bond of energy and emotion that links people in the real world, too.

Rainbow. The rainbow is a sign of a covenant, a sacred obligation.

Keywords

Upright: Peace, joy, happiness, contentment, love, family life, peace and quiet, honor, virtue

Reversed: Unhappiness, sorrow, arguments, disputes, betrayal, breakups, wrath, anger, irritation

Writing Prompts

Write about:

- a family with young children

- a cottage

- a rainbow

- the calm after a storm

- a far-reaching promise

Page of Cups

THE PAGE OF CUPS IS a dreamer. He's a young man with an old soul and the heart of a poet. He's an artist, well suited to literary pursuits, songwriting, lyric composition . . . anything that demands an undercurrent of emotion.

Still waters run deep, and the Page of Cups is a bottomless spring of thought and contemplation. In fact, according to tarot tradition, the Page of Cups *is* water—in human form. He personifies the fluid undercurrents that define the suit of cups. Because he's young and immature, his emotions can rise and fall with the tides.

Key Symbols

Youthful Enthusiasm. Like all pages, the Page of Cups is young, with childlike enthusiasm and an unbounded capacity to learn.

Speedy Delivery. During the Renaissance, pages were the youngest members of the royal court, frequently serving as messengers. Because the suit of cups is concerned with spiritual life, the Page of Cups specializes in delivering messages with an emotional impact.

Student of the Month. Pages were also students, learning their future roles through apprenticeships. The Page of Cups focuses on emotional lessons.

Swim with the Fishes. The Page of Cups is pictured standing on the shore of a rolling ocean. He holds a cup with a fish; the fish seems to be talking, and because the Page of Cups is the personification of water, he speaks the language of the seas.

260

Keywords

Upright: A kind, sympathetic, romantic, tender, sweet, gentle, dreamy, and imaginative young person—but also one who is sometimes unlucky in love.

Reversed: An insincere person who tries to win support through flattery. Jealousy, hypersensitivity, and melancholy.

Writing Prompts

Write about:

- an emotional message
- an emotional lesson
- the language of the seas
- an underwater society
- a flood

Knight of Cups

THE KNIGHT OF CUPS IS gallant, graceful, and generous. He is imaginative—even visionary. More than anything, he is a romantic idealist who believes that beauty is truth, and truth is beauty.

Unfortunately, the Knight of Cups is so romantic that he will fall in love with every beautiful woman who crosses his path. He will leave you with a long, lingering kiss on your doorstep, and he'll promise to call. He'll mean it, too—but once he's back on his horse and another beautiful woman crosses his path, he'll simply forget.

Key Symbols

Water, Water Everywhere. The Knight of Cups is a handsome knight in shining armor. He seems to raise his cup in salute as he and his white horse stand on the bank of a wide, clear river that is fed by a rushing waterfall.

A Quiet Hero. During medieval times, knights were adventurers and rescuers, sworn to defend the weak and helpless while they journeyed to fulfill a quest. The Knight of Cups doesn't seem particularly adventurous. Instead, he is a dreamer and a visionary, who rides gracefully and quietly, and his winged helmet symbolizes the misty clouds of his imagination.

Astrological Symbolism. Astrologically, the four knights of the tarot are associated with the four mutable signs of the zodiac. The Knight of Cups represents the mutable water sign of Pisces, which makes him sensitive and introspective.

Elemental Symbolism. Elementally speaking, the four knights of the tarot are all fiery. They simply combine the element of fire with the element of their own suit. In that regard, the Knight of Cups embodies the steamy combination of fire with water.

Historic Significance. Years ago, the Knight of Cups was said to herald a visit from a friend who would bring unexpected money.

Keywords

Upright: Romantic adventure, poetry, artistic creativity, a dreamer, a visionary
Reversed: An evil, merciless man; mischief, trickery, fraud, duplicity, swindle

Writing Prompts

Write about:

- a romantic hero

- a visionary

- a traveling poet

- an emotional adventure

- an emotional rescue

Queen of Cups

THE QUEEN OF CUPS EFFORTLESSLY balances marriage and family—and for many, she represents the perfect wife and mother. She's a wellspring of love and devotion. She's caring, giving, nurturing, sensitive, protective, and kind.

The Queen of Cups is innately sensitive to other people's feelings. She is naturally intuitive, and she's exceptionally psychic. In fact, she's so empathic that at times she can seem like a mind reader. She can read oracles and interpret dreams, and she's well equipped to make a career as a professional counselor or a therapist.

She's also creative and artistic. At home, she's an accomplished cook who seems to specialize in hearty soups and stews, along with cookies, cakes, and pies.

Key Symbols

Queen of Water. Like all of the tarot's queens, the Queen of Cups is a mature woman, gracious and wise in the ways of the world. Queens, of course, are rulers—but their rule is based on the feminine principles of safeguarding and nurturing their realms. The Queen of Cups is charged with safeguarding and nurturing the suit of Cups, which corresponds to the watery world of emotions.

Water Signs. Almost every symbol in the card reinforces the Queen's connection with water. From her seashell-shaped throne, apparently carved from mother of pearl, she gazes contemplatively into the depths of her golden chalice. Her silvery satin gown flows gracefully, as do the waves of her golden hair. She is surrounded by water, with a reflective, clear lake both behind and in front of her.

Astrological Symbolism. Astrologically, the four queens of the tarot are associated with the four cardinal signs of the zodiac. The Queen of Cups represents the cardinal water sign of Cancer, which makes her a natural wife and mother.

Elemental Symbolism. Elementally speaking, the four queens are all watery. Each one combines the element of water with the element of her suit. As a result, the queen of the watery suit of Cups embodies the placid combination of water with even more water.

Historic Symbolism. Historically, the Queen of Cups card was said to foretell a rich marriage for a man and a distinguished marriage for a woman.

Keywords

Upright: A fair woman; good, honest, devoted, intelligent, warm, nurturing, healing, protective, sensitive, psychic, intuitive; a counselor or therapist; the perfect wife and mother

Reversed: A meddling, suffocating, or overbearing woman

Writing Prompts

Write about:

- a "perfect" wife and mother—with a secret

- an empath

- an oracle in the classic sense of the word: a person, not a fortunetelling device

- a woman who smothers those she loves, killing them with kindness

- a seaside home

King of Cups

THE KING OF CUPS IS a kind and gentle man. He's just and fair, often associated with business, law, science, or the ministry. He's frequently connected to art and science, too. When he sits on his throne, he seems lost in thought—but his quiet, calm demeanor disguises a fierce and passionate nature.

Oddly enough, the King of Cups was also said to be a man in a powerful position who could be shifty in his business dealings. Historically, the King of Cups was a cautionary card, warning of ill-will on the part of a man of position; he could be a hypocrite, only pretending to help.

Today, however, many tarot readers believe that the King of Cups represents a devoted husband and father, committed to his wife and family, and protective of their feelings.

Key Symbols

King of Water. Like all of the kings in the tarot deck, the King of Cups is a seasoned, experienced man. He has successfully completed the mission he undertook as the former Knight of Cups. He was rewarded with the keys to the kingdom, and he now rules the entire realm—as well as its armies, which defend and conquer in the name of the throne.

A Watery World. Almost every symbol in the card reinforces the King's connection to water. He leans forward on his floating throne, which is carved with seashells and seahorses. He's wearing a fish-shaped pendant, a blue tunic, and a long, flowing cape. He holds a golden scepter in his left hand and a golden chalice in his right. Behind him, a merchant sailing ship glides across the waves and a dolphin leaps above the seafoam.

Astrological Symbolism. Astrologically, the four kings of the tarot are associated with the four fixed signs of the zodiac. The King of Cups represents the fixed fire sign of Scorpio, which makes him an intensely passionate individual.

Elemental Symbolism. Elementally, the four kings of the tarot are all airy intellectuals. They simply combine the element of air with the corresponding element of their own suit. In that regard, the King of Cups embodies the vaporous combination of air with water.

Historic Significance. According to tradition, the King of Cups might be something of a hypocrite who offers help without intending to follow through. In modern interpretations, however, the King of Cups is a fitting counterpart to the Queen of Cups, in which case he may be a loving, caring husband and father.

Keywords

Upright: A good, honest man; kind, generous, wise, compassionate, artistic, cultured, inspired, tolerant, intuitive, empathic, and sensitive

Reversed: Idleness, untruthfulness, dishonesty, shiftiness, double-dealing, two-timing, alcoholism

Writing Prompts

Write about:
- a fundamentalist minister who believes passionately in evolution
- a sea world veterinarian
- a faith healer
- a hypocrite
- King Neptune

Ace of Swords

THE ACE OF SWORDS IS the first card in the suit of swords, the suit that corresponds to the ancient element of air. It's the embodiment of intellect and thought.

In most tarot decks, the four aces share a similar design: a giant hand parts the swirling mists of a silver cloud, holding the emblem of the suit. In this case, that emblem is a gleaming silver sword, held aloft like the sword Excalibur from the legends of King Arthur. Its steely blade glints in the sun. The tip pierces a crown adorned with olive and palm branches.

Like the Ace of Wands, the Ace of Swords is held in the right hand, which symbolizes action. (The Ace of Cups and the Ace of Pentacles are both held in the left hand, which symbolizes receptivity.) Whoever holds the sword is invisible: the weapon seems to float on the air currents that correspond to the airy nature of this suit.

Key Symbols

Start Fresh. All of the aces represent new beginnings; this one heralds a new beginning on an intellectual level. The aces also symbolize gifts. In this case, learning, higher thought, logic, and communication are yours for the taking.

Something's in the Air. The airy Ace of Swords cuts to the heart of any issue. It represents the essence of reason, thought, understanding, and verbal communication. The sword also represents an ability to cut through any clouds of confusion, to pierce any veil of mystery or misunderstanding.

An Aggressive Defense. The sword is a longstanding symbol of justice, liberation, and truth. The goddess of justice holds a sword. So did medieval knights, who were sworn to protect and defend those who couldn't fight for themselves. In a tarot reading, the Ace of Swords could represent an aggressive defense or a just offense.

Reward Offered. The Ace of Swords is a forceful card. It denotes triumph, conquest, victory, and success on the battlefield. That battlefield, of course, is metaphoric and could relate to any arena: work, home, love, money, or health. The olive and palm branches symbolize victory and peace through strength.

A King's Crown. The crown symbolizes leadership and authority, but on a higher level it symbolizes the power that created the universe.

Fertile Thinking. Like all the aces, the Ace of Swords can represent the potential for creation. Occasionally it might indicate a pregnancy: the sword's tip penetrates the base of a crown, suggesting the physical act of impregnation. The image could foretell a literal pregnancy or suggest that a new idea is about to be conceived.

Astrological Symbolism. Astrologically, the Ace of Swords is associated with all of the powers of air—the element associated with Gemini, Libra, and Aquarius.

Historic Significance. Historically, the Ace of Swords was said to portend either great prosperity or great misery. Reversed, the card was believed to symbolize a broken engagement, for a woman, because of her own lack of prudence.

Keywords

Upright: Decisiveness, intellect, logic, judgment, discrimination, triumph, potency
Reversed: Dullness, indecision, illogic, poor judgment, impotence

Writing Prompts

Write about:

- a magic weapon

- Excalibur

- an argument

- the long arm of the law

- a stabbing pain

Two of Swords

THE TWO OF SWORDS is one of the strangest images in the tarot deck: A lone woman, dressed in a long gown, perches on a stone bench as regally as if she were sitting on a throne. Her arms are laid across her chest like a corpse's, and she tries to maintain a tenuous equilibrium by balancing two heavy swords against her shoulders. The sky above her is dark and cloudy, lit only by a sliver of the crescent moon.

Key Symbols

Tough Choices. When the Two of Swords appears in a reading, it typically represents a difficult decision—a choice between two conflicting thoughts, ideas, or emotions.

Reconciliation. The card could symbolize a need to reconcile two disparate views.

Limited Vision. The woman's blindfold symbolizes the loss of sight. She can still use her other four senses, however—as well as her sixth sense, intuition, which is symbolized by the moon.

Quiet Thoughts. The blindfold might also symbolize the unconscious or subconscious mind.

Truce. The Two of Swords could symbolize a moment of peace—even a temporary truce or ceasefire during times of war. Some readers believe it symbolizes courage.

Historic Significance. Historically, the Two of Swords was said to represent friendship and harmony as well as gifts for a woman or influential protection for a man in search of help. Some also said that the Two of Swords symbolized interaction and dealings with rogues.

Keywords

Upright: Decision, choices, equilibrium, balance, initiation
Reversed: Blindness, indecision, disloyalty, treachery, lies

Writing Prompts

Write about:

- a decision

- a truce

- a blindfold

- a crescent moon

- a seaside meditation

Three of Swords

THE THREE OF SWORDS HARDLY needs to be interpreted or explained to most people: it's the picture of heartbreak and overwhelming grief. It's a living, beating heart, still filled with blood and capable of supporting life. For the moment, however, its owner must wonder if that life is still worth living.

Key Symbols

When it Rains, it Pours. The image itself is simple: a disembodied heart is suspended in a cloudy sky where rain falls like tears.

Stabbed in the Heart. Three razor-sharp swords stab the heart at regularly spaced intervals.

Divorce. The Three of Swords often refers to separation or divorce. Because there are three swords, the card may indicate a relationship destroyed by a third person, through betrayal or infidelity.

Lost Pregnancy. Occasionally, the Three of Swords symbolizes the grief and sorrow that follows a miscarriage or stillbirth. That interpretation is based on the number of swords, which represent the creative force and bond between mother, father, and child.

Chest Pain. In rare cases, the Three of Swords could suggest anxiety or panic attacks, heart disease, or surgery.

Bleeding Heart. The Three of Swords might also represent a bleeding heart—someone who sympathizes with anyone who has a sad story to tell.

Sacred Heart. The Three of Swords also looks like the Sacred Heart of Christ, bleeding of wounds inflicted by his crown of thorns. That may be one reason that early tarot scholars said the Three of Swords could represent a nun.

Keywords

Upright: Sorrow, sadness, grief, loss, divorce, infidelity, depression
Reversed: Healing, recovery, blessings in disguise

Writing Prompts

Write about:

- a broken heart

- an adulterous affair

- a miscarriage

- a stillbirth

- a rainstorm

Four of Swords

THE FOUR OF SWORDS TYPICALLY symbolizes a brief but welcome respite, retreat, or period of reflection. It can even represent a short-term illness followed by a brief period of recuperation.

Key Symbols

Lying in State. In most renditions of the card, a young knight sleeps under the soft glow of a stained glass window, arms folded in a prayerlike gesture across his chest. Alternately, the card depicts a knight in effigy, carved into the lid of a tomb. He lies flat on his back, and his hands are clasped in perpetual prayer.

Worldly Concerns. Three swords are suspended above him, either in midair or mounted on the chapel wall. They represent the ever-present worries and concerns of the world, hanging in a state of suspended animation.

Ready for Battle. A fourth sword lies near the knight, ready to be called into service on a moment's notice.

Rest and Recuperation. In the classical religious sense of the image, the knight isn't dead—he's only sleeping. An earthly battle has been won; now the soldier rests in peace and awaits his resurrection.

Helping Hand. The stained glass window in the background shows one person ministering to another.

Overnight Journeys. The Four of Swords can also represent dreams, mystic journeys, or out-of-body travel and experiences.

Initiation Ceremony. The card could symbolize the ceremony of ritual death and resurrection that some secret societies use to initiate their members.

Keywords

Upright: Rest, retreat, recuperation, recovery, relaxation
Reversed: Fatigue, illness, fever

Writing Prompts

Write about:

- what happens after death

- a cemetery

- a crypt

- the relic of a saint

- an initiation ceremony

Five of Swords

THE FIVE OF SWORDS IS the card of defeat and humiliation, in which a victorious fighter gathers the spoils of war. Two of his vanquished opponents are walking toward the horizon, heads bowed, and he watches them with a smug, self-satisfied smile on his face.

Key Symbols

Battle of the Minds. In the swords cards, battle scenes usually represent intellectual conflicts or verbal arguments.

Not a Fair Fight. The Five of Swords often symbolizes poor sportsmanship.

Blowing Over. The billowing, fast-moving clouds in the sky seem to hint at a victory that will be short-lived.

Numeric Significance. In the tarot, the five cards almost always spell trouble, indicating a crisis and the need for continuing resolve at the halfway point in the progression from one to ten. That's when events can either take a turn for the better or go horribly awry.

Historic Significance. Historically, the Five of Swords warned of an attack on someone's finances.

Keywords

Upright: Defeat, humiliation, degradation, failure, loss, dishonor, poor sportsmanship, malice, slander

Reversed: A short-lived victory

Writing Prompts

Write about:

- the agony of defeat

- a poor sport

- a sore winner

- a brief, public argument

- spoils of war

Six of Swords

The Six of Swords is one of the most compelling cards in the tarot deck, with many layers of deeply moving symbolism. It's a card of transition from one life to another, from a troubled existence to a more peaceful reality.

Key Symbols

River Crossing. A ferryman steers his craft across a small body of water, from one shore to the other. His passenger is seated quietly, clothed from head to foot in a hooded robe. Symbolically, the boat represents an individual floating along the river of life; the ferryman is a spirit guide, and the passenger is the spirit in the physical vessel of a body.

Scars in One's Soul. The bottom of the boat has been pierced by six separate swords, which stand upright like ghostly passengers. They represent old injuries, wounds, scars, and assaults, and they've become a permanent fixture. To pull them out would leave the ship full of holes.

Tour Guide. In ancient Greek mythology, Charon was the psychopomp who ferried the souls of the newly dead across the river Acheron—or the River Styx—if they could pay his fare. In fact, people were often buried with gold coins over their eyes or under their tongues so they could to pay for their passage.

Time is a River. The water behind the ferry, which symbolizes the past, is choppy and rough. The water ahead, representing the future, looks smooth.

Literal Meaning. While the Six of Swords often symbolizes a spiritual journey, it can also represent a literal journey—especially a short, pleasant trip across water.

Company News. The Six of Swords might also represent the arrival of a traveling envoy or a messenger.

Little Deaths. In many tarot decks this image has a haunting, spectral quality, sometimes suggesting a sort of death. Just as the Death card itself rarely indicates a literal, physical death, the Six of Swords may refer to a smaller, less deadly assault—such as a crudely hurled insult or the jab of a sharp word.

Historic Significance. Historically, the Six of Swords was said to herald a public declaration of love or a proposal, or an unfavorable end to a lawsuit.

Keywords

Upright: Transition, journey, voyage, travel by water
Reversed: Stasis, delay, permanence

Writing Prompts

Write about:

- the River Styx
- a trip to a distant land
- an uncharted voyage
- a journey to the underworld
- travel by water

Seven of Swords

THE SEVEN OF SWORDS DEPICTS the proverbial thief in the night. He has stolen into his enemy's camp, and he's making off with the weapons left unguarded. The enemies are oblivious to the fact that they've been invaded.

Key Symbols

Alarm System. The Seven of Swords clearly points out that someone needs to be on guard: theft, deception, and subterfuge are afoot.

Double Agent. The thief pictured in the card could be a traitor or a counterspy.

Watch What You Say. In more practical terms, the thief could be a backstabbing gossip. Swords are about communication, after all.

Camping Out. The tents represent protection from the elements, as well as a place for strategic battle planning.

Flag Day. The banners flying over the tents symbolize a rallying point for the troops.

Historic Significance. Historically, the Seven of Swords was said to be a good card. Fortunetellers in the past said it suggested a dark girl, and that it promised a peaceful life in the country. Reversed, it heralded a news release or public announcement.

Keywords

Upright: Theft, sabotage, humiliation, defeat, sneak attacks, spies, enemies, unreliable friends, plagiarism

Reversed: Courage, self-respect

Writing Prompts

Write about:

- a thief, spy, or traitor

- a gossip

- stolen property

- stolen moments

- a campground

Eight of Swords

THE EIGHT OF SWORDS REPRESENTS a damsel in distress—much like the woman in *The Perils of Pauline*. In that series of classic silent movies, a young heiress was routinely abducted and entrapped by a money-hungry villain—and just as routinely, she was rescued by a dashing hero.

Key Symbols

Damsel In Distress. While this young woman hasn't been tied to a railroad track, she has been blindfolded and tied to a tree.

Caged Like an Animal. She's encircled by swords that are reminiscent of prison bars.

Slippery Footing. The ground beneath her feet is muddy and wet; she seems to be standing in a marsh or a swamp.

Victim Mentality. The woman in the card doesn't seem to have put up much of a fight. She may be a willing victim, perhaps suffering from Stockholm Syndrome. She may be a martyr for a cause.

Passive Resistance. She's not struggling against her bonds; she stands still with her head bent. If she wants to be liberated, she'll probably have to free herself. If she can't shake the blindfold off, she might need to feel her way out of her prison by stepping gingerly through the row of swords. Alternatively, she could shimmy up to one of the swords to cut some ties—and that could be a metaphor.

Historic Significance. Historically, the Eight of Swords suggested scandal for a woman, spread by rumors and gossip. Reversed, it symbolized the departure of a relative.

Keywords

Upright: Restriction, imprisonment, bondage, entrapment, victimization, crisis, criticism, blame, misfortunes, disgrace

Reversed: Freedom, liberation, self-sufficiency

Writing Prompts

Write about:

- entrapment

- a prison

- a jail cell

- bars on a cage

- a rescue

Nine of Swords

THE NINE OF SWORDS IS the card of despair. A woman sits bolt upright in bed. She's surrounded by inky blackness, and her hands cover her face. She's in anguish. Her blanket is rumpled, as if she has been tossing and turning for hours, and nine ominous swords loom in the air above her bed.

Key Symbols

Wake-up Call. The Nine of Swords often symbolizes nightmares, phobias, insomnia, and worry—particularly the type of worry that strikes at three in the morning, waking us from a sound sleep and keeping us up while we ponder all the horrible fates that could befall us or the ones we love.

Dark Night of the Soul. The card can also represent a period of spiritual desolation—the "dark night of the soul" described by St. John of the Cross.

Three a.m. Feeding. It's always darkest just before the dawn. At three in the morning, when we're awakened by a nightmare or we find ourselves battling insomnia, our worst fears can grow to monstrous proportions.

Mini-blinds. The swords in the card almost look like a curtain of fear and oppression. If you look closely at the image, however, you will notice one important fact: the swords have no substance. There is no light reflecting off their surface, and there are no shadows to indicate depth. In other words, those swords aren't real. They are simply figments of her imagination.

Loneliness. Sadly, the anguished woman in the illustration is alone, unwilling or unable to call a friend or a partner to comfort her and keep her company.

Security Blanket. In many renditions of the card, she sleeps under an astrological quilt. She can take comfort in the fact that the heavens above protect her, and that the cycles of the star indicate that no situation is static. In fact, the world will keep turning, the planets will continue in their orbit around the sun, and light from distant constellations will remind us of the strengths associated with the signs of the zodiac.

Historic Significance. Historically, the Nine of Swords was said to refer to a minister, priest, or some other member of the clergy, as well as a temple, church, monastery, or convent. It was also said to suggest that someone's suspicions or misgivings about a shady character were well-founded.

Keywords

Upright: Nightmares, obsession, despair, insomnia, mental cruelty, grief, sorrow, loss, guilt, shame, fear, dread

Reversed: Consciousness, calm, rationality

Writing Prompts

Write about:

- a nightmare

- a premonition

- a sound in the middle of the night

- a bed, a blanket, or a quilt

- a story that comes to you in your sleep

Ten of Swords

THE TEN OF SWORDS IS one of the most gruesome cards in the tarot deck. It's the card of overkill and ruin.

Here, in the last card in the suit, all the swords have come to a final resting place. Unfortunately for the man depicted, they've landed in a gruesome line along the full length of his torso. Heavy dark clouds hang low over the horizon, where only a sliver of light shows any promise of a new day.

Key Symbols

He's Dead, Jim. A murder victim lies sprawled in a pool of his own blood. In an obvious case of overkill, he has been stabbed ten times. The murder weapons, ten swords, are still embedded in his body.

Crime of Passion. One look at the victim and there can be no mistaking that this is a crime of passion. No disinterested killer would go to such lengths.

A Clue to the Killer. The dead man's hand seems to be frozen in some sort of parting gesture.

Live By the Sword. Swords are rarely literal; in most cases, they represent words, thoughts, and verbal duels. In this case, the dead man might have succumbed to vicious personal attacks, gossip, and backstabbing.

Negative Imagery. Not surprisingly, most tarot readers interpret it as a card of suffering, pain, disillusionment, and grief.

Silver Linings. There is a bright side, however—or at least a glimmer of hope. The sun is either setting or rising at the horizon, and the clouds really do have silver linings. A new day will dawn soon.

Final Endings. In tarot, the ten cards normally represent conclusions—and when the Ten of Swords appears in a reading, those conclusions are inarguable. The figure in this card will never rise again. His spirit is free to go. He can leave the scene of the crime and move on to a higher plane.

Historic Significance. Historically, fortunetellers were careful to point out that the Ten of Swords was not a card of violent death. However, it sometimes did suggest imprisonment or treason—especially if it was followed by an Ace and a King. The card also bears a certain resemblance to Julius Caesar's murder.

Keywords

Upright: Ruin, defeat, grief, disruption, desolation, sadness, distress, lies, spite, gossip
Reversed: Advantage, power, authority

Writing Prompts

Write about:

- a crime of passion

- a murder

- physical pain

- gossip

- a backstabbing friend or colleague

Page of Swords

The Page of Swords is a young man with his head in the clouds. Like all pages, he has a childlike enthusiasm and an unbounded capacity to learn. He is a reader, a writer, and a talker. He's precocious—practically a prodigy. He is thoughtful and imaginative, and he's naturally drawn to teachers, scientists, and philosophers.

The Page of Swords is also perpetually observant and alert. He doesn't miss a thing. If he isn't officially in the loop, he'll conduct a little investigative research on his own to find out what everyone else in the castle is doing.

His outlook is as crisp and clear as the summer sky. In fact, according to tarot tradition, the Page of Swords *is* air—in human form. He's the embodiment of the fast-moving energy that connects the suit of Swords to the world of intellect and communication. In other words, the Page of Swords is a graphic example of how air can take human form.

Key Symbols

The Sky's the Limit. Like all pages, the Page of Swords is youthful, with childlike enthusiasm and an unbounded capacity to learn.

Air Mail. During the Renaissance, pages were the youngest members of the royal court. It was their job to take news from one person to another. Because the suit of Swords is concerned with intellectual life, the airy Page of Swords specializes in delivering intellectual messages.

Honor Student. Pages were also students, learning their future roles through apprenticeships. The intellectual Page of Swords is a model student; he's a reader and a thinker.

Lost in Thought. The Page of Swords is a lithe, active young man who holds a sword in both hands. He looks as though he's walking across a rugged landscape, under a sky filled with billowing clouds. His hair is blowing in the wind, and he seems to pause for a moment, as though he's heard a sound carried on the breeze. He looks lost in thought, but he leans slightly forward on one leg, as if he's about to start running.

Historic Significance. Historically, the Page of Swords was connected to spies, surveillance, undercover operatives, and secret service employees.

Keywords

Upright: Intelligence, keen powers of observation, vigilance
Reversed: Spies, revealed secrets

Writing Prompts

Write about:

- an intellectual message

- an intellectual lesson

- an airhead

- a voice heard on the wind

- a snippet of song

Knight of Swords

THE KNIGHT OF SWORDS IS probably the one who best matches most people's conception of a knight. He is a skillful, brave warrior—more of a fighter than a lover. His armor is always polished, and his horse is always ready to ride.

He's a whirlwind who rides in with a clap of thunder and a flash of lightning. The atmosphere around him is charged with passion and intensity. At any moment, the storm could break, the skies will clear, and he'll be looking for a place to dry off.

The Knight of Swords is a quick thinker. He's intelligent, articulate, and analytical. He's also enthusiastic, energetic, and brave. His courage sometimes borders on the foolhardy—almost as though he thinks he's immortal.

The Knight of Swords didn't just memorize the code of chivalry—he helped write it. He is truly a knight's knight.

Key Symbols

Air Assault. Elementally speaking, the four knights of the tarot are all fiery. They simply combine the element of fire with the element of their own suit. In that regard, the Knight of Swords embodies the combustible mix of fire with air. He might be able to ride like the wind, but he's also full of hot air.

Full Speed Ahead. The Knight of Swords rides at full speed, as if he's scattering his enemies. He brandishes a heavy sword over his head as his galloping steed charges toward his destination. They're moving fast: the horses' hooves are kicking up a storm of rocks and dust, and the knight's cape billows behind him.

Synergy. Experienced riders will tell you that when they are on their horses, their minds and bodies work in perfect harmony. Horse and rider no longer feel like two separate creatures. Their individual strengths and talents combine. The horse knows the rider's will from a gentle nudge or whispered command. The rider can sense how and where the horse will move and shift his weight accordingly. The Knight of Swords is one of those riders who move in perfect union with their animals—and his mind moves as quickly as his mount.

Astrological Symbolism. Astrologically, the four knights of the tarot are associated with the four mutable signs of the zodiac. The Knight of Swords represents the mutable air sign of Gemini, which makes him versatile and quick-thinking.

Historic Significance. Historically, the Knight of Swords was said to herald a struggle with a rival. Reversed, it was said to foretell a dispute with an imbecile. It sometimes refers to a soldier or man of arms, predicting that he will be involved in heroic action. The Knight of Swords is a prototypical hero of romantic chivalry—like Galahad, one of King Arthur's knights.

Keywords

Upright: Skill, bravery, battle, combat, defense, opposition, resistance

Reversed: Boredom, sarcasm, incompetence, ineptitude, foolishness, folly, stupidity, impertinence, extravagance, ridicule, fraud, mischief, cunning

Writing Prompts

Write about:

- a soldier on the battlefield of ideas

- a hero who offends the politically correct

- an investigator

- an intellectual adventure

- an intellectual rescue

Queen of Swords

THE QUEEN OF SWORDS EMBODIES all of the qualities of the airy Swords cards. She's probably the most intelligent woman in the tarot deck. She's a quick thinker and a clear communicator. She's intensely perceptive and keenly observant. She's got a rapier wit and a sharp tongue to match.

She's not afraid to fight for the ideals that matter to her. If she's on your side, the Queen of Swords is a loyal defender and friend. If not, she won't hesitate to cut you down to size. She didn't get to be the Queen of Swords by staying quiet, and you can count on her to make her observations and thoughts clear in any company.

She's also been tempered—made harder—by time and experience. Historically, the Queen of Swords was thought to represent a widow, but these days she can represent anyone who has suffered a devastating emotional loss, including the loss of a lover or a child. The Queen of Swords has also been associated with miscarriage and infertility.

Key Symbols

Queen of Air. Like all of the tarot's queens, the Queen of Swords is a mature woman, gracious and wise in the ways of the world. Queens, of course, are rulers—but their rule is based on the feminine principles of safeguarding and nurturing their realms. The Queen of Swords is charged with safeguarding and nurturing the suit of Swords, which corresponds to the airy world of the intellect.

Air Signs. Almost every symbol in the card reinforces the Queen's connection with air. She's surrounded by open sky, and trees bend and blow in the wind. Carved on her throne are flying birds and winged angels. She holds her left hand out, as if to gauge which direction the wind is blowing, and she holds her sword aloft in her right hand—which is her dominant hand, so it symbolizes action.

Astrological Symbolism. Astrologically, the four queens of the tarot are associated with the four cardinal signs of the zodiac. The Queen of Cups represents the cardinal air sign of Libra, which makes her a gracious and charming leader.

Elemental Symbolism. Elementally speaking, the four queens are all watery. Each one combines the element of water with the element of her suit. As a result, the queen of the airy suit of Swords embodies the vaporous combination of water with air.

Historic Significance. While the Queen of Swords' historic status as a widow makes her well acquainted with heartbreak, her personal tragedies don't keep her from enjoying the good things in life. According to some accounts, she likes to dance at parties.

Keywords

Upright: Eloquence, grace, charm, logic, intelligence, power, discernment, analysis, science, professionalism, objectivity, self-reliance, intellect, political instincts

Reversed: Anger, aloofness, willfulness, hatred, cruelty, slyness, sharp tongue, bigotry, hypocrisy, deceit

Writing Prompts

Write about:
- a widow
- a divorcee
- a mother-in-law
- a sharp-tongued woman
- a party girl

King of Swords

THE KING OF SWORDS IS a firm friend or a powerful enemy. He is an authoritative leader and commander; he makes intellectual decisions based on solid logic. He's a man of action with a keen mind that generates a steady stream of ideas.

In most versions of the card, the imposing King of Swords leans forward with a scowl on his face and a clenched fist resting on the arm of his throne. He wears a full suit of chain mail armor topped with a blue tunic and a red cape. He looks as though he's about to stand up and make a point with the heavy sword in his hand.

The King of Swords is active, clever, subtle, fierce, delicate, courageous, skillful, and inclined to domineer. He can tend to overvalue small things. At times, he can also be deceitful, tyrannical, and crafty.

Key Symbols

King of Air. Like all of the kings in the tarot deck, the King of Swords is a seasoned, experienced man. He has successfully completed the mission he undertook as the former Knight of Swords. He was rewarded with the keys to the kingdom, and he now rules the entire realm—as well as its armies, which defend and conquer in the name of the throne.

Sky Kingdom. The airy symbols that surround the king reinforce his connection to his element. Butterflies and wings are carved on his throne, and the ground at his feet is scattered with wind-blown leaves.

Elemental Symbolism. Elementally, the four kings of the tarot are all airy intellectuals. They simply combine the element of air with the corresponding element of their own suit. In that regard, the King of Swords embodies the rarefied combination of air with air.

Astrological Symbolism. Astrologically, the four kings of the tarot are associated with the four fixed signs of the zodiac. The King of Swords represents the fixed fire sign of Aquarius, which makes him a forward-thinking, socially conscious monarch.

Historic Significance. Historically, the King of Swords was thought to indicate that it was time to put an end to a ruinous lawsuit. Traditionally, the card was said to represent lawyers, doctors, surgeons, and senators.

Keywords

Upright: Judgment, power, command, authority, law
Reversed: Cruelty, perversity, barbarity, evil

Writing Prompts

Write about:

- a lawyer

- a legislator

- a politician

- a tyrant

- a surgeon

Ace of Pentacles

THE ACE OF PENTACLES IS the first card in the suit of pentacles, the suit that corresponds to the ancient element of earth. It's the embodiment of physical existence. It also promises a world of possibilities, ranging from new beginnings on the material plane to an accumulation of spiritual treasures.

Key Symbols

Mint Condition. All of the aces represent new beginnings; the Ace of Pentacles symbolizes a fresh start on a physical level. The aces also symbolize gifts. In this case, wealth and good health are yours for the taking.

Real Estate. The Ace of Pentacles is a practical card. No other card is as grounded or down-to-earth—because the Ace of Pentacles is earth itself. The card sometimes heralds a new life—which could be the birth of a baby, or simply a new lease on life through better health and a more optimistic attitude. Because pentacles represent money, the Ace could also symbolize the start of a new career, a raise, a promotion, or a rewarding investment. And because pentacles correspond to the physical world, the Ace could even suggest the acquisition of land or a new home. There is nothing more tangible than real estate; it's an investment that's grounded in real property, as opposed to paper money, stock certificates, or bonds, which have no value in and of themselves. It's not always a physical symbol, either: the Ace of Pentacles can also describe treasured ideals and spiritual values.

A Garden of Earthly Delights. The garden shown in the card symbolizes rest and reflection, order over chaos, and refuge, and the wall around the garden represents safety and protection.

Circles of Meaning. The design on the pentacle is a Pythagorean symbol. The star symbolizes the five senses, while the circle represents the spirit that unites them. The pentacle in the card is the same sort of orb that emperors and kings once held as symbols of their reign.

Vaporous Matter. The clouds symbolize higher thought and a separation between the worlds.

Historical Significance. In *The Pictorial Key to the Tarot*, Arthur Edward Waite called the Ace of Pentacles the most favorable card in the deck because it symbolizes wealth and abundance on many levels. The card sometimes suggests that people will have the resources they need to pursue their dreams and manifest their spiritual, emotional, and intellectual ideals. The Ace of Pentacles also portends physical pleasure, comfort, and luxury.

Astrological Symbolism. Astrologically, the Ace of Pentacles is associated with all of the powers of earth—the element associated with Taurus, Virgo, and Capricorn.

Keywords

Upright: Perfection, happiness, contentment, comfort, joy, ecstasy, financial rewards, gold, money, treasure, reward, prosperity, income

Reversed: Love of money as the root of all evil; misuse of resources; squandered wealth

Writing Prompts

Write about:

- a magic coin
- a lucky penny
- seed money
- a crystal ball
- a fertilized egg

Two of Pentacles

THE TWO OF PENTACLES IS a card of balance and change. It depicts the constant juggling act that most people perform as they try to synchronize their schedules, and the balancing act they attempt when it's time to pay bills.

Key Symbols

Juggling Act. The juggler in the Two of Pentacles is part clown, part court jester, and part showman. He's juggling only two balls, but he's moving them in a complicated pattern, weaving them in and out of a ribbon in the shape of a lemniscate, the figure-eight symbol of infinity. (The lemniscate also figures prominently in the Magician and Strength cards.) The juggling suggests a perpetual ebb and flow of gain and loss, weakness and strength—a life in a steady state of flux.

Balance of Nature. Because the suit of pentacles relates to money and material existence, this card may refer to balancing two jobs, or trying to live in two worlds—work and home, for example—or even trying to make income and expenses balance at the end of every month.

Two-stepping. Occasionally, the Two of Pentacles could suggest the two-timing nature of someone who juggles more than one relationship or strings two people along.

Dance Partners. The design is reminiscent of the cosmic dance of the sun and the moon, like a man and a woman, circling each other in the heavens.

Humble Opinions. The Two of Pentacles might also symbolize a character's "two cents' worth."

Keywords

Upright: Harmony, balance, dexterity, juggling

Reversed: Agitation, trouble, embroilment, embarrassment, awkward positions, confusion, concern, worry, difficulties

Writing Prompts

Write about:

- a juggling act

- a tap dance

- a traveling performer

- two separate scenes that mesh together

- two separate points of view in your story

Three of Pentacles

THE THREE OF PENTACLES IS the card of artistry. It depicts a stonemason—a master of his art—carving out a world far more orderly and beautiful than the world he was born into. He's following the divine guidance of a bishop and a monk who hold the blueprint of his creation.

Key Symbols

A Work of Art. As a young sculptor puts the finishing touches on a life-size statue in the sanctuary, a bishop and a monk discuss the artist's progress. The card depicts the process of giving substance and form to our spiritual ideas and beliefs. The sculptor is designing a work of art that will serve as a tangible reminder of God's grace and presence.

Tools of the Trade. In the wrong hands, the sculptor's hammer and chisel could be weapons of destruction. In the artist's grip, however, they become instruments of creation. He chips away at the unforgiving matter of time and space, carving out a new reality for himself.

Artistic Genius. The stonemason's artistry elevates him: he stands higher than his observers do. The imagery seems to reinforce the belief that many artists and writers have about their work: while they are fully engaged in the act of creating, they say, the work doesn't feel as though it's coming from inside them. Instead, they feel that the work is coming through them, as if they're channeling a vision and a consciousness far greater than their own.

Light from Above. Three stained glass windows shaped like pentacles seem to frame the sculpture in a halo of heavenly light.

A Spiritual Setting. The setting, a church, is an obvious allusion to the house of God. Less apparent, however, is the additional reminder that our physical bodies are also temples; we are all spiritual beings in physical form.

Holy Trio. The three pentacles under the arch call for the integration of body, mind, and spirit.

Historic Significance. Historically, if the Three of Pentacles came up in a man's reading, it would portend celebrity for his eldest son. Early tarot scholars also related the card, when it was reversed, to children, childhood, or childlike impulses.

Keywords

Upright: Skill, creativity, talent, ability, renown, nobility, elevation, dignity, rank, aristocracy, power, fame and fortune

Reversed: Mediocrity, puerility, pettiness, weakness, humility

Writing Prompts

Write about:

- a time in which you seemed to feel words flow through you, rather than from you

- the difference between artistry and craftsmanship

- taking direction

- accepting criticism

- writer's block

Four of Pentacles

THE FOUR OF PENTACLES IS the card of the miser—a stern-looking king who seems unwilling to share any piece of himself. He sits far removed from the outside world, clutching one golden coin to his chest. Two coins are planted firmly under his feet, and a fourth is perched on top of his head.

Key Symbols

The Midas Touch. The miserly king looks a lot like King Midas—and the image could serve as a warning about balance and proportion. Remember that while everything Midas touched turned to gold, it was a curse—not a blessing. In fact, his obsession with wealth actually cost him his daughter.

Four Elements. The four coins in the card represent the miser's material possessions, as well as his mind, heart, and soul. The four coins actually symbolize the four realms of the Minor Arcana: spiritual, emotional, intellectual, and physical.

Moneybag. The miser is actually sitting on a treasure chest, filled with even more of his precious belongings.

Priority Express. The figure in the card is clearly focused on his material and physical existence. He's obsessed with making sure his money and property are all in order; he also may be concerned about his physical health and well-being.

Body Language. The miser's body language couldn't be any clearer. He wants you to back off—and stay back, far away from the pentacle he's guarding in his lap.

Historic Significance. The Four of Pentacles does guarantee a certain measure of financial security and stability. Historically, the card was said to herald pleasant news from a lady, for a bachelor. Reversed, it was believed to represent a cloister, monastery, or convent.

Keywords

Upright: Material gain, possessiveness, asset management, determination, borders, self-protection, boundaries, limits, isolation

Reversed: Delay, opposition, hindrances, obstruction, obstacles, loss

Writing Prompts

Write about:

- selfishness

- withholding

- greed

- restraint

- isolation

Five of Pentacles

THE FIVE OF PENTACLES IS a card of crippling poverty—as well as the fear it inspires. Two beggars make their way through wind and snow past the lighted stained glass window of a church.

Key Symbols

Vow of Poverty. In *The Pictorial Key to the Tarot*, Arthur Edward Waite said the beggars in the card were mendicants—monks who lived a life of poverty and preaching. The mendicants were so committed to poverty that they didn't even have monasteries, like most other religious orders at the time. They lived and worked in the streets, depending solely on the charity of others.

Material Trouble. The mendicants in the card are dirty, hungry, and handicapped by time and circumstances. They hobble through wind and drifting snow. They're making their way past a church, where a bright light glows from within, but it's hard to know if they realize that help is at hand. With any luck, they're making their way to the entrance, where sanctuary and warmth await. Waite called this card "Material Trouble."

No Leg to Stand On. One of the figures hobbles on crutches—he is so bereft, he literally doesn't have a leg to stand on. In the tarot, images of sheer poverty like this one are metaphors for spiritual poverty.

Damaged Goods. Both of the figures in the card seem to have been wounded—perhaps by the tenets of organized religion, by ministers and clerics who betrayed the very faith they claimed to represent.

Shame and Blame. The Five of Pentacles could also refer to people who feel they can never measure up spiritually, who feel guilt and shame, or who feel condemned to make their way through a cold world without the warmth and support of a spiritual group.

Helping Hands. The two figures are passing a church, a symbol of refuge, haven, and help from above. The light is on inside, so the door is probably open.

Historic Significance. One archaic interpretation of the card had to do with love and lovers—wives and husbands, lovers, mistresses, and paramours. It could even suggest a sweet, pure, and chaste relationship between a chivalrous man and a refined woman.

Keywords

Upright: Poverty, material troubles, fear, anxiety, loss, destitution, bankruptcy, ruin, disorder, disgrace, chaos

Reversed: Troubles in love, debauchery and licentiousness, discord, disharmony, conflict

Writing Prompts

Write about:
- a window
- a light
- a church
- a soup kitchen
- an encampment of homeless people

Six of Pentacles

THE SIX OF PENTACLES IS the card of charity, benevolence, and goodwill. The merchant pictured in the card is obviously successful in his work, and he seems to enjoy his ability to share his wealth. The scales he holds, reminiscent of the scales of Justice, illustrate the concept of social justice.

Key Symbols

Legal Tender. The Six of Pentacles is closely connected to industry and commerce. Money doesn't grow on trees, as they say—it's earned, through business and investment. When those ventures pay off, some people think of charity and philanthropy as a means of giving back to society.

Fair Trade. The businessman in the Six of Pentacles is committed to fairness and ethical trading. His scale is legal for trade.

Just Deserts. The merchant in the card also seems to recognize that he has been more fortunate than most. He knows that all rights—and privileges—entail an equal measure of responsibility. He demonstrates the belief that gifts should be shared, not hoarded. All told, the image is a testimony to his goodness of heart as well as his success in life.

Kind Words. He also seems to be talking to the people he's helping, which is a reminder that a kind word can be worth its weight in gold.

Poverty Mentality. The beggars are dressed a lot like the two mendicants who were pictured in the previous card, the Five of Pentacles. They're both dirty and bedraggled and wrapped in old blankets. One's head is covered, which could symbolizes some sort of damage to his thought process. (As is the case with a lot of homeless people, the beggar might even suffer from some sort of mental illness or instability.)

Energy Exchange. On a less obvious level, the Six of Pentacles also reminds us that money isn't the root of all evil—but the love of money can be. It also hints at the love-hate relationship that many people have with money, and by extension, the discomfort some people feel when they are on the receiving end of a compliment, a favor, or a gift. When anything of value changes hands, money is simply a way to measure the energy that's being exchanged between two parties.

Can't Buy Me Love. Occasionally, the Six of Pentacles might suggest that someone may be trying to buy love or is begging for attention or affection.

Keywords

Upright: Business, commerce, trade, charity, presents, gifts, favors

Reversed: Envy, jealousy, unsatisfied ambition, class warfare, taxation without representation, forced redistribution of wealth

Writing Prompts

Write about:

- a beggar
- a charity
- a merchant
- an outstretched hand
- a Goodwill store

Seven of Pentacles

THE SEVEN OF PENTACLES IS the card of patience, perseverance, and anticipation, as a young farmer gazes at a crop of
seven ripening pentacles. While harvest day is approaching,
at this point he's still poised between failure and success.

Key Symbols

Seed Money. While money itself doesn't grow on trees,
the Seven of Pentacles does suggest that it's possible to grow
one's finances through careful planting and cultivation. The
card could even refer to seed money.

Growth Fund. The card could also refer to the brief period of stagnation and inertia that can sometimes follow the
initial excitement and enthusiasm of starting a new project.

Patience. Remember that you can't rush Mother Nature,
and that patience is a virtue.

Counting Chickens. While success seems imminent, the card might be a warning
of sorts: the young man could be dreaming about the rich harvest he expects, but that
thinking could be premature. Late-summer storms occasionally rumble through and
flatten even the hardiest of crops. All in all, the image could suggest the old adage
"Don't count your chickens before they hatch."

Historical Significance. Historically, the Seven of Pentacles was believed to symbolize arguments, quarrels, and fights—or, alternatively, the qualities of innocence and
ingenuity. The card was also thought to represent a raise, promotion, or some other im-
provement in position for a lady's future husband.

Keywords

Upright: Money, finance, business, barter, gain, profit, financial success
Reversed: Money worries, anxiety about a loan, impatience, apprehension, suspicion, disappointment, failed harvest

Writing Prompts

Write about:

- a buried seed

- ripening fruit

- an idea sprouting

- a stakeout

- a scarecrow

Eight of Pentacles

THE EIGHT OF PENTACLES IS the card of prudence and preparation. A woodworker seated at his workbench is carving a series of pentacles. A skilled craftsman, he seems to be continually perfecting his skills—and at the same time, he's managing to produce marketable wares. He displays his products prominently, and he works in full view of customers and passerby.

Key Symbols

An Honest Day's Pay. Remember the artist in the Three of Pentacles? Here is his counterpart, the craftsman or artisan, who actually gets paid for his work. Granted, the craftsman's creations probably aren't as rarefied as the artist's—but what the artisan lacks in quality he makes up for in quantity.

Arts and Crafts. He might not be strictly spiritual—but he's definitely more practical. In fact, as a craftsman, he's probably more likely than a starving artist to generate income, put food on the table, and keep a roof over his head—all without sacrificing his creativity. Ultimately, he may even be *more* spiritual, because he's better suited to the task of keeping body and soul together.

Making Money. In many versions of the card, a stonemason carves a series of pentagrams on a series of golden disks. He is literally making money.

Self-protection. He wears a heavy leather smock to protect himself from chips and shards of wood or stone.

Historic Significance. Historically, the Eight of Pentacles symbolized intelligence, lovingly applied to material matters—such as agriculture and engineering. Another historic interpretation of the card says that it represents a young businessman or a dark girl.

Keywords

Upright: Art, craft, artistry, craftsmanship, workmanship, apprenticeship, tutelage, study, mastery, practicality, a money-making opportunity, practical use of a skill or a talent, artistic creations for sale or trade, work for hire

Reversed: Loss of ambition, cunning, intrigue, vanity, greed, troubles with a loan, "penny wise and pound foolish"

Writing Prompts

Write about:

- a carving

- a woodworker

- a craft fair

- a trade show

- the difference between artistry and craft

Nine of Pentacles

THE NINE OF PENTACLES IS a card of comfort and prosperity. In a well-manicured garden, an elegant woman stands with a falcon on her arm. She is alone, but she doesn't seem lonely. In fact, she looks as though she enjoys her solitude.

Key Symbols

Financial Security. The Nine of Pentacles often symbolizes financial security, perhaps through an inheritance or wisely planned investments. It suggests both good luck and good management of one's resources.

To the Manor Born. In the distance, we can just barely see the manor, the main house on an estate. The woman's presence in the manor's garden is a sign of wealth and privilege.

Opportunity Knocks. The woman in the card seems to have a history of putting herself in the right place at the right time, as well as a knack for making her own opportunities.

Material Comforts. She is surrounded by wealth, luxury, and the comforts of material security. The nine pentacles that give the card its name are growing on the grapevines that surround her. The coming harvest will help assure her continued comfort and prosperity. She will have wine in the winter, and fruit for her bread.

Security Fence. The trellised grapevines that surround her reinforce her sense of security. Like a wall, they symbolize protection from the outside world. This woman also seems to know her limitations. In fact, she has set her boundaries. She has chosen what she'll allow in and what she'll keep out.

Custom Design. Gardens symbolize rest and reflection, order over chaos, and refuge. The woman in this card has tamed nature; her mind has superimposed its own design on the world around her.

Animal Control. She holds a trained falcon on her leather-gloved hand. Even though the falcon is a bird of prey—as well as a hunting weapon that's notoriously difficult to master—she handles the bird with a natural grace and ease.

Keywords

Upright: Material well-being, riches, inheritance, pleasure, prudence, safety, success, accomplishment, certitude, discernment; solitude and peace

Reversed: Theft, deception, loneliness, restlessness

Writing Prompts

Write about:

- comfort
- wealth
- privilege
- social status
- solitude

Ten of Pentacles

THE TEN OF PENTACLES IS a card of extended family. In the courtyard of a medieval dwelling, three generations are gathered: a young couple, their small child, and a white-haired, bearded grandfather.

Key Symbols

The wealth of detail in the Ten of Pentacles is as rich as you would expect in a card that suggests prosperity and satisfaction—not only on the material level, but also in the emotional realm.

Family Life. In most readings, the Ten of Pentacles suggests the richness of family life. It symbolizes inheritance, not only of resources, but also of wisdom, experience, family values, and beliefs, all passed from generation to generation.

Tree of Life. The people in the card are positioned behind an emblem of ten pentacles, which is shaped like the Kabbalistic Tree of Life.

Social Security. The old man is wearing an elegant cloak, which implies wealth, social status, and security.

Go Greyhound. The dogs also hint at the family's status: they are greyhounds, a breed that used to be reserved for noblemen and aristocrats.

Structural Stability. The young couple is standing under an arch, an ancient architectural construct that still stands as one of the strongest, long-lasting designs for any building. The structure suggests a permanence and support for their relationship.

House in Order. In the classic Celtic Cross spread, one position is reserved for a card known as your "house." By design, the card that lands in that position describes the people closest to you, the ones who see you every day and know you well. In many respects, the Ten of Pentacles illustrates the "house" concept perfectly, simply by depicting several generations of a single family gathered under a single roof.

Respect and Protect. There's a brick wall between the young couple and their patriarch, which suggests a healthy boundary between them.

Historic Significance. Historically, the Ten of Pentacles symbolized gambling, games of chance, and loss.

Keywords

Upright: Riches, family life, home, household, inheritance, pension, legacy
Reversed: Disharmony, discord, strife, arguments with family members

Writing Prompts

Write about:

- an old man and his dog

- a wall

- a young boy at play

- family tradition

- intergenerational relationships

Page of Pentacles

THE PAGE OF PENTACLES IS a young man with both his feet on the ground. He is nurturing, generous, and kind. He is also studious, diligent, and persevering. He may even be a child prodigy. Despite his high level of skill, however, he is usually extremely careful, even cautious, and he doesn't take many risks.

In fact, according to tarot tradition, the Page of Pentacles *is* earth—in human form. He embodies the grounded energy that connects the suit of Pentacles to the world of matter and physical existence. In other words, the Page of Pentacles is a graphic example of how earth can take human form.

Key Symbols

Salt of the Earth. Like all pages, the Page of Pentacles is youthful, with childlike enthusiasm and an unbounded capacity to learn. He stands with an oversized pentacle in his hand, as if displaying a work of art. Wrapped in a green cloak, he stands in a green valley. His feet are both firmly planted on the ground; he's moving slowly, focused only at the treasure in his hands.

Package Delivery. During the Renaissance, pages were the youngest members of the royal court. It was their job to take news from one person to another. Because the suit of Pentacles is concerned with physical life, the Page of Pentacles specializes in delivering messages with physical impact.

Learning to Run. The Page of Pentacles is still immature, so his physical ability is not fully developed. He's young and strong, but his fine motor skills are still unrefined. Indoors, he's like a bull in a china shop. Outdoors, he's in his element: he can walk for miles across the open countryside. Hiking and camping are two of his favorite pastimes.

Historic Significance. Historically, the Page of Pentacles was said to refer to a dark youth, a young officer or soldier, or a child.

Keywords

Upright: Study, physical development, news about physical existence
Reversed: Delays in physical development and maturity

Writing Prompts

Write about:

- a camper

- a hiker

- a physical message

- a physical lesson

- an earthy young person

Knight of Pentacles

THE KNIGHT OF PENTACLES DOESN'T fit most people's pre-conceptions of knights. He doesn't move fast, he's not especially flirtatious, and when the rest of the knights ride off on adventures, he usually stays behind to take care of the kingdom's routine border patrols. His mission in life seems to be taking care of the ordinary details and everyday responsibilities that the other knights overlook.

In fact, some people think the Knight of Pentacles is actually sort of dull. He's steady, reliable, practical, patient, slow-moving, and methodical. He pays an almost slavish attention to detail. He is earthy and grounded—so well grounded that it takes him a lot of time to get moving and pick up speed. He is slow to anger, but furious when he's finally enraged.

Key Symbols

Down-to-Earth. Elementally speaking, the four knights of the tarot are all fiery. They simply combine the element of fire with the element of their own suit. In that regard, the Knight of Pentacles embodies the rather uneventful combination of fire with earth.

Slow Motion. The Knight of Pentacles seems to have traded his valiant steed for a heavy black workhorse. He's paused at the bank of a river while he seems to ponder the pentacle in his outstretched hand. Both he and his horse are at rest; neither one is moving.

Slow Growth. On the other side of the river, several fields have been cultivated and new crops are beginning to sprout.

Astrological Symbolism. Astrologically, the four knights of the tarot are associated with the four mutable signs of the zodiac. The Knight of Pentacles represents the mutable fire sign of Virgo, which makes him conscientious and conservative.

Historical Significance. Historically, a reversed Knight of Pentacles was said to foretell a brief period of unemployment.

Keywords

Upright: Solidity, usefulness, responsibility, practicality
Reversed: Inertia, idleness, stagnation

Writing Prompts

Write about:

- a sturdy young man
- a couch potato
- a long-term plan
- a physical adventure
- a physical rescue

Queen of Pentacles

THE QUEEN OF PENTACLES IS more than just earthy and grounded. She is intensely physical, sensual, primal, lusty, and tactile. Like the emblem of her suit, she is well-rounded.

Because the suit of Pentacles is associated with money and material possessions, the Queen of Pentacles is also connected to riches, wealth, and opulence. She's resourceful; when she invests her time and energy in a project, it turns into gold.

Practical and sensible, she's a natural healer who could go so far as to have a career as a doctor or nurse. She especially likes to work with children so she can see them grow. At home, she has a green thumb. She has plants in every window and gardens in her yard. The Queen of Pentacles also likes luxury and physical comforts, enjoyments that could lead her to be an interior decorator or designer.

Key Symbols

Queen of Earth. Like all of the tarot's queens, the Queen of Pentacles is a mature woman, gracious and wise in the ways of the world. Queens, of course, are rulers—but their ruler is based on the feminine principles of safeguarding and nurturing their realms. The Queen of Pentacles is charged with safeguarding and nurturing the suit of Pentacles, which corresponds to the earthy world of material and physical reality.

She is also quiet, kind, and unassuming. While she is practical, she can be extremely generous. She has a big heart, and she is liberal with her time, her emotions, and her resources.

Earth Signs. Almost every symbol in the card reinforces the Queen's connection with earth. She sits in a garden of delights, much like the Empress, her counterpart in the Major Arcana. Rams' heads decorate the arms of her throne, a reference to the earthy sign of Capricorn. She's sheltered from the harsh light of the sun by an arbor of fruit-bearing trees. She can see many worlds in the pentacle she holds.

Astrological Symbolism. Astrologically, the four queens of the tarot are associated with the four cardinal signs of the zodiac. The Queen of Pentacles represents the cardinal earth sign of Capricorn, which makes her a savvy businesswoman who can cultivate a wide range of resources for her people.

Elemental Symbolism. Elementally speaking, the four queens are all watery. Each one combines the element of water with the element of her suit. As a result, the queen of the earthy suit of Pentacles embodies the fertile combination of water and earth.

Historical Significance. Historically, the Queen of Pentacles was said to foretell presents from a wealthy relative, and a rich and happy marriage for a young man.

Keywords

Upright: A dark woman, wealth, security, generosity, magnificence, confidence, candor
Reversed: Evil, suspicion, suspense, fear, mistrust, suspicion

Writing Prompts

Write about:
- a gardener
- a florist
- a dark and mysterious woman
- a secret pregnancy
- a wealthy woman

King of Pentacles

THE KING OF PENTACLES IS a levelheaded businessman who manages the affairs of his kingdom with mathematical precision. He is conscientious, wise, and practical—and he has a flair for ingenious solutions to complicated problems.

It usually takes him a long time to get angry—but once roused, he can be furious. The rest of the time, he may seem emotionless, imperturbable, and insensitive.

The King of Pentacles likes to help others gain financially and materially from their work and relationships. He cultivates alliances and partnerships that are deep and long lasting.

Key Symbols

Earth King. Like all of the kings in the tarot deck, the King of Pentacles is a seasoned, experienced man. He has successfully completed the mission he undertook as the former Knight of Pentacles. He was rewarded with the keys to the kingdom, and he now rules the entire realm—as well as its armies, which defend and conquer in the name of the throne.

Kingdom of Earth. The earthy symbols that surround the king reinforce his connection to his element. His throne is a massive, hewn structure, as heavy and immovable as the earth itself. It's embellished with bull's heads, a symbol of earth and Taurus. The king is also surrounded by grapevines, a sign of wealth, abundance, and material satisfaction.

Astrological Symbolism. Astrologically, the four kings of the tarot are associated with the four fixed signs of the zodiac. The King of Pentacles represents the fixed earth sign of Taurus, which makes him a steady, reliable monarch.

Elemental Symbolism. Elementally, the four kings of the tarot are all airy intellectuals. They simply combine the element of air with the corresponding element of their own suit. In that regard, the King of Pentacles embodies the somewhat dry and dusty combination of air with earth.

Historic Significance. Historically, the King of Pentacles was tied to mathematical gifts, achievements, and success. Reversed, it symbolized a vicious old man, or a dangerous man. Traditionally, the King of Pentacles was said to represent dark men, along with merchants, employers, and professors of math, science, and physics.

Keywords

Upright: A savvy and successful businessman, wealth, investment, business acumen, mathematical ability, and success

Reversed: Vice, weakness, ugliness, perversity, corruption, peril

Writing Prompts

Write about:

- a king

- a physical scientist

- a self-made man

- a power broker

- an irresistible force that comes up against an immovable object

Conclusion

I hope this guide has given you a firm foundation for incorporating tarot cards into your writing practice. With any luck, you've found a few ideas to improve your current writing projects—as well as inspiration for even more stories, poems, books, and articles down the road. While this book is ending, you're only just beginning an exciting journey into the world of tarot.

I'd love to hear about any success you have in working with the cards. If you'd like to share your work—or let me know about your next published piece based on the cards— just send me an email! My address is *corrine@corrinekenner.com*.

Good luck, and happy writing!

—Corrine Kenner
www.corrinekenner.com

A Glossary of Tarot Terms and Symbols

A

Abbey—refuge; holy place; symbol of the divine within one's self.

Above—the Higher Self.

Above/Below—heaven and earth.

Abyss—depth; the origin and ending of the world; the underworld; the unconscious.

Acorn—potential.

Adam Kadmon—the primordial man.

Adam and Eve—the primordial couple.

Air—one of the four elements; active; masculine; corresponds to the Minor Arcana suit of Swords and the intellect.

Air Signs—the "thinkers" of the Zodiac: Gemini, Libra, and Aquarius.

Alchemy—Greek and Arab attempts to make gold; symbolic of salvation. The four stages include (1) prime matter, symbolic of origins and guilt; (2) the first transmutation, symbolic of early efforts at transformation; (3) purification, symbolic of passion; and (4) gold, symbolic of spiritual attainment.

Allegory—a descriptive story that includes symbolic or hidden meaning, used for imparting ideas and principals.

Alpha and Omega—first and last letters of the Greek alphabet; beginnings and endings.

Altar—a focus for worship, sacrifice, and spirituality; refuge and sanctuary.

Amulet—a charm carried to ward off evil.

Anchor—Christian symbol of salvation and hope.

Angels—invisible forces; Four archangels appear in tarot: Raphael, angel of air (The Lovers); Michael, angel of fire (Temperance); Gabriel, angel of water (Judgement); and Uriel, angel of earth (The Devil).

Animals—divine forces; human characteristics.

Ankh—ancient Egyptian cross of life, with the perfect balance of masculine (Osiris) and feminine.

Antlers—the divine masculine; the father god.

Anubis—ancient Egyptian jackal-headed god of wisdom; represents the evolution of consciousness.

Anvil—earthly matter.

Ape—Thoth, Egyptian god of wisdom.

Apple—health; healing.

Arcana—plural of the Latin Arcanum.

Archer—offers direction; symbol of the astrological sign Sagittarius.

Archetypes—innate ideas or patterns in the psyche, expressed as symbols and images. Carl Jung's description of archetypes include the *anima*, the feminine aspect of a man's personality; the *animus*, the masculine aspect of a woman's personality; the *mother*, which typifies a nurturing, emotional parent; the *father*, a physical, protective parent; the *trickster*, or rebel; and the *shadow*, the hidden, antisocial dark side of human nature, as well as the *hero*, the *maiden*, and the *wise old man*.

Armor—defense; protection.

Ashes—spiritual purification.

Ass—humility; patience; courage.

Astrological Correspondences:

- **Aries**: The Emperor
- **Taurus**: The Hierophant
- **Gemini**: The Lovers
- **Cancer**: The Chariot

- **Leo**: Strength
- **Virgo**: The Hermit
- **Libra**: Justice
- **Scorpio**: Death
- **Sagittarius**: Temperance
- **Capricorn**: The Devil
- **Aquarius**: The Star
- **Pisces**: The Moon

Aura—energy field.

B

Backpack—tools; karma.

Bandages—newborn's swaddling and corpse's shroud; wounds.

Basket—womb.

Bat—blindness; darkness; chaos; leathery bat wings offer a striking contrast to pristine angel wings.

Bear—lunar animal; prime matter; unconscious; the Great Mother.

Beard—masculinity; strength; wisdom; power.

Bed—sexuality; intimacy; rest; illness; nurturing.

Bee—creative activity; monarchy; social organization.

Bell—joy; victory.

Bird—the soul; good news; soaring spirit.

Black—negative; passive; receptive.

Blindfold—lack of information; sometimes relates to Justice.

Blood—sacrifice; passion.

Blue—associated with spirituality.

Boar—magic and prophecy.

Boat—cradle; womb; the body.

Boaz and Joachim—The pillars of light and darkness, mercy and severity, strength and stability, or spirit and matter that held the veil in the Temple of Solomon, the first Temple of Jerusalem. Boaz was King David's great-grandfather. Joachim was a high priest.

Book—education; knowledge; life; the universe.

Bow and Arrow—sunlight; pangs of love.

Box—feminine; maternal; unconscious.

Branch—see garland.

Bread—fertility; communion with others; staff of life; money.

Breast—love; nurturing; mothering.

Bridge—connection between worlds; transition from life to death and from the secular to the divine.

Broom—cleansing power; unity of male and female.

Buckle—self-defense; protection.

Bud—new beginning.

Bull—symbol of the astrological sign Taurus.

Butterfly—transformation.

C

Caduceus (a winged wand entwined by two serpents)—symbol of Mercury, messenger of the gods; the wand represents power, the snakes represent wisdom, and the wings represent diligence; also, the wand represents earth, the wings represent air, and the serpents represent fire and water.

Canal—passage; childbirth.

Candle—faith in spiritual things; enlightenment; the light and spirit of the individual.

Canyon—vast unconsciousness.

Cartomancy—the art of divination with cards.

Castle—physical and spiritual refuge; stronghold of good or evil; a place of guarded treasure; to be watchful; embattled; otherworldly.

Cat—domesticity; liberty; vanity; witch's familiar.

Cauldron—vessel of magical change; the womb.

Cave—the feminine; the unconscious; an entrance to the underworld; initiation.

Celtic Cross—a popular tarot spread, designed in the shape of a cross, with additional cards laid alongside for additional information.

Cernunnos—Celtic horned god.

Chain—bondage; restriction; communication.

Chakras—seven energy centers of the body.

Chalice—human heart; holy grail; womb.

Chalice (covered)—heaven and earth.

Chariot card—the young charioteer is in command of his physical and emotional drives, symbolized by the two opposing forces that pull the Chariot.

Chariot—the human body.

Charioteer—the self.

Chasm—division between worlds.

Child—innocence; the future.

Church—refuge; holy place; symbol of the divine within one's self.

Circle—completion; infinity; enclosure; the feminine; heaven; the sun; nothingness; the fifth element, Spirit.

Clarifier—an additional card used to enhance or explain the primary cards in a spread.

Cliff—division between worlds.

Cloak—veil; separation; something hidden.

Clocks—under the law of time; or something that is possible but not yet firmly in the future.

Clouds—mysterious and sacred; a symbol of higher thought.

Cold—solitude.

Colors:

Black, the color of night, is linked to darkness and sleep, when our consciousness fades and our unconscious thoughts and emotions take control of our dreams. Black is mysterious. It can even be elegant and authoritative. Black is also the color of mourning, depression, darkness, and anxiety, and it can symbolize the darker forces of nature, like upheaval and destruction.

Blue, like the sea and the sky, symbolizes depth and calm, a tranquil environment for meditation and reflection.

Brown, the color of bare earth, symbolizes the potential of fallow soil. It can represent grounding, stability, and practicality. Brown can also symbolize poverty and dirt.

Gray, a mixture of black and white, is the color of shadows and shade, along with fog. It can symbolize depression and confusion, or simply a steady drizzle.

Green is the color of nature, growth, healing, and fertility. It symbolizes creativity and prosperity. In the United States, green is the color of money and financial success. Green can also symbolize envy, jealousy, and greed.

Indigo, like the midnight heavens, symbolizes cosmic mysteries. For those who find themselves lost in its inky depths, indigo inspires contemplation, wisdom, spiritual realization, and cosmic wisdom.

Orange, like a blazing fire or a sunset on a tropical island, symbolizes the flames of desire and burning passions. Orange typically represents vitality and enjoyment, vigor, physical health, enthusiasm, and enjoyment.

Pink, a lighter shade of red, indicates passions that have cooled—or an interest still blushing into existence. Shades of pink and rose are soothing, calming, and symbolize acceptance, friendship, forgiveness, love, romance, peace, and harmony.

Red, the color of wine or blood, symbolizes passion, love, and sex. Red is also the color of Mars, the planet of energy and aggression. It can represent danger, anger, and alarm.

Silver, the color of the moon, symbolizes reflection.

Violet, the traditional color of royalty, symbolizes leadership and divinity, as well as luxury, wealth, and sophistication.

White, like the clouds, symbolizes innocence, pure spirituality, intuition, and psychic ability. It can also seem sterile, cold, clinical, and easily marred.

Yellow, like the sun, symbolizes energy, clear thinking, and consciousness. Yellow is also the color of Mercury, the planet of speed and communication. Yellow represents optimism, radiance, and brilliance. Yellow can sometimes symbolize cowardice and weakness.

Collective Unconscious—Carl Gustav Jung's term for the underground stream of psychic energy and shared archetypes that link all people to each other.

Columns—duality; choice; civilization.

Conflict—a troubling or opposing force in the querent's life.

Corn—fertility.

Cornucopia—the union of male and female; horn of plenty.

Court cards—the page (or knave), knight, queen, and king of the four suits of the Minor Arcana.

Crab—symbol of the astrological sign Cancer.

Crane—justice; longevity.

Crest—thought.

Crescent Moon—symbol of Isis, the ancient Egyptian queen of heaven; also the symbol of virgin goddesses; the newborn; the ship of light that carries the soul through the dark night into dawn.

Crocodile—duality; capable of living on land and in water.

Cross—protection.

Cross, Blue—spiritual leader.

Cross, Celtic—popular tarot layout; fertility; union of heaven and earth.

Cross, Inverted—humility; tree of life.

Cross, Red—health; healing; and medicine.

Cross, Rosy—fertility; spilled blood of Christ; seven stages of initiation.

Cross, Solar—equal arms indicate union of male and female; positive and negative.

Cross, Yellow—philosopher or philosophy.

Crossed Keys—unlock knowledge and truth. The gold depicts solar energy; the silver depicts lunar energy; St. Peter, as the Hierophant, held the keys that made him the founder of Christ's church on earth.

Crossroads—choice.

Crow—messenger.

Crown—attainment and mastery.

Crux Ansata (the Egyptian ankh)—union of male and female; heaven and earth; eternity; immortality.

Crystal—transmits and magnifies energy.

Cube—earth; material world; four elements.

Cups—the second suit; symbolizes emotional life.

Curtain—separation of worlds.

D

Daffodils—springtime.

Dagger—phallus; masculinity.

Dance—union of space and time; creation; metamorphosis.

Dawn—new beginnings.

Day/Daylight—clarity; reason.

Death—end of an era; sacrifice; destruction; leads to rebirth.

Death card—Not the frightening specter that most of us expect, the card of Death is one of transition. It foretells the completion of one stage of life and the exciting beginning of a new phase.

Devil—subconscious desires; materialism.

Devil card—with tongue firmly in cheek, the Devil of the Major Arcana shows us that a selfish devotion to material possessions and ill-conceived passions ties us down and keeps us from true happiness.

Desert—asceticism; deprivation; transcendence; abstract thought.

Dew—spiritual illumination; approaching dawn.

Directions:

- **East** air; associated with the suit of Swords.
- **South** fire; associated with the suit of Wands.
- **West** water; associated with the suit of Cups.
- **North** earth; associated with the suit of Pentacles.

Disk—spherical bodies, especially the earth but also the sun and the moon; the heavens; the pentacle.

Dog—faithful companion; loyalty; protector, guardian; conscience; tamed beast.

Dolphin—salvation.

Door—access; opportunity; new situation; a barrier which only initiates may unlock and pass through; transition.

Dot—seed; beginning; origin; the number one.

Dove—peace; harmony; innocence; devotion; spirit; soul; Holy Spirit.

Dragon—adversary.

Drum—the heart; the spoken word.

Duality—balance; equilibrium; opposing forces; choices; attraction of opposites.

E

Eagle—keen vision and comprehension; symbol of the astrological sign Scorpio; John the Baptist.

Earth—concrete physical manifestation.

Earth Signs—the "maintainers" of the Zodiac: Taurus, Virgo, Capricorn.

Earthquake—sudden change for better or worse.

Eclipse—drama.

Egg—potential; the world.

Eight—infinity (the lemniscate); caduceus; eternal spiral; regeneration.

Elements—the four ancient elements (fire, water, air, and earth) correspond to each of the tarot's four suits: fire for wands, water for cups, air for swords, and earth for pentacles. (Some tarot readers assign a fifth element, spirit, to the Major Arcana cards.)

Elephant—physical strength.

Emperor card—the archetypical father, the authoritative Emperor brings order out of chaos so that civilization can prosper.

Empress card—the archetypical mother, the Empress nurtures and protects all of nature, including humankind.

Esoteric— secret; intended for and understood by only a chosen few.

Eve—primordial woman; mother of all.

Exoteric—public; suitable for the uninitiated.

Eye of Horus—symbol of the watchful Egyptian lord of the skies.

F

Falcon—untamed will.

Feather—wind; flight; words.

Feather, Red—victory.

Fire—one of four ancient elements; represents spirit, will, inspiration, desire; purifying force.

Fire Signs—the "initiators" of the Zodiac: Aries, Leo, Sagittarius.

Fish—creative inspiration; ideas; Jesus; symbol of the astrological sign Pisces.

Five—the five senses; the five appendages of man; five vowels.

Flag—victory.

Flame—spirit; will.

Fleur-de-lis—illumination; royalty; the triple majesty of God; the trinity of body, mind, and spirit.

Flute—erotic or funereal anguish; masculine shape, feminine sound; associated with shepherds.

Fool Card—technically, the Fool is the Major Arcana's only unnumbered card. A wanderer, most tarot experts agree that the Fool represents each of us—naive travelers through life, off on a grand adventure, out to learn whatever experience and the tarot can teach us.

Fool's Journey—The procession of the Fool through the cards of the Major Arcana is often said to be an allegorical description of our journey through life, starting with the Fool and culminating with the World card.

Forces—in tarot, the term "forces" refers to people and circumstances that may help or hinder the querent. Such forces also are delineated as either positive, negative, or hidden.

Forest—the unconscious.

Fortress—refuge, protection, safety.

Fountain—life force; access to hidden secrets.

Four—wholeness; stability; four suits of the Minor Arcana; four elements; four cardinal points; four seasons; four ages of man; four horsemen of the apocalypse.

Fox—slyness.

Fruit—fertility; completion; temptation.

Fylfot cross—a type of solar cross with "feet" that represents harmony and movement.

G

Garden—control of nature; cultivation of the human soul.

Gargoyles—captive cosmic forces.

Garland—universal connections; links; fellowship; completion.

Gazelle—the soul.

Girdle—strength; connection.

Globe—dominion.

Globe, Winged—sublimation of matter through evolution.

Glove—traditionally, the right-hand glove is removed before a superior.

Glyph—a mark or a symbol (i.e., astrological glyphs).

Gnome—elemental creature of earth.

Gnosis—spiritual knowledge.

Goat—symbol of the astrological sign Capricorn.

Gold—solar energy; material treasure.

Golden Dawn—a mystical organization that popularized the tarot and other occult studies at the turn of the last century. Members included Arthur Edward Waite and Pamela Colman Smith, creators of the Rider-Waite-Smith tarot, and Aleister Crowley, designer of the Thoth tarot deck.

Grapes—abundance; celebration.

Grapevines—growth; coming harvest.

Green—material; healing.

Griffin (half eagle, half lion)—guardian of the tree of life; vigilance; used to represent both the Messiah and the antichrist.

H

Halo—living people are portrayed with square or hexagon halos; dead saints are pictured with round halos; God is portrayed with a triangular halo.

Hammer—power, strength, force of might.

Hand—open or closed in giving or restraint; raised in blessing or binding oath.

Hanged Man card—He sacrifices his comfort and passions for a time, like the Norse god Odin, knowing that better things will occur as a result.

Hare—love; fertility; the menstrual cycle; the moon.

Harp—passage to the next world.

Hat—thought, intellect.

Hearth—the home; feminine receptacle for masculine fire; love; security.

Heat—sexuality; maturity.

Hermaphrodite—integration.

Hermes Trismegistus—"Hermes the thrice great"; Greek name for Thoth.

Hermetic—derived from Hermes Trismegistus and his lore; magical; alchemical.

Hermit card—far removed from the hustle and bustle of everyday life, The Hermit reflects on spiritual concerns. He carries his light of wisdom as a beacon for others to follow.

Hexagram—six-pointed star; combination of material and spiritual.

Hierophant—high priest.

Hierophant card—a symbol of traditional authority and influence, the hierophant is a spiritual link to humanity's higher powers.

High Priestess card—secretive and guarded, the High Priestess knows the secrets life holds, but shares them only with the wise.

Holy Grail—the mythological object pursued by King Arthur's knights; Christ's chalice at the last supper; receptacle for Christ's blood.

Hood—spiritual secrets.

Horn—an enemy's approach; the end of the world.

Horse—controlled life force; solar animal.

Hourglass—mortality; passage of time; cyclical nature of the universe; God's grace descending onto the earth.

House—the human body; floors of a house symbolize levels of consciousness; rooms symbolize private thoughts; windows symbolize possible understanding and communication.

I

Ibis—ancient Egyptian bird, symbolic of thought and inspiration.

IHVH—Hebrew initials of the holy name of God; also symbolic of the four Minor Arcana suits.

Iris—Greek mythological personification of the rainbow connecting heaven and earth.

J

Jester—a fool; the inverse counterpart of the king.

Jewels—spiritual truths; status; power; riches.

Judgement card—all is revealed, as the Judgement card reminds us to forgive and be forgiven.

Jupiter—planet of luck and expansion.

Justice card—when blindfolded, the goddess of Justice is blind to superficial concerns. With her eyes unveiled, Justice sees all. In most renditions of the card, she holds a two-edged sword, a reminder that fairness cuts both ways.

K

Kabbala (also spelled cabala, cabbala, kabala, kabbalah, qabala)—an ancient Jewish system used to explain the order and workings of the universe.

Karma—cause and effect; the effect of past actions on the present and on future choices.

Key—a new opening; change.

Keys—the numbered Major Arcana cards; often referred to as keys to higher knowledge.

King—active expression of the highest qualities of the suit.

Knife—vengeance; instinct.

Knight cards—fast-moving people and events related to each suit.

Knight on a Horse—mind over matter.

Knot—infinity; bondage; luck.

Kundalini—the path of energy as it moves through the chakras.

L

Lake— the occult; mystery; contemplation; consciousness; revelation.

Lamb—martyrdom; sacrifice; Jesus.

Lamp/Lantern—intelligence; wisdom; the light and spirit of the individual.

Laurel wreath—victory, triumph; immortality.

Layout—the spread, pattern, or design a reader selects to lay out the cards for a reading.

Leaves—growth, life, and vitality.

Left—negative; feminine; receptive.

Lemniscate (figure 8)—infinity.

Lightning—a flash of illumination; a bolt from the blue; divine power; inspiration; intuition.

Lilith—Adam's first wife, banished for her refusal to submit to him.

Lily—transformation; afterlife.

Lily, Water—symbol of the element of water.

Lily, White—purity.

Line, Horizontal—balance; stability.

Line, Vertical—growth; phallic; masculine; active; connects heaven and earth; wand.

Lingam—Eastern phallic-shaped symbol of masculine energy (see Yoni).

Lion—symbol of the astrological sign Leo; the sun; the ego; courage; untamed will; St. Mark.

Lotus—spiritual awakening; in India, Brahma's dwelling place and the manifestation of his work.

Lovers card—while an appearance by this couple could encourage any hopeless romantic, The Lovers also signify a choice to be made between two equally strong desires.

Lyre—wisdom; moderation; prophecy; the seven strings connote the mystical properties of the number seven.

M

Ma'at—Egyptian goddess of justice.

Magician card—the Magician represents an individual in control of life's tools and techniques, like those on the table in front of him. Typically, they include a cup, a sword, a pentacle, and a wand—the four symbols of the Minor Arcana.

Magus—magician; wise man.

Major Arcana—the tarot's twenty-two "Greater Secrets"; often represent cosmic forces beyond our control.

Mandela—geometric, circular design, representative of the divine.

Mars—planet of energy, aggression, and warlike emotions.

Master Numbers—11, 22, 33, 44 indicate the highest quality of the numbers themselves.

Meadow—sanctuary; rest; rejuvenation.

Mermaid—idealized, elusive form of female beauty; vanity; fickleness.

Minor Arcana—the tarot's fifty-six "Lesser Secrets"; often represent mundane events and forces within our control.

Miter—the official headdress of the pope, bishops, abbots, and ancient Jewish high priests.

Moon—reflects light; inspires thought; measures time and cycles of life; astrologically, the emotions and intuition; subconsciousness.

Moon card—deeply rooted in the unconscious, the dreamlike moon symbolizes secrets and mysteries that may not be understood—or even recognized.

Moon Phases—new; waxing; full; waning.

Mountain—meeting of heaven and earth; ascent; struggle; obstacles.

Mushrooms—decay and regeneration; home to fairies.

Music—the pure manifestation of will.

N

Necklace—unity; continuity; erotic links

Neptune—watery planet of illusion.

Nimbus—halo or aura.

Night—mystery; the unconscious; passive; feminine; anticipatory.

Nine—months of pregnancy.

Number Symbolism—the Major Arcana card descriptions in Part III include a key number section explaining the symbolism of numbers appearing in cards. In particular, see pages 125–179.

Numerology—the language of numbers.

Nymphs—spirits of running water, fountains, springs, and waterfalls; the immature feminine; temptation, multiplicity; may preside over some aspects of fertility, birth, and death.

O

Octagon—spiritual regeneration; the intermediary between the square and the circle.

Oracle—a tool for divination; anyone who practices divination.

Orange—color of balance and seeking.

Orb—dominion; the world; temporal power; when surmounted with a cross, a sign of spiritual authority.

Ouroboros—the snake swallowing its tail is a symbol of totality, immortality, and infinity.

Outcome—the final card in any spread is often referred to as a "likely outcome." Because the tarot offers us the chance to change the future as a result of a reading, however, that outcome is never set in stone.

Oval—female genitalia.

Owl—spiritual wisdom.

P

Page cards—messages, news; beginnings; and young people related to the suit.

Palm—masculine, active energy.

Pansy—five petals represent man and thought.

Peacock—immortality.

Pelican—self-sacrifice.

Pentacle—materialism; values; treasures.

Pentagram—an unending symbol of perfection and wholeness. Each point symbolizes one of the five appendages of the human body head, arms, and legs, as well as the four ancient elements and the element of spirit.

Phallus—perpetuation of life, power, and propagation.

Phoenix—mythical Egyptian bird which sets itself aflame and then is reborn from its own ashes; destruction and recreation; linked to both the sun and the moon.

Pillars—duality; choice; civilization.

Pine Tree—a sturdy character.

Pip—a numbered card of the Minor Arcana.

Planets:

- **Sun** Illumination, the self, the ego.
- **New Moon** (1st Quarter) Inspiration, beginnings.
- **Waxing Moon** (2nd Quarter) Growth, development.
- **Full Moon** (3rd Quarter) Maturity, completion.
- **Waning Moon** (4th Quarter) Reflections, planning.
- **Mercury** Speed, communication.
- **Venus** Love, attraction, spiritual treasure, fertility.
- **Mars** Energy, aggression, self–defense, action.
- **Jupiter** Luck, growth, expansion, enthusiasm.
- **Saturn** Discipline, limits, boundaries, tradition.
- **Uranus** Independence, rebellion, freedom.
- **Neptune** Glamour, illusions, sensitivity.
- **Pluto** Death, regeneration, unavoidable change.

Plow—fertilization; cultivation.

Pluto—endings; death; regeneration; change.

Pomegranate—countless seeds symbolize fertility and diversity.

Pregnancy—creativity.

Primroses—fall season.

Purple—color of spirituality.

Pyramid—earth in its material aspects; suggest trinity of thought, action, and deed.

Q

Queen—passive expression of the highest qualities of the suit.

Querent—the person who receives a tarot reading. The word querent is derived from "query," which means "inquiry" or "question."

Query—The question or focus of a tarot reading.

Quilt—synthesis; comfort; protection.

R

Rabbit—fertility; spring.

Rags—wounded spirit; holes in the soul.

Rainbow—God's promise of protection.

Ram—symbol of the astrological sign Aries.

Reader—the person who reads the cards.

Reins—intelligence; will.

Reversals—cards that appear upside down in a spread. They typically demand special consideration during a reading.

Ribbons—symbolic of immortality; victory; fulfillment.

Right—active; positive; masculine.

River—time; change.

Rock—permanence; stability; solidity.

Rope—lifeline; attachment; organization.

Rose—love; appreciation.

Rose, Red—passion.

Rose, White—purity.

Rota—Latin for wheel; anagram of tarot.

S

Salamander—elemental creature of fire.

Saturn—planet of limitations, restrictions, time.

Scales—justice; balance; symbol of the astrological sign Libra.

Scarab—renewal; regeneration; endurance.

Scorpion—symbol of the astrological sign Scorpio.

Scrolls—hidden mysteries; divine law.

Scythe—harvest; mutilation; death.

Seal of Solomon—two triangles form a six-pointed star, a symbol of spiritual potential and the connection between the conscious and unconscious.

Seasons:

- **Spring** Wands
- **Summer** Cups
- **Fall** Swords
- **Winter** Pentacles

Sephira—the ten spheres on the Kabbalistic Tree of Life. Each sphere represents one facet of God's being.

- **Crown** (Kether) the Godhead; the Source.
- **Wisdom** (Chokmah) God the Father.
- **Understanding** (Binah) God the Mother.
- **Mercy** (Chesed) God the Merciful and Benevolent.
- **Severity** (Geburah) Almighty God; God the Forceful.
- **Beauty** (Tiphareth) God the Balancer and Healer.
- **Victory** (Netzach) God the Inspiration.
- **Splendor** (Hod) God the Intellectual.
- **Foundation** (Yesod) God the Etheric; Earthly heaven.
- **Kingdom** (Malkuth) The physical world.

Serpent—energy; wisdom; knowledge; temptation; forked tongue (deceit); a serpent biting his tail represents infinity and endless transformation.

Seven—seven heavens; seven planets; seven musical notes; seven chakras; seven gifts of the Holy Spirit; seven stages of initiation; seven days of creation; seven deadly sins.

Shadow—alter ego; primitive instinct.

Sheaf—unification; integration; and strength.

Shell—fertility; protection; defense.

Ship—wealth; crossing; a rudder symbolizes steering ability and safe passage; sails symbolize the creative breath; oars represent creative thoughts and words and the source of action.

Shoes—base nature.

Shuffle—to mix the tarot cards, either poker style, hand over hand, or in a face-down slush pile on the table.

Signature—binding agreement; contract.

Significator—a card representing a querent, question, or situation. Other cards in the spread typically represent the *situation*, the *foundation* of the issue at hand, the *past*, the *present*, and the *future* of the situation, and the *most likely outcome* of the querent's current path.

Silver—lunar energy.

Six—the human soul.

Skeleton—death; putrification and decay.

Skull—death's head; mortality.

Sky—dome-shaped heaven.

Smoke—combines air and fire, symbolizing the path of fire to heavenly salvation.

Snow—sterility; cold; rigidity.

Spark—creation.

Sphinx—a combination of four creatures—a human head, a bull's body, lion's feet, and eagle's wings—that represents all four elements and symbolizes the riddle of human existence.

Spider—creativity; aggression; a spider in the center of a web symbolizes the spiral structure of the universe; the Great Mother in her devouring aspect

Spinning—giving life.

Spiral—the flow of energy through the universe.

Spread—the layout, pattern, or design a reader selects to spread the cards for a reading.

Square—most stable of all forms; firm foundations; strength; stability.

Staff—power; authority; support; instrument of punishment.

Stag—wisdom.

Star—hope; idealism; inspiration.

Star card—the card of faith and hope, the Star is a shining light in the darkness.

Star, Five-Sided—(see Pentagram).

Star, Eight-sided—cosmic order and radiant energy of life.

Star, Six-sided—union of male and female; intersection of material and spiritual; seal of Solomon.

Stairs—a climb; an ascent.

Stream—flows into the sea of cosmic consciousness.

Strength card—a woman gently holds the jaws of a powerful lion, patiently controlling a force that could otherwise eat her alive.

Styx—the Greek mythological river encircling Hades, over which Charon ferries the souls of the dead.

Suits—the four subdivisions of the Minor Arcana: wands, cups, swords, and pentacles.

Suitcases—travel; emotional baggage; karma; necessities.

Sun—illumination; gives life; astrologically, the self, the ego, consciousness.

Sun card—nothing can hide in the bright light of day, and even the dourest individuals come out to celebrate.

Sunrise—beginnings; initiation.

Sunflower—joy; attraction; solar symbol, as their heads follow the sun.

Swan—love; solitude; music; poetry; self-transformation.

Sword—intellect; conflict; justice and authority.

Sylph—elemental creature of air.

Synchronicity—meaningful coincidence.

T

Tarocchi/Tarock/Tarocco—traditional card games of Italy, Austria, and other European countries, played with a seventy-eight-card tarot deck.

Temperance card—with dexterity and grace, Temperance demonstrates how balance can serve as a bridge to wholeness.

Temple—refuge; holy place; symbol of the divine within one's self.

Ten—completion; perfection; ten fingers and toes.

Tent—impermanence; movement; travel; battlefield; communion with nature.

Tetragrammaton—the unutterable name of God, made up of the Hebrew letters Yod, Heh, Vau, Heh.

Thirteen—bad luck; number of witches in a coven; the number of men at the last supper; number of full moons in a calendar or lunar year.

Thoth—ancient dog-headed Egyptian god of wisdom; scribe of the gods; married to Ma'at, goddess of justice.

Three—body, mind, and spirit; birth, life, and death; past, present, and future; holy trinities.

Three-Leaf Clover—the Holy Trinity.

Throne—monarchy; wisdom; divinity.

Ticket—exclusive entrance.

Tide—the ebb and flow of life; the emotions.

Tomb—gateway to another life.

Tower—man's creation.

Tower card—should we build ourselves up too high, the Tower card warns that a bolt from the blue could shake us to our very foundations.

Tree of Knowledge of Good and Evil—bears five fruits, representing the five senses.

Tree of Life—the roots are planted in heaven and the branches extend to earth. Its twelve fruits represent the twelve facets of personality, as well as the months of the year and the disciples of Christ.

Tree—the mind.

Triangle—interest in metaphysics; see Three.

Trickster—cultural variant of the Fool.

Triple Goddess—maiden, mother, and crone; comparable to other triple deities such as father, son, and holy spirit.

Trump cards—the cards of the Major Arcana.

Twins—symbol of the astrological sign Gemini.

Two—duality; partnerships; choices; combinations; creative power; echo; reflection; conflict; occasionally a graphic female symbol.

Typhon—the serpent; the five senses.

U-V

Undine—elemental creature of water.

Unicorn—chastity; purity; lunar; feminine.

Uranus—planet of rebellion and the unexpected.

Valley—fertility; cultivation; water.

Veil—hidden emotions, actions, thoughts, and ideas.

Venus—planet of love; morning and evening star.

Virgin—symbol of the astrological sign Virgo.

Virtues—the cardinal virtues of ancient Greece were philosophy, justice, prudence, fortitude, and temperance. Justice, Strength, and Temperance are represented in the Major Arcana.

W

Wand—channel for spirit and creative energy; creative power.

Water Lilies—eternal life.

Water Signs—the "feelers" of the Zodiac: Cancer, Scorpio, Pisces.

Water-Bearer—symbol of the astrological sign Aquarius.

Wave—swelling emotional force and energy.

Web—the snare of Satan.

Wells—offer water and refreshment from the womb of Mother Earth; source of wish fulfillment.

Wheat—abundance; growth; harvest.

Wheel—cycle of cosmic expression; the year; time.

Wheel of Fortune card—because nothing is certain but change itself, the Wheel of Fortune reminds us all that what goes up must also come down.

White—positive; active.

Wine—celebration; harvest; blood.

Wolf—untamed; wild; uncivilized; underlying violence and fear.

World card—a card of completion and success, the World is the last stop on the Fool's journey.

Wreath—victory.

X-Y-Z

Yin-Yang—Chinese symbol of the balance between masculine and feminine; active and passive.

Yggdrasil—the World Tree of Norse mythology.

Yod—Hebrew letter; the hand of God; divine intervention; gift; drop of light; descent of life force from spirit into material.

Yoni—Eastern symbol of receptive, feminine energy (see Lingam).

Zero—non-being; the cosmic egg; the wheel of the year; the circle of life; completion.

Zodiac—literally, "circle of animals."

Zodiac Signs:

- **Aries** (the ram): (March 21—April 20) The initiator; ruled by Mars.
- **Taurus** (the bull): (April 21—May 20) The maintainer; ruled by Venus.
- **Gemini** (the twins): (May 21—June 20) The questioner; ruled by Mercury.
- **Cancer** (the crab): (June 21—July 20) The nurturer; ruled by the Moon.
- **Leo** (the lion): (July 21—August 20) The loyalist; ruled by the Sun.
- **Virgo** (the virgin): (August 21—September 20) The modifier; ruled by Mercury.
- **Libra** (the scales): (September 21—October 20) The judge; ruled by Venus.
- **Scorpio** (the scorpion): (October 21—November 20) The catalyst; ruled by Pluto.
- **Sagittarius** (the archer): (November 21—December 20) The adventurer; ruled by Jupiter.
- **Capricorn** (the goat): (December 21—January 20) The pragmatist; ruled by Saturn.
- **Aquarius** (the water bearer): (January 21—February 20) The reformer; ruled by Uranus.
- **Pisces** (the fish): (February 21—March 20) The visionary; ruled by Neptune.

Index

Tarot Journaling

Using the Celtic Cross to
Unveil Your Hidden Story

CORRINE KENNER

A tarot journal can help you learn more about the cards, but it can also teach you a great deal about yourself. Beginning tarot students are advised to keep a tarot journal, and many experienced tarot readers are devoted to the practice. The only book of its kind, *Tarot Journaling* covers everything needed to create, keep, and preserve a personal tarot journal.

Readers will discover hundreds of ideas to inspire and enliven their tarot journals, including considerations when choosing journaling materials, how to save time when recording readings, techniques for getting past writer's block, tips for turning negative energy into a positive brainstorming tool, and innovative ideas for protecting privacy. *Tarot Journaling* offers readers the tools to record and reflect upon the stories told by the cards—the stories of our lives.

978-0-7387-1618-3
216 pp., 6 x 9 $12.95

To order, call 1-877-NEW-WRLD
Prices subject to change without notice
Order at Llewellyn.com 24 hours a day, 7 days a week!

Simple Fortunetelling
with Tarot Cards
Corrine Kenner's Complete Guide

CORRINE KENNER

Some call tarot a tool for meditation and self-development. Others claim these seventy-eight cards offer a glimpse of the future. So, which is right?

According to Corrine Kenner, all of the above! Practical, fun, and easy-to-use, this guide will show you how to combine wisdom from the cards with your intuition and common sense to achieve a new understanding of the past, present, and future. Kenner introduces the basics—why tarot works, its colorful history, spreads, ethics, giving readings—along with practical techniques for timing predictions and enhancing your psychic skills. The personality of each card is brought to life through myth and legend, numerical and astrological symbolism, and keywords gleaned from legendary occult scholars. You'll soon learn how to read these classic images and, with practice, divine meaning from signs and symbols in everyday life, too.

978-0-7387-0964-2
336 pp., 7½ x 9⅛, illus. $16.95

Tall Dark Stranger
Tarot for Love & Romance

CORRINE KENNER

For centuries, the love-struck, lovesick, and lovelorn have consulted the tarot—a tradition still thriving today. *Tall Dark Stranger* makes it easy for anyone to explore matters of the heart through tarot. There is even a guide to tarot terms and symbols.

Corrine Kenner's tour of the tarot begins with its colorful, romantic history. She goes on to describe the deck itself—explaining its structure, suits, symbolism, archetypes, and astrological associations—while relating its special significance in love and relationships. The second part of the book is devoted to the nitty-gritty of tarot readings: choosing a deck, preparing for a reading, asking appropriate questions, timing events, and interpreting cards and spreads. By the end of the book, readers will have a powerful edge in conquering the ever-mysterious ways of love.

978-0-7387-0548-4
312 pp., 7½ x 9⅛, illus. $15.95

What Tarot Can Do for You
Your Future in the Cards

BARBARA MOORE

T. S. Eliot may have called it "a wicked pack of cards," but the Tarot is used by many today as a tool for effective divination and spiritual exploration. Just like the mysterious reader who turns over the cards to reveal your future, the pages of *What Tarot Can Do for You* reveals the rich world of images and symbols that can enhance and enchant your life.

See how the Tarot can foretell coming events, create solutions to problems, add variety and depth to your meditations, and focus your spellworking. From using the Tarot for self-improvement to healing to journaling, this book will show you the benefits of several activities associated with Tarot and give examples of each process.

978-0-7387-0173-8
192 pp., 5³⁄₁₆ x 8, illus.   **$7.95**

To Write to the Author

If you wish to contact the author or would like more information about this book, please write to the author in care of Llewellyn Worldwide and we will forward your request. Both the author and publisher appreciate hearing from you and learning of your enjoyment of this book and how it has helped you. Llewellyn Worldwide cannot guarantee that every letter written to the author can be answered, but all will be forwarded. Please write to:

Corrine Kenner
℅ Llewellyn Worldwide
2143 Wooddale Drive, Dept. 978-0-7387-1457-8
Woodbury, MN 55125-2989, U.S.A.

Please enclose a self-addressed stamped envelope for reply,
or $1.00 to cover costs. If outside U.S.A., enclose
international postal reply coupon.

Many of Llewellyn's authors have websites with additional information and resources. For more information, please visit our website at:

www.llewellyn.com